CHARTER SCHOOLS and THEIR ENEMIES

OTHER BOOKS BY THOMAS SOWELL:

Basic Economics

Discrimination and Disparities

A Conflict of Visions

Intellectuals and Society

CHARTER SCHOOLS
and
THEIR ENEMIES

Thomas Sowell

BASIC BOOKS

New York

To those children whose futures

hang in the balance

Basic Books
Hachette Book Group
1290 Avenue of the Americas, New York, NY 10104
www.basicbooks.com

Printed in the United States of America

Originally published in hardcover and ebook by Basic Books in June 2020

First Edition: June 2020

Published by Basic Books, an imprint of Perseus Books, LLC, a subsidiary of Hachette Book Group, Inc. The Basic Books name and logo is a trademark of the Hachette Book Group.

The Hachette Speakers Bureau provides a wide range of authors for speaking events. To find out more, go to www.hachettespeakersbureau.com or call (866) 376-6591.

The publisher is not responsible for websites (or their content) that are not owned by the publisher.

Library of Congress Control Number: 2020936857

ISBNs: 978-1-5416-7513-1 (hardcover), 978-1-5416-7514-8 (ebook)

LSC-C

10 9 8 7 6 5 4 3 2 1

CONTENTS

PREFACE

In a sense, this story began back in the early 1970s, at a gathering of various conservative and neoconservative intellectuals, hosted by Irving Kristol, then editor of a high-quality quarterly publication called *The Public Interest*.

After a round of convivial recollections from those present about how we had begun our careers on the political left or, as in my case, the far left as a Marxist, Irving raised a very serious question about how some way could be found to improve the substandard educational levels of most black schoolchildren. At that point I said something like, "You are talking as if good education for black children is something that has never happened before, and that has to be created from scratch."

This immediately caught his attention, and he asked me to tell him where this had happened, and how. I gave him a brief sketch of the history of all-black Dunbar High School in Washington, D.C., during the era from 1870 to 1955, and the various achievements of its graduates in elite colleges during that era, as well as in careers that led many of them to pioneer as the first black federal judge, the first black general, and the first black Cabinet member, among other distinctions.

His interest very much aroused, Irving urged me to research and write about this, and volunteered to finance the research. Out of this came an article titled, "Black Excellence: The Case of Dunbar High School," which appeared in the Spring 1974 issue of *The Public Interest*. Two years later, I wrote another article for *The Public Interest* about a number of successful black schools, in various parts of the country, titled "Patterns of Black Excellence."

If I thought that, amid all the research and writings about failing black schools, many scholars and policy-makers would be interested in black schools that succeeded, I was sadly mistaken. Many scholars and policy-makers already had their own explanations for the failures of black schools, and their own "solutions" for that problem. What I had written was, to them, at best a passing distraction, if not something that needed to be discredited, so that they could get on with promoting their own prescriptions, policies and programs.

Chief Justice Earl Warren had already declared racially separate schools to be "inherently unequal" in the Supreme Court's landmark *Brown v. Board of Education* decision in 1954, so racial segregation was the prevailing explanation of substandard black educational achievements.

The fact that all-black Dunbar High School was only about a mile away from the Supreme Court where the Chief Justice made his historic pronouncement, and that Dunbar, at that time, sent a higher proportion of its graduates on to college than any white public high school in the city,[1] was a fact that was probably unknown to those crusading for racial "integration" in the schools, and that fact probably would not have made any difference to them, even if they had known it.

Many people had already made up their minds, and did not want to be confused by facts. Years of mandatory busing of black children to white schools, in order to achieve racial "integration" was the logical corollary of what Chief Justice Warren had said, though the *Brown v. Board of Education* decision did not itself prescribe mandatory busing. The busing crusade produced heated controversies, bitter racial polarization and dangerous confrontations in the streets, with schoolchildren caught in the middle of it all— but little, if any, net benefit to the educational levels of black children.

Eventually, the busing crusade faded in futility. But something very different later appeared on the horizon— the idea that low-income parents should be allowed to choose where their children went to school, just as high-income parents already could, by sending their children to private schools if the local public school was unsatisfactory. Extending choice to parents in general could be done in a variety of ways, including vouchers that could cover tuition at low-cost, private schools such as some Catholic parochial schools.

That was just one option among many. There were also magnet schools, homeschooling and tuition tax credits, for example. Eventually, one of the most strikingly successful kinds of schools that emerged from this experimentation was the charter school— a special public school freed from some of the rigidities of the regular public schools, and allowed to receive government financial support only so long as its students' educational outcomes met various educational criteria.

Not all charter schools turned out to be successful, just as not all traditional public schools turned out to be successful— or all failures, for that matter. But particular charter schools, and especially some particular networks of charter schools, located in low-income black and Hispanic neighborhoods, achieved educational results not only far above the levels achieved by most public schools in those neighborhoods, but sometimes even higher educational results than those in most schools located in affluent white neighborhoods.

No one expected that. Anyone who might have predicted such an outcome beforehand would have been considered to be hopelessly unrealistic.

This story might seem to have had a happy ending— at least for that fraction of minority students attending successful charter schools. But, in fact, even the most successful charter schools have been bitterly attacked by teachers unions, by politicians, by the civil rights establishment and assorted others. How can success be so unwelcome? It is apparently not unwelcome to parents of low-income minority students. In New York City alone, there are more than 50,000 children on waiting lists to get into charter schools.[2] Yet New York's mayor has announced an end to the expansion of charter schools and threatened restrictions on those already functioning. It is much the same story in California— and in many other places in between.

Understanding why and how educational success has been such unwelcome news to so many people and institutions is the purpose of this book. With growing political threats to charter schools across the country, the stakes could not be higher for poor and minority youngsters, for whom a good education is their biggest opportunity for a better life. That in itself is enough to make this a story well worth understanding by all people of good will, despite whatever other differences they might have.

Thomas Sowell
The Hoover Institution
Stanford University

Chapter 1

COMPARISONS AND COMPARABILITY

Depending on who you read or listen to, charter schools are either a striking success[1] or a "failed and damaging experiment"[2]— or even just "fads."[3] With all the voluminous educational statistics available, it might seem strange that such extremely different conclusions, and controversies arising from these differences, should exist and persist. Nevertheless, these controversies have continued to rage for years, with growing intensity, as charter schools have expanded from a barely noticeable part of the educational scene when they began in the 1990s to thousands of schools with millions of students today.

Public charter schools are public schools not created by the existing government education authorities, but by some private groups who gain government approval by meeting various preconditions set by authorizing agencies.[4] These agencies issue charters enabling these schools to operate as public schools eligible for taxpayer money and to enroll public school students who apply.

By allowing more autonomy and flexibility in public charter schools than in the more tightly controlled traditional public schools, it was hoped that new educational policies and practices that emerge from this experiment might produce some better educational results. In that case, traditional public schools would have these new policies and practices available to use if they chose to, thereby benefitting the much larger number of students in the traditional public school sector. If, however, a charter school has educational outcomes that fail to satisfy the authorities, those authorities can revoke its charter and end its access to taxpayer money and public school students.

One important difference, however, is that students are not assigned to go to public charter schools, as they are assigned to attend particular traditional public schools. Those students whose parents want them to go to particular charter schools can seek admission to those charter

schools, usually by entering a lottery. Choosing students by lottery—
rather than by their ability or their educational track record— is
supposed to keep the students in the two kinds of schools more or
less comparable, so as to keep the experiment valid and its conclusions
applicable to public schools in general.

One major complication in studies comparing public charter
schools with traditional public schools is that the racial, ethnic, and
socioeconomic backgrounds of students in the charter schools as a
whole turn out to be very different from those of students in traditional
public schools as a whole.

COMPARABLE   STUDENTS

Nationwide, white students plus Asian students are a majority of
the students in traditional public schools, while black students plus
Hispanic students are a majority of the students in charter schools,
which are often located in low-income minority communities.[5] On
a wide range of educational tests, over the years white and Asian
students as a whole have scored significantly higher than black and
Hispanic students as a whole.[6] Therefore comparisons of charter
school and traditional public school outcomes on various tests are a
problem, because their respective students are from groups with a long
history of different educational results. There is also a long history of
different educational results with children from low-income families
and high-income families.

Under these circumstances, it can be hard to know how much of
whatever differences there may be in educational outcomes, as between
charter schools and traditional public schools, are due to the schools
themselves and how much are due to their different mix of students
from different ethnic and socioeconomic backgrounds.

A striking example of how racial or ethnic differences among
students can make it hard to determine the effectiveness of different
schools— whether in terms of charter schools or in other contexts—
is a study of educational test score differences among the 50 states.

Students in Iowa scored higher on those tests than students in Texas. *But whites in Texas scored higher than whites in Iowa; blacks in Texas scored higher than blacks in Iowa; Asians in Texas scored higher than Asians in Iowa; and Hispanics in Texas scored higher than Hispanics in Iowa.*[7] How then could Iowa students as a whole have scored higher than Texas students as a whole? Simply because "Iowa's student population is predominantly white"[8] and students in Texas include far more minority students, mostly low-income minorities.

While gross statistics might suggest that Iowa had better schools than Texas, an ethnic breakdown of the population taking those tests would suggest the direct opposite. For similar reasons, comparing educational outcomes in charter schools as a whole with educational outcomes in traditional public schools as a whole can be like comparing apples and oranges— unless there is some way to compare particular schools' educational results when educating truly comparable students.

Since such comparability is simply not there in gross statistical comparisons of public charter schools as a whole with other public schools as a whole, the approach here will be to compare individual charter schools with individual traditional public schools that are as similar as possible. Among the wide variety of statistics available on educational test results in charter schools and traditional public schools, the ones given the greatest weight here will be statistics comparing students in particular schools meeting all three of the following criteria:

1. There is a similar ethnic composition of students[9] in a particular charter school being compared to a particular traditional public school serving the same local population.
2. The students in both schools are taught in the very same building, thus reducing whatever effect differences in particular buildings, or in the neighborhoods around those buildings, might be. This also reduces the likely range of dispersion in the locations of the homes from which students come, as well as the likely dispersion of their socioeconomic backgrounds.

3. The charter school and the traditional public school have one or more classes at the same grade level in the same building, so that students in these particular classes can be compared in their results when taking the same tests.

Schools meeting all three requirements simultaneously are by no means common. But, if our goal is to compare educational results *among truly comparable students* in truly comparable circumstances, whether those students are in charter schools or in traditional public schools, then this may be as close as we can come to achieving that.

Uncommon as it may be to find large numbers of such situations in a given community, New York City is exceptional in having a substantial number of charter schools and traditional public schools meeting all three requirements. In school year 2017–2018, there were more than 23,000 New York City students in particular classes meeting all these requirements in these particular schools.[10] So New York City has a substantial sample of ethnically and socioeconomically comparable students whose educational outcomes can be compared.

THE DATA

Each school year, the New York State Education Department gives the same tests in "English Language Arts" and in mathematics to public school students— whether in public charter schools or in traditional public schools— in grades 3 through 8. So it is possible to make comparisons of students' results on these tests in the same grade levels in particular charter schools with particular traditional public schools located in the same buildings. The New York State Education Department publishes not only aggregate test scores of classes in these schools but also the ethnic breakdown of the students and the percentage of them who meet its definition of "economically disadvantaged."

That still leaves the question of how to select which of the innumerable pairings of classes to examine. If the pairings are chosen by simply cherry-picking examples, all the efforts to achieve comparability will have been wasted, since different people can obviously choose different examples.

One viable option is to simply make available *all* the data from all of the classes in New York City where a charter school has been housed in the same building with one or more traditional public schools which have some classes at the same grade levels, and students with a similar racial or ethnic background. That is done here in the Appendix. But while it is a viable option to make available all test score data, demographic data, and socioeconomic data for students in these situations, it is *not* a viable option to discuss all these data individually, without expanding the study to the dimensions of an encyclopedia. Moreover, charter schools differ among themselves, just as traditional public schools do, and these differences also require discussion and analysis.

Selecting which charter schools to examine in detail *by some principle*, as distinguished from arbitrary cherry-picking, can be done in a number of ways. The way chosen here is to examine those particular charter school networks with multiple schools having classes in *the largest number of buildings* in New York City where they are housed with one or more traditional public schools whose grade levels coincide. Here the sample chosen for detailed study in Chapter 2 are all charter school networks with students in *five or more buildings* in New York City that they share with traditional public schools having students at the same grade levels.

For the sake of ethnic comparability, the paired schools in our sample must also meet the criterion of having a majority of their students who are either black and/or Hispanic. A finer ethnic breakdown for each school can be found in Appendix II.

Such data provide separate samples from different charter school networks, and from different school locations within each network. As a result, the statistical influence of the peculiarities of any particular school or any particular neighborhood on the data can be reduced or at least recognized.

People who would prefer some other method of choosing samples to examine in detail are free to make their own selection from the voluminous data in the Appendix. All these data are from the New York State Education Department, and the definitions used in the tables are their definitions.

By choosing to examine in some detail those charter school networks with classes located in five or more buildings in New York City, a large amount of data can be examined from a small number of charter school networks. In this case, there turned out to be five charter school networks in New York City that met the three specified requirements in school year 2017–2018, and had classes housed in five or more buildings with traditional public schools having classes at the same grade levels. These networks were the KIPP (Knowledge Is Power Program) charter schools, and charter schools in the Success Academy, Explore Schools, Uncommon Schools and Achievement First networks.

After examining the performances of these particular charter school networks in some detail in Chapter 2, there will be a more summary examination there of the performances of *all* charter schools in New York City that met the same three criteria for inclusion in the citywide sample.

Chapter 2

CHARTER SCHOOL RESULTS

W hile our main concern is finding out what educational outcome differences there are between students in public charter schools and students in traditional public schools, the detailed data in our sample also reveal differences in test scores between different charter school networks, between different schools in the same networks, between classes in the same schools, as well as similar differences among traditional public schools. All these differences can be found in the tables in this chapter, by those who are interested, even if not all these things are discussed in the text.

Data on the ethnic makeup of charter school students and traditional public school students paired with them in the same buildings are available in Appendix II, and are summarized in passing in this chapter. In both kinds of schools, these are ethnic data for students in the specific classes being compared, *not* data on the ethnic makeup of students in the entire buildings in which they are housed. Our samples are defined by the classes whose test scores are being compared, not by all the students in the buildings.

Two tests given annually by the New York State Education Department, to both public charter school students and students in traditional public schools, are officially designated as the English Language Arts test and the Mathematics test.

The students' scores on these statewide tests are broken down into four categories by the New York State Education Department. The lowest test scores are officially defined as being in Level 1, and the highest test scores are defined as being in Level 4. Students who score in Level 3 are designated as being "proficient," according to the standards for whatever grade they are in, and those whose scores are in Level 4 are designated as being *above* "proficient" for that grade. These definitions are repeated under each table of statistics showing

7

test score results. The main point here is simply that Level 1 is at the bottom and Level 4 is at the top.

"Proficient"— Level 3— is a crucial measure. While students who fall below that level are likely to be promoted to the next grade anyway, in many or most traditional public schools, their prospects of mastering those subjects in higher grades that build on what was taught in the same subjects in lower grades— mathematics being a clear example— are obviously not good. That is especially so if they score in the bottom category, Level 1, two levels below "proficient." Therefore statistics on test scores in Level 1 are also crucial, and will also be a special focus here. To score two levels below "proficient" in arithmetic makes it unlikely to be able to master algebra in later years. Cumulative deficits can be extremely hard to overcome, even by conscientious and intelligent youngsters.

In a world where higher mathematics is required in many professions— not just for scientists, engineers or statisticians, but increasingly also for economists, psychologists, sociologists and others*— an inability to master mathematics means that doors of opportunity into a wide range of professions are silently closing in the background as children go through elementary school without achieving proficiency in arithmetic. Having children talking in school about how they are going to become doctors or pilots, when they have not mastered fractions or decimals, is a cruel hoax— as they can discover later in life as adults, when it is too late.

---

*   Even in professions where mathematics is not in daily use, the progress of the profession over time means that a doctor, for example, must keep up with new developments, and cannot keep treating patients on the basis of what was learned in medical school, years earlier. To keep up with new medications, technologies and treatments requires studying empirical data on the results of these things, which are often expressed in sophisticated statistical analyses which the doctor must be equipped mathematically to understand.

KIPP CHARTER SCHOOLS

The KIPP charter schools are the largest non profit network of charter schools in the country. The first of KIPP's more than 200 schools, now scattered from coast to coast, began in Houston in 1994 and the second, a year later, in New York City's South Bronx. Both schools serve predominantly minority youngsters from low-income families, as do other schools in the KIPP network.

In New York City, there were 11 KIPP charter schools in school year 2017–2018, including 5 located in the same buildings with one or more traditional public schools serving the same community, and having some classes at the same grade level in both kinds of schools. In each of these 5 KIPP charter schools, at least 95 percent of the students in our sample were either black or Hispanic in 2017–2018. This was also true of the ethnic breakdown in the traditional public schools housed in the same buildings.[1] Most of the students in both the KIPP charter schools and in the traditional public schools housed with them were classified as "economically disadvantaged" by the New York State Education Department.[2]

High Scores in English

In school year 2017–2018 a majority of KIPP charter school students scored at Level 3 ("proficient") or above on the English Language Arts test in 10 of their 14 grade levels in the five buildings they shared with students in traditional public schools.[3] A majority of the traditional public school children in these same five buildings scored at Level 3 ("proficient") or above in just *one* of their 20 grade levels. Some of these buildings contained more than one traditional public school, which is why there were more grade levels for traditional public school students than for KIPP charter school students. Details are shown in Table 1A.

TABLE 1A: NEW YORK STATE ENGLISH LANGUAGE ARTS TEST RESULTS, 2017–2018

SCHOOLS HOUSED TOGETHER	CLASS GRADE LEVEL	LEVEL 1 RESULTS (Percent)	LEVEL 2 RESULTS (Percent)	LEVEL 3 RESULTS (Percent)	LEVEL 4 RESULTS (Percent)
ALEXANDER HUMBOLDT SCHOOL	3rd grade	28	37	33	1
KIPP charter school	3rd grade	7	19	68	7
MARIA TERESA SCHOOL	6th grade	52	24	19	5
Patria Mirabal School	6th grade	42	37	13	7
KIPP charter school	6th grade	3	17	37	42
MARIA TERESA SCHOOL	7th grade	44	36	17	3
Patria Mirabal School	7th grade	37	41	19	3
KIPP charter school	7th grade	11	42	35	12
MARIA TERESA SCHOOL	8th grade	13	40	28	19
Patria Mirabal School	8th grade	23	37	30	10
KIPP charter school	8th grade	0	30	44	26
NEW DESIGN MIDDLE SCHOOL	6th grade	56	33	11	0
KIPP charter school	6th grade	14	29	28	29
NEW DESIGN MIDDLE SCHOOL	7th grade	57	26	15	2
KIPP charter school	7th grade	14	37	42	7
NEW DESIGN MIDDLE SCHOOL	8th grade	18	55	18	8
KIPP charter school	8th grade	2	26	35	36

Performance Levels: Level 1: Well Below Proficient   Level 2: Below Proficient   Level 3: Proficient   Level 4: Above Proficient
SOURCE: New York State Education Department

TABLE 1A: ENGLISH LANGUAGE ARTS (continued)

SCHOOLS HOUSED TOGETHER	CLASS GRADE LEVEL	LEVEL 1 RESULTS (Percent)	LEVEL 2 RESULTS (Percent)	LEVEL 3 RESULTS (Percent)	LEVEL 4 RESULTS (Percent)
SCHOOL OF INTEGRATED LEARNING	6th grade	14	24	22	39
KIPP charter school	6th grade	19	24	32	25
SCHOOL OF INTEGRATED LEARNING	7th grade	22	31	35	12
KIPP charter school	7th grade	25	38	26	11
SCHOOL OF INTEGRATED LEARNING	8th grade	18	41	23	18
KIPP charter school	8th grade	13	26	37	24
WILLIAM LLOYD GARRISON SCHOOL	5th grade	51	32	10	7
KIPP charter school	5th grade	25	31	27	17
WILLIAM LLOYD GARRISON SCHOOL	6th grade	53	29	10	7
Lou Gehrig School	6th grade	48	28	23	1
KIPP charter school	6th grade	9	20	23	48
WILLIAM LLOYD GARRISON SCHOOL	7th grade	54	28	14	4
Lou Gehrig School	7th grade	58	34	8	0
KIPP charter school	7th grade	10	35	46	9
WILLIAM LLOYD GARRISON SCHOOL	8th grade	24	57	13	6
Lou Gehrig School	8th grade	51	39	8	3
KIPP charter school	8th grade	8	15	42	35

Performance Levels: Level 1: Well Below Proficient Level 2: Below Proficient Level 3: Proficient Level 4: Above Proficient
SOURCE: New York State Education Department

Low Scores in English

Among students who scored down at the bottom in Level 1 on the English Language Arts test, the percentage of traditional public school students scoring at the bottom exceeded the percentage of KIPP charter school students who scored that low, in all but two of the grade levels in the five school buildings where both sets of students were housed. In most cases the percentage of traditional public school students who scored that low was some *multiple* of the percentage of KIPP charter school students who scored that low. In the two grade levels where the percentage of traditional public school students scoring at the bottom was less than the percentage of the KIPP charter school students at that same level, the differences were small (19 percent versus 14 percent and 25 percent versus 22 percent).

Overall, KIPP students clearly did better on the English Language Arts test in these five buildings than traditional public school students in the same grades. None of the KIPP charter school grade levels had 40 percent or more of their students scoring down at the bottom in Level 1. But 11 of the 20 grade levels in the various traditional public schools scored that low. These included 8 grade levels where more than half the students scored down in Level 1.

High Scores in Mathematics

On the New York State Education Department's Mathematics test in school year 2017–2018, a majority of the KIPP charter school students scored at the "proficient" Level 3 or above in 12 of their 14 grade levels. In the two exceptions, 50 percent and 49 percent of KIPP students reached the "proficient" Level 3 or above in mathematics. Among the students in the traditional public schools in the same buildings, a majority reached the "proficient" Level 3 and above in just *one* grade level out of 20. (Details in Table 1B)

Low Scores in Mathematics

Among students scoring down at the bottom in Level 1 on the mathematics test, the percentages of those in the traditional public

TABLE 1B: NEW YORK STATE MATHEMATICS TEST RESULTS, 2017–2018

SCHOOLS HOUSED TOGETHER	CLASS GRADE LEVEL	LEVEL 1 RESULTS (Percent)	LEVEL 2 RESULTS (Percent)	LEVEL 3 RESULTS (Percent)	LEVEL 4 RESULTS (Percent)
ALEXANDER HUMBOLDT SCHOOL	3rd grade	25	31	30	14
KIPP charter school	3rd grade	7	15	41	37
MARIA TERESA SCHOOL	6th grade	50	29	18	4
Patria Mirabal School	6th grade	41	25	22	13
KIPP charter school	6th grade	6	10	49	35
MARIA TERESA SCHOOL	7th grade	35	35	19	11
Patria Mirabal School	7th grade	37	35	20	8
KIPP charter school	7th grade	16	21	31	31
MARIA TERESA SCHOOL	8th grade	23	38	18	22
Patria Mirabal School	8th grade	37	48	13	1
KIPP charter school	8th grade	6	23	29	41
NEW DESIGN MIDDLE SCHOOL	6th grade	85	5	10	0
KIPP charter school	6th grade	4	21	34	41
NEW DESIGN MIDDLE SCHOOL	7th grade	71	22	7	0
KIPP charter school	7th grade	6	13	13	68
NEW DESIGN MIDDLE SCHOOL	8th grade	61	24	12	3
KIPP charter school	8th grade	4	12	16	68

Performance Levels: Level 1: Well Below Proficient Level 2: Below Proficient Level 3: Proficient Level 4: Above Proficient
SOURCE: New York State Education Department

TABLE 1B: MATHEMATICS (continued)

SCHOOLS HOUSED TOGETHER	CLASS GRADE LEVEL	LEVEL 1 RESULTS (Percent)	LEVEL 2 RESULTS (Percent)	LEVEL 3 RESULTS (Percent)	LEVEL 4 RESULTS (Percent)
SCHOOL OF INTEGRATED LEARNING	6th grade	18	27	39	16
KIPP charter school	6th grade	23	28	32	17
SCHOOL OF INTEGRATED LEARNING	7th grade	43	30	16	11
KIPP charter school	7th grade	28	22	30	20
SCHOOL OF INTEGRATED LEARNING	8th grade	8	45	27	20
KIPP charter school	8th grade	14	24	22	40
WILLIAM LLOYD GARRISON SCHOOL	5th grade	70	16	10	5
KIPP charter school	5th grade	20	26	33	20
WILLIAM LLOYD GARRISON SCHOOL	6th grade	52	31	13	3
Lou Gehrig School	6th grade	72	21	7	0
KIPP charter school	6th grade	15	14	34	37
WILLIAM LLOYD GARRISON SCHOOL	7th grade	69	24	5	1
Lou Gehrig School	7th grade	85	10	5	0
KIPP charter school	7th grade	15	10	37	37
WILLIAM LLOYD GARRISON SCHOOL	8th grade	44	43	10	3
Lou Gehrig School	8th grade	77	19	3	1
KIPP charter school	8th grade	10	17	32	40

Performance Levels: Level 1: Well Below Proficient   Level 2: Below Proficient   Level 3: Proficient   Level 4: Above Proficient
SOURCE: New York State Education Department

schools were, in most grade levels, again some *multiple* of the percentage of KIPP charter school students who scored that low. In none of the grade levels did as many as 30 percent of the KIPP students score at the bottom in Level 1. But half or more of the students in traditional public schools in the same buildings scored down in Level 1 in ten of their twenty grade levels. There were as many as 85 percent scoring at the bottom in two of those grade levels.

In short, the disparity in outcomes was even greater in mathematics than in English. This is not uncommon as a general pattern. Some have suggested that this is because students' language skills depend on both the home and the school, while their mathematics skills are usually acquired only in school. But, whatever the reason, the pattern turns up often. Table 1B has more detailed information on the mathematics test results in 2017–2018.

Conclusion

Overall, the KIPP charter school students considerably outperformed most of their traditional public school neighbors in the same grade levels in the same five buildings in New York City in school year 2017–2018. In mathematics, the results were especially grim for the traditional public school students, most of whom failed to reach the "proficient" Level 3 in all but one of their 20 grade levels, and at least half failed to score above Level 1 in ten of their twenty grade levels.

SUCCESS ACADEMY CHARTER SCHOOLS

Although the KIPP schools were the largest non-profit network of public charter schools in the country in school year 2017–2018, there were more Success Academy charter schools in New York City, where Success Academy schools have been concentrated. The first of the Success Academy charter schools was established in Harlem in 2006. Over the years, the Success Academy network established charter schools in other New York City low-income minority neighborhoods, such as Bedford-Stuyvesant and the South Bronx.

As of 2017, there were 46 Success Academy charter schools in New York City, with a total of more than 15,000 students.[4] Of these schools, there were 13 Success Academy charter schools located in the same buildings with one or more traditional public schools, and having some classes at the same grade levels as those of their traditional public school neighbors.

In all of these thirteen Success Academy charter schools, at least 92 percent of the students in our sample were either black or Hispanic in school year 2017–2018. In the traditional public schools with classes located in the same buildings, at least 89 percent of the students in our sample were either black or Hispanic. A majority of these students in both Success Academy charter schools and traditional public schools housed with them were classified as "economically disadvantaged" by the New York State Education Department.[5]

By the time the first Success Academy charter school was founded in 2006, there was more than a decade of other charter schools' experiences that its founder— Eva Moskowitz— could draw on, instead of having to learn everything the hard way, by trial and error. As she put it, "I drew on lessons from other pioneers in the charter movement including KIPP, Achievement First, and Uncommon."[6]

Whatever the combination of things that went into the creation of the Success Academy network, its students' performances on tests of English and mathematics have been even more striking, and more uniform, than those of the KIPP charter schools— and more than most other charter schools— in New York City.

High Scores in English

On the New York State Education Department's English Language Arts test in 2017–2018, all 30 Success Academy charter school grade levels of classes located in thirteen school buildings with various traditional public schools, had a majority of their students scoring at the "proficient" level or above. These majorities ranged from 82 percent to 100 percent. Of the 36 grade levels in the traditional

TABLE 2A: NEW YORK STATE ENGLISH LANGUAGE ARTS TEST RESULTS, 2017–2018

SCHOOLS HOUSED TOGETHER	CLASS GRADE LEVEL	LEVEL 1 RESULTS (Percent)	LEVEL 2 RESULTS (Percent)	LEVEL 3 RESULTS (Percent)	LEVEL 4 RESULTS (Percent)
BENJAMIN FRANKLIN SCHOOL	3rd grade	18	34	45	3
Success Academy charter school	3rd grade	1	12	77	11
BENJAMIN FRANKLIN SCHOOL	4th grade	24	43	26	7
Success Academy charter school	4th grade	0	7	39	54
BRONX WRITING ACADEMY	6th grade	43	20	17	21
Jordan L. Mott Junior High School	6th grade	39	32	22	7
Success Academy charter school	6th grade	0	0	15	85
BRONX WRITING ACADEMY	7th grade	44	33	21	2
Jordan L. Mott Junior High School	7th grade	50	39	12	0
Success Academy charter school	7th grade	0	3	58	38
BRONX WRITING ACADEMY	8th grade	35	40	19	6
Jordan L. Mott Junior High School	8th grade	40	43	13	4
Success Academy charter school	8th grade	0	0	33	67
CROWN ELEMENTARY SCHOOL	3rd grade	22	32	42	4
Success Academy charter school	3rd grade	0	3	75	21
CROWN ELEMENTARY SCHOOL	4th grade	26	48	21	5
Success Academy charter school	4th grade	0	5	58	37

Performance Levels: Level 1: Well Below Proficient   Level 2: Below Proficient   Level 3: Proficient   Level 4: Above Proficient
SOURCE: New York State Education Department

TABLE 2A: ENGLISH LANGUAGE ARTS (continued)

SCHOOLS HOUSED TOGETHER	CLASS GRADE LEVEL	LEVEL 1 RESULTS (Percent)	LEVEL 2 RESULTS (Percent)	LEVEL 3 RESULTS (Percent)	LEVEL 4 RESULTS (Percent)
FREDERICK DOUGLASS ACADEMY II	6th grade	36	36	27	0
Wadleigh Performing and Visual Arts	6th grade	36	32	20	12
Success Academy charter school	6th grade	0	14	44	42
FREDERICK DOUGLASS ACADEMY II	7th grade	31	38	25	6
Wadleigh Performing and Visual Arts	7th grade	35	40	25	0
Success Academy charter school	7th grade	5	14	62	20
FREDERICK DOUGLASS ACADEMY II	8th grade	29	43	14	14
Wadleigh Performing and Visual Arts	8th grade	25	42	33	0
Success Academy charter school	8th grade	0	1	49	50
HENRY H. GARNET SCHOOL	5th grade	46	34	16	4
Success Academy charter school	5th grade	0	9	41	50
HERNANDEZ/HUGHES SCHOOL	3rd grade	24	32	41	3
Success Academy charter school	3rd grade	1	9	61	29
HERNANDEZ/HUGHES SCHOOL	4th grade	13	39	39	10
Success Academy charter school	4th grade	0	12	53	35
MAHALIA JACKSON SCHOOL	3rd grade	52	36	12	0
Success Academy charter school	3rd grade	0	8	81	12
MAHALIA JACKSON SCHOOL	4th grade	34	40	19	6
Success Academy charter school	4th grade	0	14	53	33
MOSAIC PREPARATORY ACADEMY	5th grade	35	30	24	11
Success Academy charter school	5th grade	3	16	36	46

Performance Levels: Level 1: Well Below Proficient   Level 2: Below Proficient   Level 3: Proficient   Level 4: Above Proficient
SOURCE: New York State Education Department

TABLE 2A: ENGLISH LANGUAGE ARTS (continued)

SCHOOLS HOUSED TOGETHER	CLASS GRADE LEVEL	LEVEL 1 RESULTS (Percent)	LEVEL 2 RESULTS (Percent)	LEVEL 3 RESULTS (Percent)	LEVEL 4 RESULTS (Percent)
PS 138 BROOKLYN	3rd grade	4	13	80	2
Success Academy charter school	3rd grade	0	8	71	21
PS 138 BROOKLYN	4th grade	4	19	50	28
Success Academy charter school	4th grade	0	14	58	28
PS 138 BROOKLYN	5th grade	29	21	26	25
Success Academy charter school	5th grade	0	15	38	46
PS 138 BROOKLYN	6th grade	33	28	20	19
Success Academy charter school	6th grade	0	5	23	73
STEM INSTITUTE OF MANHATTAN	3rd grade	25	50	20	5
Success Academy charter school	3rd grade	0	4	72	24
STEM INSTITUTE OF MANHATTAN	4th grade	22	44	22	11
Success Academy charter school	4th grade	0	1	46	53
URBAN ASSEMBLY ACADEMY FOR FUTURE LEADERS	6th grade	52	36	12	0
Success Academy charter school	6th grade	0	3	21	76
URBAN ASSEMBLY ACADEMY FOR FUTURE LEADERS	7th grade	41	39	19	2
Success Academy charter school	7th grade	0	12	46	42
URBAN ASSEMBLY ACADEMY FOR FUTURE LEADERS	8th grade	26	45	24	5
Success Academy charter school	8th grade	0	5	41	54

Performance Levels: Level 1: Well Below Proficient   Level 2: Below Proficient   Level 3: Proficient   Level 4: Above Proficient
SOURCE: New York State Education Department

TABLE 2A: ENGLISH LANGUAGE ARTS (continued)

SCHOOLS HOUSED TOGETHER	CLASS GRADE LEVEL	LEVEL 1 RESULTS (Percent)	LEVEL 2 RESULTS (Percent)	LEVEL 3 RESULTS (Percent)	LEVEL 4 RESULTS (Percent)
URBAN ASSEMBLY BRONX ACADEMY OF LETTERS	6th grade	45	31	18	6
Success Academy charter school	6th grade	0	6	32	63
URBAN ASSEMBLY BRONX ACADEMY OF LETTERS	7th grade	35	48	14	2
Success Academy charter school	7th grade	0	8	75	18
URBAN ASSEMBLY BRONX ACADEMY OF LETTERS	8th grade	37	31	21	11
Success Academy charter school	8th grade	0	2	36	62
WILLIAM FLOYD SCHOOL	3rd grade	29	38	29	4
Success Academy charter school	3rd grade	0	7	68	25
WILLIAM FLOYD SCHOOL	4th grade	24	48	26	2
Success Academy charter school	4th grade	0	13	50	37

Performance Levels: Level 1: Well Below Proficient   Level 2: Below Proficient   Level 3: Proficient   Level 4: Above Proficient
SOURCE: New York State Education Department

public schools housed in the same thirteen buildings with them, *only three* had a majority of their students in any grade level scoring at "proficient" and above.

Among the Success Academy charter school students in nine of the grade levels, there was a majority of students scoring *in Level 4 alone*— above "proficient"— on the English Language Arts test. These majorities ranged from 53 percent to 85 percent. In *none* of the 36 grade levels in the traditional public schools in the same thirteen buildings was there a majority of students scoring in Level 4. Among the traditional public schools, the highest percentage reaching Level 4 was 28 percent of fourth-graders in P.S. 138 in Brooklyn. Its general record on the English Language Arts test was good in the third, fourth and fifth grades, where a majority of its students scored at the "proficient" Level 3 or above. (Details in Table 2A)

Low Scores in English

Among students scoring down at the bottom in Level 1, on the English test, there were *zero percent* of Success Academy charter school students scoring that low in 26 of their 30 grade levels. The highest proportion scoring that low, among the remaining 4 grade levels of Success Academy students, was 5 percent. Among the 36 grade levels in the traditional public schools housed in the same buildings, the lowest percentage of students scoring at the bottom in Level 1 was 4 percent and the highest was 52 percent.

High Scores in Mathematics

On the statewide mathematics test, a majority of the Success Academy charter school students in all grade levels in all thirteen buildings scored at the "proficient" level or above. Indeed, a majority of these Success Academy students scored in Level 4 alone (above "proficient") in mathematics *in every grade level*. These majorities scoring in Level 4 in mathematics ranged from 71 percent to 99 percent.

Among the traditional public schools in the same thirteen buildings, just four grade levels out of thirty had a majority of their students scoring at the "proficient" level or above. None had a majority scoring at Level 4. The highest proportion of traditional public school students scoring at Level 4 was, in mathematics as in English, in P.S. 138 in Brooklyn, where 31 percent of its fourth-graders scored that high in school year 2017–2018.

Low Scores in Mathematics

Turning to the students who scored at the bottom, in Level 1 on the 2017–2018 mathematics test, in every grade level in all thirteen buildings the proportion of students in traditional public schools exceeded the proportion of Success Academy students who scored that low. In 22 of 26 grade levels, *zero percent* of Success Academy students scored at that low level in mathematics. Meanwhile, the proportion of traditional public school students scoring that low ranged from 4 percent to 74 percent. Among Success Academy charter school students in these same thirteen buildings, the highest proportion scoring at the bottom in Level 1 on the mathematics test was 3 percent in one grade level in one school. (Details in Table 2B)

At the bottom, as at the top, an exception among the traditional public schools was P.S. 138 in Brooklyn. Among its third-graders, fourth-graders and fifth-graders, the students scoring down in Level 1 were 11 percent, 4 percent and 15 percent, respectively, though 27 percent of its sixth-graders scored that low.

Conclusion

The educational outcomes in the Success Academy charter schools and in the traditional public schools housed with them in the same thirteen buildings can be readily summarized: Success Academy charter schools have had an overwhelmingly higher rate of educational success in tests of both English and mathematics. Among the traditional public schools, P.S. 138 in Brooklyn had a creditable record in both English and mathematics, though not in the same league with Success Academy charter schools. Back in 2013, a higher percentage of the fifth-graders in a Success Academy charter school in Harlem passed the New York State Mathematics examination than any other public

TABLE 2B: NEW YORK STATE MATHEMATICS TEST RESULTS, 2017–2018

SCHOOLS HOUSED TOGETHER	CLASS GRADE LEVEL	LEVEL 1 RESULTS (Percent)	LEVEL 2 RESULTS (Percent)	LEVEL 3 RESULTS (Percent)	LEVEL 4 RESULTS (Percent)
BENJAMIN FRANKLIN SCHOOL	3rd grade	24	25	28	22
Success Academy charter school	3rd grade	0	1	27	72
BENJAMIN FRANKLIN SCHOOL	4th grade	35	37	18	9
Success Academy charter school	4th grade	0	1	3	96
BRONX WRITING ACADEMY	6th grade	44	23	25	8
Jordan L. Mott Junior High School	6th grade	46	34	17	2
Success Academy charter school	6th grade	0	0	2	98
BRONX WRITING ACADEMY	7th grade	51	32	13	4
Jordan L. Mott Junior High School	7th grade	67	26	6	1
Success Academy charter school	7th grade	0	0	2	98
CROWN ELEMENTARY SCHOOL	3rd grade	41	24	27	8
Success Academy charter school	3rd grade	0	0	8	92
CROWN ELEMENTARY SCHOOL	4th grade	36	34	16	13
Success Academy charter school	4th grade	0	1	5	94

Performance Levels: Level 1: Well Below Proficient   Level 2: Below Proficient   Level 3: Proficient   Level 4: Above Proficient
SOURCE: New York State Education Department

TABLE 2B: MATHEMATICS (continued)

SCHOOLS HOUSED TOGETHER	CLASS GRADE LEVEL	LEVEL 1 RESULTS (Percent)	LEVEL 2 RESULTS (Percent)	LEVEL 3 RESULTS (Percent)	LEVEL 4 RESULTS (Percent)
FREDERICK DOUGLASS ACADEMY II	6th grade	50	30	20	0
Wadleigh Performing and Visual Arts	6th grade	40	36	20	4
Success Academy charter school	6th grade	0	0	22	78
FREDERICK DOUGLASS ACADEMY II	7th grade	44	25	19	13
Wadleigh Performing and Visual Arts	7th grade	40	40	15	5
Success Academy charter school	7th grade	2	2	9	88
HENRY H. GARNET SCHOOL	5th grade	62	20	15	4
Success Academy charter school	5th grade	0	1	20	79
HERNANDEZ/HUGHES SCHOOL	3rd grade	29	26	29	17
Success Academy charter school	3rd grade	1	0	3	96
HERNANDEZ/HUGHES SCHOOL	4th grade	29	39	26	6
Success Academy charter school	4th grade	0	0	11	89
MAHALIA JACKSON SCHOOL	3rd grade	54	33	7	6
Success Academy charter school	3rd grade	0	0	21	79
MAHALIA JACKSON SCHOOL	4th grade	38	31	25	6
Success Academy charter school	4th grade	0	5	19	76
MOSAIC PREPARATORY ACADEMY	5th grade	41	32	19	8
Success Academy charter school	5th grade	3	3	17	77

Performance Levels: Level 1: Well Below Proficient   Level 2: Below Proficient   Level 3: Proficient   Level 4: Above Proficient
SOURCE: New York State Education Department

TABLE 2B: MATHEMATICS (continued)

SCHOOLS HOUSED TOGETHER	CLASS GRADE LEVEL	LEVEL 1 RESULTS (Percent)	LEVEL 2 RESULTS (Percent)	LEVEL 3 RESULTS (Percent)	LEVEL 4 RESULTS (Percent)
PS 138 BROOKLYN	3rd grade	11	9	53	27
Success Academy charter school	3rd grade	0	2	27	71
PS 138 BROOKLYN	4th grade	4	28	37	31
Success Academy charter school	4th grade	0	4	15	81
PS 138 BROOKLYN	5th grade	15	35	35	16
Success Academy charter school	5th grade	0	1	14	85
PS 138 BROOKLYN	6th grade	27	29	26	19
Success Academy charter school	6th grade	0	5	9	86
STEM INSTITUTE OF MANHATTAN	3rd grade	57	22	22	0
Success Academy charter school	3rd grade	0	0	5	95
STEM INSTITUTE OF MANHATTAN	4th grade	43	32	18	7
Success Academy charter school	4th grade	0	0	1	99
URBAN ASSEMBLY ACADEMY FOR FUTURE LEADERS	6th grade	74	21	6	0
Success Academy charter school	6th grade	0	0	2	98
URBAN ASSEMBLY ACADEMY FOR FUTURE LEADERS	7th grade	64	22	15	0
Success Academy charter school	7th grade	0	0	20	80

Performance Levels: Level 1: Well Below Proficient   Level 2: Below Proficient   Level 3: Proficient   Level 4: Above Proficient
SOURCE: New York State Education Department

TABLE 2B: MATHEMATICS (continued)

SCHOOLS HOUSED TOGETHER	CLASS GRADE LEVEL	LEVEL 1 RESULTS (Percent)	LEVEL 2 RESULTS (Percent)	LEVEL 3 RESULTS (Percent)	LEVEL 4 RESULTS (Percent)
URBAN ASSEMBLY BRONX ACADEMY OF LETTERS	6th grade	70	23	5	3
Success Academy charter school	6th grade	0	1	13	86
URBAN ASSEMBLY BRONX ACADEMY OF LETTERS	7th grade	63	24	9	3
Success Academy charter school	7th grade	0	0	12	88
WILLIAM FLOYD SCHOOL	3rd grade	26	15	45	15
Success Academy charter school	3rd grade	1	3	19	77
WILLIAM FLOYD SCHOOL	4th grade	40	43	14	2
Success Academy charter school	4th grade	0	0	6	94

Performance Levels: Level 1: Well Below Proficient   Level 2: Below Proficient   Level 3: Proficient   Level 4: Above Proficient
SOURCE: New York State Education Department

school fifth-graders in the entire state of New York. This included, as the *New York Times* put it, "even their counterparts in the whitest and richest suburbs, Scarsdale and Briarcliff Manor."[7]

EXPLORE SCHOOLS CHARTER SCHOOLS

There were six buildings in which charter schools in the Explore Schools network were housed with traditional public schools in 2017–2018. There were 20 grade levels in these six buildings that these charter schools and traditional public schools had in common. At least 90 percent of the students in the Explore Schools charter schools in these six buildings were either black or Hispanic, as were 90 percent or more of the traditional public school students in four of these six buildings. In the other two buildings, 86 percent of the traditional public school students in our sample were either black or Hispanic. A majority of the students in both kinds of schools were classified as "economically disadvantaged" by the New York State Education Department.[8]

High Scores in English
On the English Language Arts test in school year 2017–2018, the charter schools in the Explore Schools network had a majority of their students reach the "proficient" level or above in only four of the 20 grade levels in these buildings. The traditional public schools housed with them had a majority of their students reach levels of "proficient" or above in only two of their 20 grade levels on that same test.

Low Scores in English
Among students scoring down at the bottom, in Level 1, on the English Language Arts test, the range for the Explore Schools students was from 2 percent to 43 percent. Among the various traditional public schools in the same buildings, their students' range was from 3 percent to 77 percent. (Details in Table 3A)

TABLE 3A: NEW YORK STATE ENGLISH LANGUAGE ARTS TEST RESULTS, 2017–2018

SCHOOLS HOUSED TOGETHER	CLASS GRADE LEVEL	LEVEL 1 RESULTS (Percent)	LEVEL 2 RESULTS (Percent)	LEVEL 3 RESULTS (Percent)	LEVEL 4 RESULTS (Percent)
BROOKLYN ARTS AND SCIENCE ELEMENTARY SCHOOL	3rd grade	15	54	28	2
Explore Schools charter school	3rd grade	26	26	44	4
BROOKLYN ARTS AND SCIENCE ELEMENTARY SCHOOL	4th grade	40	30	18	12
Explore Schools charter school	4th grade	31	39	20	9
BROOKLYN ARTS AND SCIENCE ELEMENTARY SCHOOL	5th grade	62	23	15	0
Explore Schools charter school	5th grade	43	21	20	16
EBBETS FIELD MIDDLE SCHOOL	6th grade	77	10	10	3
Explore Schools charter school	6th grade	38	44	10	8
EBBETS FIELD MIDDLE SCHOOL	7th grade	48	27	20	5
Explore Schools charter school	7th grade	22	36	38	4
EBBETS FIELD MIDDLE SCHOOL	8th grade	35	33	23	9
Explore Schools charter school	8th grade	2	43	40	15
ISAAC BILDERSEE JUNIOR HIGH SCHOOL	6th grade	52	28	12	8
Explore Schools charter school	6th grade	33	21	20	26
ISAAC BILDERSEE JUNIOR HIGH SCHOOL	7th grade	45	36	16	3
Explore Schools charter school	7th grade	22	49	22	7
ISAAC BILDERSEE JUNIOR HIGH SCHOOL	8th grade	24	57	12	7
Explore Schools charter school	8th grade	12	41	36	12

Performance Levels: Level 1: Well Below Proficient Level 2: Below Proficient Level 3: Proficient Level 4: Above Proficient
SOURCE: New York State Education Department

TABLE 3A: ENGLISH LANGUAGE ARTS (continued)

SCHOOLS HOUSED TOGETHER	CLASS GRADE LEVEL	LEVEL 1 RESULTS (Percent)	LEVEL 2 RESULTS (Percent)	LEVEL 3 RESULTS (Percent)	LEVEL 4 RESULTS (Percent)
MS 394 SCHOOL	3rd grade	13	58	29	0
Explore Schools charter school	3rd grade	21	39	37	4
MS 394 SCHOOL	4th grade	35	29	21	15
Explore Schools charter school	4th grade	15	36	40	9
MS 394 SCHOOL	5th grade	34	45	15	6
Explore Schools charter school	5th grade	23	42	22	13
MS 394 SCHOOL	6th grade	48	22	12	18
Explore Schools charter school	6th grade	31	29	19	21
MS 394 SCHOOL	7th grade	22	30	40	8
Explore Schools charter school	7th grade	27	43	25	4
MS 394 SCHOOL	8th grade	14	42	22	22
Explore Schools charter school	8th grade	15	37	41	7
PARKSIDE PREPARATORY ACADEMY	6th grade	42	20	25	13
Explore Schools charter school	6th grade	28	30	25	18
PARKSIDE PREPARATORY ACADEMY	7th grade	26	34	27	13
Explore Schools charter school	7th grade	24	35	33	7
PARKSIDE PREPARATORY ACADEMY	8th grade	13	31	33	24
Explore Schools charter school	8th grade	2	39	46	14
RYDER ELEMENTARY SCHOOL	3rd grade	21	37	43	0
Explore Schools charter school	3rd grade	3	36	50	10
RYDER ELEMENTARY SCHOOL	4th grade	3	39	34	23
Explore Schools charter school	4th grade	5	33	36	26

Performance Levels: Level 1: Well Below Proficient Level 2: Below Proficient Level 3: Proficient Level 4: Above Proficient
SOURCE: New York State Education Department

Whether measured by test scores at the top or at the bottom, these are disappointing outcomes for both kinds of schools. Not all charter schools are educationally successful. But the painful fact is that even those charter schools whose outcomes are disappointing often nevertheless do better than the traditional public schools housed with them in the same buildings.

High Scores in Mathematics

On the New York State Mathematics test given in 2017–2018, a majority of the charter school students in the Explore Schools network reached the "proficient" level or above in just 6 of their 20 grade levels, though they reached 50 percent in two other grade levels. Students in the various traditional public schools housed in the same buildings did even worse on the mathematics test than on the English Language Arts test. *None* of their 20 grade levels in these six buildings had a majority of the traditional public school students achieving "proficiency" in mathematics. Their highest proportion reaching the "proficient" level or above in mathematics was 39 percent. (Table 3B)

In a few grade levels the Explore Schools students did well on the mathematics test. In five grade levels, from 60 percent to 86 percent of these charter school students scored at the "proficient" level or above.

Low Scores in Mathematics

Among the students scoring down at the bottom, in Level 1, on the New York State Education Department's Mathematics test, the range for the Explore Schools students was from 3 percent to 55 percent. Among the traditional public school students in the same buildings, the proportion of those scoring down at the bottom ranged from 23 percent to 68 percent. While there was only one grade level in which more than half the Explore Schools students scored at the bottom, in Level 1, more than half of the traditional public school students in the same buildings scored down in Level 1 in 10 of their 20 grade levels.

There were some grade levels in some Explore Schools where the charter school students did well. In 7 of their 20 grade levels, less than 20 percent of the Explore Schools students scored at the bottom in

TABLE 3B: NEW YORK STATE MATHEMATICS TEST RESULTS, 2017–2018

SCHOOLS HOUSED TOGETHER	CLASS GRADE LEVEL	LEVEL 1 RESULTS (Percent)	LEVEL 2 RESULTS (Percent)	LEVEL 3 RESULTS (Percent)	LEVEL 4 RESULTS (Percent)
BROOKLYN ARTS AND SCIENCE ELEMENTARY SCHOOL	3rd grade	55	23	15	6
Explore Schools charter school	3rd grade	33	17	35	15
BROOKLYN ARTS AND SCIENCE ELEMENTARY SCHOOL	4th grade	66	22	10	2
Explore Schools charter school	4th grade	33	26	19	22
BROOKLYN ARTS AND SCIENCE ELEMENTARY SCHOOL	5th grade	68	27	2	2
Explore Schools charter school	5th grade	48	21	18	13
EBBETS FIELD MIDDLE SCHOOL	6th grade	63	15	17	5
Explore Schools charter school	6th grade	24	44	22	9
EBBETS FIELD MIDDLE SCHOOL	7th grade	57	28	13	2
Explore Schools charter school	7th grade	18	32	36	14
EBBETS FIELD MIDDLE SCHOOL	8th grade	44	16	23	16
Explore Schools charter school	8th grade	13	27	48	12
ISAAC BILDERSEE JUNIOR HIGH SCHOOL	6th grade	60	19	15	6
Explore Schools charter school	6th grade	55	17	20	9
ISAAC BILDERSEE JUNIOR HIGH SCHOOL	7th grade	49	32	17	3
Explore Schools charter school	7th grade	37	28	28	7
ISAAC BILDERSEE JUNIOR HIGH SCHOOL	8th grade	45	42	10	3
Explore Schools charter school	8th grade	46	32	17	5

Performance Levels: Level 1: Well Below Proficient Level 2: Below Proficient Level 3: Proficient Level 4: Above Proficient
SOURCE: New York State Education Department

TABLE 3B: MATHEMATICS (continued)

SCHOOLS HOUSED TOGETHER	CLASS GRADE LEVEL	LEVEL 1 RESULTS (Percent)	LEVEL 2 RESULTS (Percent)	LEVEL 3 RESULTS (Percent)	LEVEL 4 RESULTS (Percent)
MS 394 SCHOOL	3rd grade	36	36	24	3
Explore Schools charter school	3rd grade	26	23	37	14
MS 394 SCHOOL	4th grade	44	26	18	12
Explore Schools charter school	4th grade	32	34	19	15
MS 394 SCHOOL	5th grade	57	32	8	4
Explore Schools charter school	5th grade	46	24	19	12
MS 394 SCHOOL	6th grade	67	24	4	6
Explore Schools charter school	6th grade	35	33	15	17
MS 394 SCHOOL	7th grade	59	24	14	2
Explore Schools charter school	7th grade	27	31	18	24
MS 394 SCHOOL	8th grade	33	35	15	17
Explore Schools charter school	8th grade	28	33	20	19
PARKSIDE PREPARATORY ACADEMY	6th grade	45	35	12	7
Explore Schools charter school	6th grade	14	25	39	23
PARKSIDE PREPARATORY ACADEMY	7th grade	53	26	16	4
Explore Schools charter school	7th grade	17	35	24	24
PARKSIDE PREPARATORY ACADEMY	8th grade	46	28	21	5
Explore Schools charter school	8th grade	7	33	30	30
RYDER ELEMENTARY SCHOOL	3rd grade	49	34	16	0
Explore Schools charter school	3rd grade	3	10	37	49
RYDER ELEMENTARY SCHOOL	4th grade	23	39	17	21
Explore Schools charter school	4th grade	9	22	22	47

Performance Levels: Level 1: Well Below Proficient   Level 2: Below Proficient   Level 3: Proficient   Level 4: Above Proficient
SOURCE: New York State Education Department

Level 1. That includes 3 grade levels where the percentages were in single digits. But there was nothing comparable in any of the traditional public schools housed in the same buildings.

Conclusion

By and large, in these six buildings, both the charter school students from the Explore Schools network and students from the various traditional public schools housed with them in these same buildings, failed to achieve "proficiency"— as defined by the New York State Education Department— in most of the grade levels, on both the English test and the mathematics test. Although this performance was well below that of the other four New York City charter school networks examined in this chapter, nevertheless a higher proportion of Explore Schools students achieved "proficiency" in more grade levels than did students in the traditional public schools housed with them in the same buildings.

This painful situation suggests the grim alternatives available for students in some low-income minority neighborhoods.

UNCOMMON SCHOOLS CHARTER SCHOOLS

The Uncommon Schools network of charter schools is not confined to New York City, but that is where they have had their most classes housed in the same buildings with traditional public school classes at the same grade levels. In school year 2017–2018, there were ten such buildings in New York City with classes at the same grade levels in both the Uncommon Schools charter schools and in one or more traditional public schools. It so happened that all of these schools were located in the borough of Brooklyn.

As for the ethnic composition of the students in the Uncommon Schools charter school samples in the ten buildings where they were housed together with traditional public schools, more than 90 percent of the students in both kinds of schools were either black or Hispanic in school year 2017–2018. A majority of both the Uncommon Schools

TABLE 4A: NEW YORK STATE ENGLISH LANGUAGE ARTS TEST RESULTS, 2017–2018

SCHOOLS HOUSED TOGETHER	CLASS GRADE LEVEL	LEVEL 1 RESULTS (Percent)	LEVEL 2 RESULTS (Percent)	LEVEL 3 RESULTS (Percent)	LEVEL 4 RESULTS (Percent)
CHRISTOPHER AVENUE COMMUNITY SCHOOL	3rd grade	22	35	41	3
Uncommon Schools charter school	3rd grade	1	14	68	17
CHRISTOPHER AVENUE COMMUNITY SCHOOL	4th grade	11	54	29	7
Uncommon Schools charter school	4th grade	2	18	39	41
CHRISTOPHER AVENUE COMMUNITY SCHOOL	5th grade	58	25	13	4
Uncommon Schools charter school	5th grade	12	37	28	23
CHRISTOPHER ELEMENTARY SCHOOL	5th grade	67	21	8	4
Uncommon Schools charter school	5th grade	36	30	23	11
EAGLE ACADEMY FOR YOUNG MEN II	6th grade	51	32	11	7
Mott Hall IV	6th grade	38	38	19	6
Uncommon Schools charter school	6th grade	17	26	25	32
EAGLE ACADEMY FOR YOUNG MEN II	7th grade	27	50	22	1
Mott Hall IV	7th grade	23	50	20	8
Uncommon Schools charter school	7th grade	16	35	35	13
EAGLE ACADEMY FOR YOUNG MEN II	8th grade	27	47	25	2
Mott Hall IV	8th grade	20	54	15	11
Uncommon Schools charter school	8th grade	12	31	43	14

Performance Levels: Level 1: Well Below Proficient   Level 2: Below Proficient   Level 3: Proficient   Level 4: Above Proficient
SOURCE: New York State Education Department

TABLE 4A: ENGLISH LANGUAGE ARTS (continued)

SCHOOLS HOUSED TOGETHER	CLASS GRADE LEVEL	LEVEL 1 RESULTS (Percent)	LEVEL 2 RESULTS (Percent)	LEVEL 3 RESULTS (Percent)	LEVEL 4 RESULTS (Percent)
GEORGE E. WIBECAN PREPARATORY ACADEMY	3rd grade	42	37	18	3
Uncommon Schools charter school	3rd grade	2	18	63	17
GEORGE E. WIBECAN PREPARATORY ACADEMY	4th grade	48	33	14	5
Uncommon Schools charter school	4th grade	1	11	40	47
GREGORY JOCKO JACKSON SCHOOL	5th grade	44	32	22	2
Uncommon Schools charter school	5th grade	24	30	27	18
GREGORY JOCKO JACKSON SCHOOL	6th grade	53	22	20	5
Uncommon Schools charter school	6th grade	12	33	36	19
GREGORY JOCKO JACKSON SCHOOL	7th grade	48	35	11	7
Uncommon Schools charter school	7th grade	12	44	33	10
GREGORY JOCKO JACKSON SCHOOL	8th grade	36	43	17	4
Uncommon Schools charter school	8th grade	8	30	46	16
HERMAN SCHREIBER SCHOOL	5th grade	31	29	22	17
Uncommon Schools charter school	5th grade	28	42	24	6
LEONARD DUNKLY SCHOOL	5th grade	41	50	6	3
Uncommon Schools charter school	5th grade	25	44	25	7

Performance Levels:　Level 1:　Well Below Proficient　Level 2:　Below Proficient　Level 3:　Proficient　Level 4:　Above Proficient
SOURCE: New York State Education Department

TABLE 4A: ENGLISH LANGUAGE ARTS (continued)

SCHOOLS HOUSED TOGETHER	CLASS GRADE LEVEL	LEVEL 1 RESULTS (Percent)	LEVEL 2 RESULTS (Percent)	LEVEL 3 RESULTS (Percent)	LEVEL 4 RESULTS (Percent)
MATH, SCIENCE & TECHNOLOGY MIDDLE SCHOOL	6th grade	44	34	13	9
Uncommon Schools charter school	6th grade	16	30	26	28
MATH, SCIENCE & TECHNOLOGY MIDDLE SCHOOL	7th grade	32	33	22	13
Uncommon Schools charter school	7th grade	13	29	46	12
MATH, SCIENCE & TECHNOLOGY MIDDLE SCHOOL	8th grade	18	40	28	13
Uncommon Schools charter school	8th grade	3	38	41	17
MIDDLE SCHOOL FOR ART AND PHILOSOPHY	6th grade	35	39	9	18
Uncommon Schools charter school	6th grade	11	26	33	30
MIDDLE SCHOOL FOR ART AND PHILOSOPHY	7th grade	41	29	28	2
Uncommon Schools charter school	7th grade	18	38	40	5
MIDDLE SCHOOL FOR ART AND PHILOSOPHY	8th grade	18	43	28	11
Uncommon Schools charter school	8th grade	10	38	32	20
PAUL ROBESON SCHOOL	5th grade	39	44	11	6
Uncommon Schools charter school	5th grade	9	32	28	31

Performance Levels: Level 1: Well Below Proficient   Level 2: Below Proficient   Level 3: Proficient   Level 4: Above Proficient
SOURCE: New York State Education Department

students and the students in traditional public schools housed with them were classified as "economically disadvantaged" by the New York State Education Department.

High Scores in English

On the English Language Arts test in 2017–2018, a majority of the charter school students in the Uncommon Schools network scored at the "proficient" and above levels in 15 of their 22 grade levels. Among the various traditional public schools in the same buildings, at *none* of their 25 grade levels did a majority of the students reach "proficient" or above on the English test. The proportion of students in these traditional public schools who reached the levels of "proficient" or above ranged from 9 percent to 44 percent. (Table 4A)

Low Scores in English

Among students who scored down at the bottom in Level 1 on the English Language Arts examination, in every grade level the proportion of students in these various traditional public schools exceeded the proportion of students in the Uncommon Schools charter schools who scored that low. The smallest difference was between 31 percent of the fifth-graders in a traditional public school and 28 percent of the Uncommon Schools fifth-graders in the same building. The largest difference was between the 48 percent of fourth-graders in one traditional public school class who scored in Level 1 and the 1 percent of Uncommon Schools fourth-graders who scored that low in the same building.

High Scores in Mathematics

On the New York State Mathematics test in 2017–2018, a majority of the charter school students in the Uncommon Schools network scored at "proficient" and above in 13 of the 18 grade levels in the ten buildings that they shared with traditional public school students. In three of those grade levels, a majority of the Uncommon Schools students scored at the top, in Level 4 alone. Among students in the various traditional public schools housed in the same buildings, in

TABLE 4B: NEW YORK STATE MATHEMATICS TEST RESULTS, 2017–2018

SCHOOLS HOUSED TOGETHER	CLASS GRADE LEVEL	LEVEL 1 RESULTS (Percent)	LEVEL 2 RESULTS (Percent)	LEVEL 3 RESULTS (Percent)	LEVEL 4 RESULTS (Percent)
CHRISTOPHER AVENUE COMMUNITY SCHOOL	3rd grade	29	26	29	16
Uncommon Schools charter school	3rd grade	3	7	31	59
CHRISTOPHER AVENUE COMMUNITY SCHOOL	4th grade	29	39	14	18
Uncommon Schools charter school	4th grade	0	9	25	66
CHRISTOPHER AVENUE COMMUNITY SCHOOL	5th grade	54	33	8	4
Uncommon Schools charter school	5th grade	10	22	35	33
CHRISTOPHER ELEMENTARY SCHOOL	5th grade	76	20	4	0
Uncommon Schools charter school	5th grade	39	15	27	19
EAGLE ACADEMY FOR YOUNG MEN II	6th grade	34	29	27	10
Mott Hall IV	6th grade	68	29	3	0
Uncommon Schools charter school	6th grade	15	24	24	37
EAGLE ACADEMY FOR YOUNG MEN II	7th grade	22	42	23	14
Mott Hall IV	7th grade	55	35	10	0
Uncommon Schools charter school	7th grade	13	20	29	38

Performance Levels: Level 1: Well Below Proficient Level 2: Below Proficient Level 3: Proficient Level 4: Above Proficient
SOURCE: New York State Education Department

TABLE 4B: MATHEMATICS (continued)

SCHOOLS HOUSED TOGETHER	CLASS GRADE LEVEL	LEVEL 1 RESULTS (Percent)	LEVEL 2 RESULTS (Percent)	LEVEL 3 RESULTS (Percent)	LEVEL 4 RESULTS (Percent)
GEORGE E. WIBECAN PREPARATORY ACADEMY	3rd grade	62	24	11	3
Uncommon Schools charter school	3rd grade	3	13	37	47
GEORGE E. WIBECAN PREPARATORY ACADEMY	4th grade	57	29	14	0
Uncommon Schools charter school	4th grade	7	6	31	57
GREGORY JOCKO JACKSON SCHOOL	5th grade	51	33	8	8
Uncommon Schools charter school	5th grade	32	21	30	17
GREGORY JOCKO JACKSON SCHOOL	6th grade	56	34	8	2
Uncommon Schools charter school	6th grade	12	24	39	26
GREGORY JOCKO JACKSON SCHOOL	7th grade	63	26	7	4
Uncommon Schools charter school	7th grade	9	19	33	39
HERMAN SCHREIBER SCHOOL	5th grade	29	21	22	28
Uncommon Schools charter school	5th grade	37	29	27	7
LEONARD DUNKLY SCHOOL	5th grade	45	36	15	3
Uncommon Schools charter school	5th grade	28	33	21	18

Performance Levels: Level 1: Well Below Proficient Level 2: Below Proficient Level 3: Proficient Level 4: Above Proficient
SOURCE: New York State Education Department

TABLE 4B: MATHEMATICS (continued)

SCHOOLS HOUSED TOGETHER	CLASS GRADE LEVEL	LEVEL 1 RESULTS (Percent)	LEVEL 2 RESULTS (Percent)	LEVEL 3 RESULTS (Percent)	LEVEL 4 RESULTS (Percent)
MATH, SCIENCE & TECHNOLOGY MIDDLE SCHOOL	6th grade	51	28	13	8
Uncommon Schools charter school	6th grade	10	36	31	23
MATH, SCIENCE & TECHNOLOGY MIDDLE SCHOOL	7th grade	36	38	23	4
Uncommon Schools charter school	7th grade	15	18	27	40
MIDDLE SCHOOL FOR ART AND PHILOSOPHY	6th grade	50	36	12	2
Uncommon Schools charter school	6th grade	26	35	23	16
MIDDLE SCHOOL FOR ART AND PHILOSOPHY	7th grade	66	26	9	0
Uncommon Schools charter school	7th grade	13	33	25	29
PAUL ROBESON SCHOOL	5th grade	44	39	11	6
Uncommon Schools charter school	5th grade	14	18	40	28

Performance Levels: Level 1: Well Below Proficient Level 2: Below Proficient Level 3: Proficient Level 4: Above Proficient
SOURCE: New York State Education Department

no grade level did a majority score as high as "proficient" or above. However, 50 percent of the fifth-graders in one traditional public school scored either "proficient" or above "proficient." (Table 4B)

Low Scores in Mathematics

Among students scoring down at the bottom in Level 1 on the mathematics test, in 17 of the 18 grade levels in which Uncommon Schools students were housed in a building with traditional public school students at the same grade level, the traditional public school students had a higher percentage of their students scoring that low. In most cases, the percentage of traditional public school students who scored in Level 1 was some multiple— as high as 62 to 3— of the percentage of Uncommon Schools students who scored that low. In the one instance where the traditional public school had a lower percentage of its students scoring at the bottom in Level 1 than did its Uncommon Schools student neighbors, the difference was small— 29 percent versus 37 percent.

Conclusion

The overall performance of charter school students in the Uncommon Schools network was substantially better than that of most of the students in most of the traditional public schools housed with them in the ten buildings they shared. In the lone exception, the Herman Schreiber School in Brooklyn had a higher percentage of its fifth-graders score at the "proficient" Level 3 and above— on both the English test and the mathematics test— than the charter school fifth-graders in the same building. But this was a clear exception to the general pattern.

ACHIEVEMENT FIRST CHARTER SCHOOLS

In school year 2017–2018, there were seven buildings in which Achievement First charter schools were housed with traditional public schools having classes at the same grade levels. As with the Uncommon Schools charter schools, these particular buildings were all in New York City's borough of Brooklyn.

As for the ethnic makeup of the students, this usually varied little between the Achievement First charter school students and the traditional public school students housed in the same buildings and taking classes at the same grade levels. Black and Hispanic students combined ranged from 94 percent to 99 percent of the students in our sample from the Achievement First charter schools in these seven buildings.

In five of the seven buildings, more than 90 percent of the students in traditional public school classes in our sample were either black or Hispanic, while in the two other buildings, the proportions were 79 percent and 86 percent, respectively. In both of these latter cases, Asian students were 17 percent and 12 percent, respectively. Whites were not as much as 5 percent of the students sampled in any of these particular classes in these schools.

A majority of these students in both kinds of schools that were housed together were classified as "economically disadvantaged" by the New York State Education Department.[9]

High Scores in English

On the English Language Arts test in 2017–2018, a majority of the Achievement First charter school students scored at the "proficient" or above levels in 17 of the 18 grade levels in the seven buildings they shared with traditional public school students at the same grade levels. Among the traditional public school students, there were just 4 grade levels out of 18 where a majority of the students scored at the "proficient" level or above in English. All 4 of these grade levels were in the same school, the Philippa Schuyler Junior High School in Brooklyn. This school's record on this test was comparable to the records of the more successful charter schools. Its majorities scoring at "proficient" or above ranged from 54 percent to 72 percent. (Table 5A)

One other traditional public school had test results similar to those of the Achievement First charter school housed in the same

TABLE 5A: NEW YORK STATE ENGLISH LANGUAGE ARTS TEST RESULTS, 2017–2018

SCHOOLS HOUSED TOGETHER	CLASS GRADE LEVEL	LEVEL 1 RESULTS (Percent)	LEVEL 2 RESULTS (Percent)	LEVEL 3 RESULTS (Percent)	LEVEL 4 RESULTS (Percent)
ADRIAN HEGEMAN SCHOOL	5th grade	49	22	21	8
Achievement First charter school	5th grade	39	35	18	8
ALEJANDRINA B. DE GAUTIER SCHOOL	3rd grade	19	63	19	0
Achievement First charter school	3rd grade	12	24	51	13
ALEJANDRINA B. DE GAUTIER SCHOOL	4th grade	46	34	17	3
Achievement First charter school	4th grade	3	19	55	23
ERNEST S. JENKYNS SCHOOL	3rd grade	36	35	26	3
Achievement First charter school	3rd grade	9	24	58	9
ERNEST S. JENKYNS SCHOOL	4th grade	28	51	18	4
Achievement First charter school	4th grade	4	33	43	20
ERNEST S. JENKYNS SCHOOL	5th grade	74	21	4	1
Achievement First charter school	5th grade	13	28	36	23
MARGARET S. DOUGLAS JUNIOR HIGH SCHOOL	6th grade	45	23	13	19
Achievement First charter school	6th grade	3	21	39	36
MARGARET S. DOUGLAS JUNIOR HIGH SCHOOL	7th grade	50	29	11	10
Achievement First charter school	7th grade	5	27	58	10
MARGARET S. DOUGLAS JUNIOR HIGH SCHOOL	8th grade	17	34	24	25
Achievement First charter school	8th grade	0	11	45	45

Performance Levels: Level 1: Well Below Proficient   Level 2: Below Proficient   Level 3: Proficient   Level 4: Above Proficient
SOURCE: New York State Education Department

TABLE 5A: ENGLISH LANGUAGE ARTS (continued)

SCHOOLS HOUSED TOGETHER	CLASS GRADE LEVEL	LEVEL 1 RESULTS (Percent)	LEVEL 2 RESULTS (Percent)	LEVEL 3 RESULTS (Percent)	LEVEL 4 RESULTS (Percent)
NEW HEIGHTS MIDDLE SCHOOL	6th grade	46	29	13	12
Achievement First charter school	6th grade	6	24	35	34
NEW HEIGHTS MIDDLE SCHOOL	7th grade	44	33	19	5
Achievement First charter school	7th grade	10	34	52	4
NEW HEIGHTS MIDDLE SCHOOL	8th grade	28	52	11	8
Achievement First charter school	8th grade	4	26	35	35
PHILIPPA SCHUYLER JUNIOR HIGH SCHOOL	5th grade	16	21	39	24
Achievement First charter school	5th grade	8	34	38	20
PHILIPPA SCHUYLER JUNIOR HIGH SCHOOL	6th grade	11	17	34	38
Achievement First charter school	6th grade	6	18	24	52
PHILIPPA SCHUYLER JUNIOR HIGH SCHOOL	7th grade	12	33	45	9
Achievement First charter school	7th grade	0	19	58	23
PHILIPPA SCHUYLER JUNIOR HIGH SCHOOL	8th grade	5	23	41	30
Achievement First charter school	8th grade	0	8	47	46
ROBERTO CLEMENTE SCHOOL	3rd grade	43	28	28	1
Achievement First charter school	3rd grade	2	17	58	23
ROBERTO CLEMENTE SCHOOL	4th grade	26	38	20	16
Achievement First charter school	4th grade	2	22	41	34

Performance Levels: Level 1: Well Below Proficient Level 2: Below Proficient Level 3: Proficient Level 4: Above Proficient
SOURCE: New York State Education Department

building. But they were similar in that neither school had a majority of their students achieve "proficiency." In this case, just 26 percent of the Achievement First fifth-graders in one building scored at the "proficient" level or above, compared to 29 percent of the traditional public school students in that same building.

The more general pattern, however, was one in which the percentage of Achievement First students scoring at the "proficient" level or above was some multiple of the percentage of traditional public school students who did so.

Low Scores in English

In all 18 grade levels that were the same for Achievement First charter students and for students in the traditional public schools housed with them, a higher percentage of the latter scored at the bottom in Level 1 on the English Language Arts test in 2017–2018. The most common pattern was that the percentage of traditional public school students who scored at the bottom in Level 1 was some multiple of the percentage of Achievement First charter school students who did so.

High Scores in Mathematics

On the New York State Education Department's Mathematics test in 2017–2018, a majority of the Achievement First charter school students scored at the "proficient" level or above in 17 of their 18 grade levels. Among the traditional public school students at the same grade levels in the same buildings, there was just one out of 18 grade levels where a majority of those students scored at the "proficient" or above levels. These were fifth-graders in the Philippa Schuyler Junior High School, 76 percent of whom scored at "proficient" or better. (Table 5B)

Achievement First charter school students had the only grade levels where a majority of the students scored at Level 4— above "proficient"— in mathematics. There were six grade levels in four schools where a majority of the Achievement First charter school students scored that high, and these majorities scoring at the top ranged from 55 percent to 80 percent.

TABLE 5B: NEW YORK STATE MATHEMATICS TEST RESULTS, 2017–2018

SCHOOLS HOUSED TOGETHER	CLASS GRADE LEVEL	LEVEL 1 RESULTS (Percent)	LEVEL 2 RESULTS (Percent)	LEVEL 3 RESULTS (Percent)	LEVEL 4 RESULTS (Percent)
ADRIAN HEGEMAN SCHOOL	5th grade	59	22	15	4
Achievement First charter school	5th grade	48	26	18	7
ALEJANDRINA B. DE GAUTIER SCHOOL	3rd grade	25	31	44	0
Achievement First charter school	3rd grade	3	17	29	50
ALEJANDRINA B. DE GAUTIER SCHOOL	4th grade	47	36	8	8
Achievement First charter school	4th grade	2	10	19	68
ERNEST S. JENKYNS SCHOOL	3rd grade	46	27	23	4
Achievement First charter school	3rd grade	6	12	36	47
ERNEST S. JENKYNS SCHOOL	4th grade	41	37	17	5
Achievement First charter school	4th grade	4	30	35	31
ERNEST S. JENKYNS SCHOOL	5th grade	74	22	4	0
Achievement First charter school	5th grade	12	23	33	32
MARGARET S. DOUGLAS JUNIOR HIGH SCHOOL	6th grade	46	26	16	11
Achievement First charter school	6th grade	2	19	49	30
MARGARET S. DOUGLAS JUNIOR HIGH SCHOOL	7th grade	61	18	10	11
Achievement First charter school	7th grade	2	8	26	64
MARGARET S. DOUGLAS JUNIOR HIGH SCHOOL	8th grade	28	30	17	25
Achievement First charter school	8th grade	0	4	41	55

Performance Levels: Level 1: Well Below Proficient Level 2: Below Proficient Level 3: Proficient Level 4: Above Proficient
SOURCE: New York State Education Department

TABLE 5B: MATHEMATICS (continued)

SCHOOLS HOUSED TOGETHER	CLASS GRADE LEVEL	LEVEL 1 RESULTS (Percent)	LEVEL 2 RESULTS (Percent)	LEVEL 3 RESULTS (Percent)	LEVEL 4 RESULTS (Percent)
NEW HEIGHTS MIDDLE SCHOOL	6th grade	54	30	11	5
Achievement First charter school	6th grade	18	31	34	17
NEW HEIGHTS MIDDLE SCHOOL	7th grade	60	24	16	0
Achievement First charter school	7th grade	5	23	39	33
NEW HEIGHTS MIDDLE SCHOOL	8th grade	59	29	13	0
Achievement First charter school	8th grade	8	20	29	44
PHILIPPA SCHUYLER JUNIOR HIGH SCHOOL	5th grade	0	24	42	34
Achievement First charter school	5th grade	0	12	41	47
PHILIPPA SCHUYLER JUNIOR HIGH SCHOOL	6th grade	20	30	37	12
Achievement First charter school	6th grade	6	20	37	36
PHILIPPA SCHUYLER JUNIOR HIGH SCHOOL	7th grade	22	34	32	12
Achievement First charter school	7th grade	1	3	21	74
PHILIPPA SCHUYLER JUNIOR HIGH SCHOOL	8th grade	27	34	25	14
Achievement First charter school	8th grade	0	2	17	80
ROBERTO CLEMENTE SCHOOL	3rd grade	57	16	19	7
Achievement First charter school	3rd grade	0	1	26	73
ROBERTO CLEMENTE SCHOOL	4th grade	38	16	23	23
Achievement First charter school	4th grade	1	27	28	44

Performance Levels: Level 1: Well Below Proficient   Level 2: Below Proficient   Level 3: Proficient   Level 4: Above Proficient
SOURCE: New York State Education Department

Low Scores in Mathematics

In 17 of the 18 grade levels in seven buildings, the percentage of traditional public school students who scored down at the bottom in Level 1 on the statewide mathematics test was larger than the percentage of Achievement First charter school students who did so. In most cases, the percentage of traditional public school students scoring at the bottom was some multiple of the percentage of Achievement First charter school students who did so.

A rare exception were the fifth-graders in the Philippa Schuyler Junior High School, who tied the Achievement First fifth-graders, with zero percent scoring in Level 1 in both schools.

Conclusion

On both the New York State English Language Arts test and the New York State Mathematics test, the Achievement First charter school students did decisively better in five of the seven school buildings where they were housed with traditional public school students. In the other two buildings, the differences were not so pronounced.

OVERVIEW

Going beyond the five charter school networks in New York City, whose students were educated in from five to thirteen buildings with traditional public school students at the same grade levels, there are other charter school networks in New York City whose students were likewise housed with traditional public school students, but in fewer buildings, as well as many individual charter schools that were not part of any network, but whose students were also educated in the same buildings with traditional public school students at the same grade levels. Detailed test score data on all these charter schools can be found in Appendix I, with demographic data in Appendix II and data on "economically disadvantaged" and other special students in Appendix III.

The question here is: To what extent were the patterns seen among the five charter school networks discussed here also found among the much larger number of charter schools in the same circumstances in the city as a whole? When considering all such charter schools in New York City, and comparing their students' test results with the test results of students in traditional public schools located in the same buildings, the patterns turn out to be strikingly similar to what we have already seen in the five charter school networks examined here in some detail.

The 65 charter schools in New York City in 2017–2018 that were located in the same buildings with traditional public schools— each with most of their students either black or Hispanic, and having one or more grade levels in common— had a total of 172 grade levels tested on the New York State English Language Arts test. In 65 percent of those grade levels, a majority of the charter school students scored at the "proficient" level or above. The 72 traditional public schools located in the same buildings had a total of 191 grade levels. In 14 percent of these grade levels, a majority of the students scored at the "proficient" and above levels on the English Language Arts test. In short, the disparity in achieving "proficiency" was nearly five to one.

On the New York State Education Department's Mathematics test, 68 percent of the charter schools' 161 grade levels had a majority of their students scoring at the "proficient" level and above. In the traditional public schools' 177 grade levels, just 10 percent had a majority of their students scoring at the "proficient" level and above. Here the disparity in achieving "proficiency" was nearly seven to one.

In many cases, the disparities in educational outcomes between New York City charter school students and traditional public school students, educated in the same buildings, were greater than the black-white educational differences so widely discussed elsewhere. This may suggest that there are many reasons for educational disparities, and the reasons for these educational outcome differences cannot be reduced to those that are mentioned most often, or most loudly.

In April 2019, for example, the *Wall Street Journal* reported on test results in New York City's charter schools in general and traditional public schools in general— that is, *not* confined to schools located in the same buildings:

The most recent state test results for grades 3–8 show that while the majority of New York students attending traditional public schools are not proficient in either math or English language arts (ELA), a majority of charter school students are.

For New York City, the charter performance is even more impressive when broken down by race. At city charters, 57% of black students and 54% of Hispanic students pass ELA, compared with 52% of white students statewide. It's the same in math, with 59% of black students and 57% of Hispanics at city charters passing, against 54% of white students statewide.[10]

In a realm where educational failure has long been the norm— schools in low-income minority neighborhoods— this is success, a remarkable success. What is equally remarkable is how unwelcome this success has been in many places. What has been especially remarkable is that it has been the most educationally successful charter schools that seem to have drawn the most hostility, both in words and in deeds.

That hostility has come from many individuals and groups, and has taken many forms. One of the most common of these forms has been a simple numerical limit, imposed by law, on the number of charter schools permitted in a given state— *utterly without regard to whether particular charter schools are producing good or bad educational outcomes*. In recent years, there have been increasing efforts to restrict, obstruct and push back the role of charter schools. California produced sweeping anti-charter-school legislation in 2019,[11] and anti-charter-school forces in New York City, among other places, have made similar headway.[12] That is a painfully sad story that needs to be understood, if this door of opportunity for minority youngsters is not to begin to be closed by charter schools' many adversaries.

Chapter 3

HOSTILITY

What reason can there be to be hostile to successful charter schools? Actually, there are millions of reasons— namely, millions of dollars. The 50,000-plus students on waiting lists for admission to charter schools in New York City,[1] where per-pupil expenditures average more than $20,000 a year,[2] represent *more than a billion dollars a year* that could be lost by the traditional public school system in New York City alone, if all the students on those waiting lists were able to get into charter schools. And that is just the initial financial loss in one city during one year.

Substantial declines in the number of students remaining in traditional public schools would also mean fewer teachers employed there, and correspondingly declining union dues, since most charter school teachers do not belong to a teachers union. The sums of money involved in union dues nationwide are billions of dollars.

Schools of education would likewise be affected negatively, if many more students were able to transfer out of traditional public schools, where degrees in education are important for advancement in a teaching career, and go into charter schools, where those degrees mean far less than a teacher's actual performance in educating students.

Although charter schools are a small part of the education sector— educating less than 10 percent of the students in kindergarten through high school nationwide[3]— the threat that they represent to a whole way of life in the much larger traditional public school system is out of proportion to their current size.

Charter schools' rate of growth, over their relatively brief existence since the 1990s, has been much higher than that in the traditional public school sector. Over the period from 2001 to 2016, enrollment in traditional public schools rose 1 percent, while enrollment in public charter schools rose 571 percent.[4] Moreover, the concentration of charter schools in low-income minority neighborhoods across the country has made them a far larger presence in those communities, with the net result that most charter school students nationwide are either black or Hispanic. Most important of all, the abysmal educational outcomes that have long been the norm in such communities have now been highlighted in the glare of disproportionately better outcomes in many charter schools in those same communities.

Not all charter schools are successful. But failing charter schools are no real threat to the education establishment's traditional public schools. Failing charter schools can have their charters revoked, cutting off their access to the taxpayers' money. This can happen more readily to a charter school than to a traditional public school that is either educationally deficient or financially corrupt. Failing charter schools can even be beneficial to the traditional public school establishment, in so far as the failures of some charter schools can be cited as reasons for restricting the growth and the operations of charter schools in general.

It is *successful* charter schools that are the real threat to the traditional unionized public schools. No charter school network examined here has been more successful educationally than the Success Academy charter schools in Harlem, Bedford-Stuyvesant, the South Bronx and other low-income minority neighborhoods in New York City— and none has been more often or more bitterly attacked in words and deeds.

POLITICAL HOSTILITY

No public official has made more sweeping or more hostile attacks on charter schools in general, and on the Success Academy charter schools in particular, than New York City's Mayor Bill de Blasio. So his words— and deeds— deserve special scrutiny. During his 2013 election campaign for the office of mayor of New York, Mr. de Blasio singled out Eva Moskowitz— founder and head of the Success Academy charter schools— as a prime target. As the *Wall Street Journal* reported:

Mr. de Blasio explicitly campaigned last year against charters— and against Ms. Moskowitz in particular. In May at a forum hosted by the United Federation of Teachers, or UFT, the potent government-employee local: "It's time for Eva Moskowitz to stop having the run of the place. . . . She has to stop being tolerated, enabled, supported." In July, on his plans to charge charters— which are independently run public schools— for sharing space with city-run public schools: "There's no way in hell Eva Moskowitz should get free rent, O.K.?"[5]

It is, of course, not Ms. Moskowitz who gets "free rent." It is the children in charter schools who need classrooms, just as children in traditional public schools need classrooms. But educational authorities seldom build schools for charter school children, as they do for children in other public schools. Instead, charter school students are often housed in existing public school buildings that have space available.

This puts the power to deny classroom space to charter schools in the hands of local school district officials, who can protect their existing traditional public schools from competition by limiting charter schools' capacity to expand and admit the many students on their waiting lists. In Boston, the number of students on waiting lists to get into charter schools there was nearly three times the number of students already in those schools. In absolute numbers, there were more than 25,000 students on waiting lists in Boston and— as already noted— more than 50,000 in New York City.[6]

Large numbers of students on waiting lists to get into charter schools are common in other cities. These include cities where there are school buildings that have been completely vacant for years, but which charter schools have been blocked from using.[7] Teachers unions have opposed letting charter schools lease or buy unused educational facilities.[8]

Teachers unions are the politically strongest of the organizations opposed to charter schools. Their millions of members and millions of dollars in political campaign contributions[9] ensure that there will be government officials— from the local to the national level— responsive to the teachers unions' agenda. That agenda includes:

1. In addition to opposition to charter schools being allowed to teach their students in existing vacant public school buildings, teachers unions have opposed letting charter school students be taught in vacant classrooms in schools where traditional public school classes are housed.[10]

2. Teachers unions have also advocated placing legal restrictions on the number of charter schools permitted to exist.[11] Many states already have such numerical limits,[12] which are wholly independent of whether the quality of charter school education is better, worse or the same as in traditional public schools. Numerical "caps" on the number of charter schools permitted to exist— *independently of their educational quality*— make no sense, except as a way of restricting the exodus of students from traditional public schools.

3. Teachers unions have advocated placing restrictions on charter schools' right to appeal adverse decisions by local school district officials to higher authorities.[13] Murderers convicted in a court of law have the right to appeal, but apparently charter schools should not.

4. Teachers unions have opposed strict student behavior rules, such as those in "no excuses" charter schools, which can lead to more suspensions or expulsions of students for disruptive or violent conduct.[14] Whether this opposition is philosophical or financial is not easy to determine. But every disruptive or violent student who is expelled, or who drops out of school after being repeatedly punished, costs the traditional public school system as much money in lost per-pupil allotments as a student who leaves to go to a charter school. If charter schools are able to maintain stricter behavioral standards than those in traditional public schools, then that can be seen as an "unfair" competitive advantage that should be ended.

5. Insistence that charter school teachers be required by law to have as many credentials— such as degrees from teachers colleges— as teachers are required to have in traditional public schools. This is depicted as an effort to guarantee that students in charter schools are taught by "qualified" teachers, even though in New York City's low-income minority neighborhoods, charter school students taught by supposedly less qualified teachers end up achieving "proficiency" far more often than students taught by teachers who have more paper credentials.

What is similar in all these different particular policies is that there are usually no *educational* benefits to students for which a fact-based claim can be made to seem even plausible— and schools supposedly exist to provide educational benefits to students. But the benefits to adults seeking to restrict the competition from charter schools seem far more obvious. Since teachers unions have millions of members and spend millions of dollars on political campaigns, they do not need logic or evidence to gain the support of elected officials who need campaign contributions to finance their re-election campaigns.

Among the arguments addressed to the public by teachers unions is that "students in charter schools roughly perform the same as students in the rest of public education," as the head of the American Federation of Teachers put it.[15] Similar statements have been made by other critics of charter schools, even though comparing charter school students as a whole with traditional public school students as a whole is comparing populations that are very different, both ethnically and socioeconomically— and which have, for generations, had very different educational outcomes.

If, as this teachers union leader said, charter schools as a whole produce about the same rate of educational success as traditional public schools— whether locally or nationally— that differs only semantically from saying that the black-white education gap has been closed in charter schools located in some low-income minority communities, such as those in New York City. But facts are far too important to let them be obscured by the particular rhetoric in which they are expressed.

Much lofty rhetoric has been deployed by teachers unions in their public relations campaigns to promote their own interests, as if they were promoting the interests of schoolchildren. But the late Albert Shanker, head of the United Federation of Teachers, was honest enough to state the plain fact: "When schoolchildren start paying union dues, that's when I'll start representing the interests of schoolchildren."[16]

Political Institutions

Enduring institutions with enduring personnel, such as teachers unions, can maintain a given set of policies and practices over time. But political institutions whose key personnel can turn over with each election seldom have such steadfastness over time. Even at a given time, government officials from different political parties can follow very different policies from one jurisdiction to another at the same time, depending on different political balances of power from place to place. Government institutions such as public schools are therefore subject to very different policies from place to place and from time to time.

Charter schools are often caught in these ever-shifting political cross currents. Favorable political climates for charter schools can turn unfavorable in the wake of just one election— and when it might turn back again is unknowable. In short, charter schools are politically embattled, and even their victories are subject to new attacks.

In New York City, as already noted, Bill de Blasio objected to Success Academy classes being held in the same buildings with traditional public school classes— even in a city where both the *New York Post* and the *Wall Street Journal* reported that there were more than 200 public school buildings that were half empty.[17] Mr. de Blasio— campaigning with teachers union support— proposed various new restrictions on charter schools, including charging them rent for the space they use in public school buildings. But this threat did not go unanswered. Success Academy founder Eva Moskowitz organized her students' parents and others, and led 17,000 people in a protest march across the Brooklyn Bridge, carrying signs that read: "Let My Children Learn."[18] It was reminiscent of an older saying: "Let My People Go."

This was a continuation of clashes over educational issues between de Blasio and Moskowitz that began when both served on the New York City Council, and would later escalate after de Blasio was elected mayor.

Although the previous New York City mayor, Michael Bloomberg, had granted Ms. Moskowitz permission to locate three more of her Success Academy schools in the same buildings with traditional public schools— nevertheless, after Bill de Blasio became mayor, as the *New York Times* put it, he "followed his word with deed, canceling plans for three of her schools in New York City while leaving virtually all other charter proposals untouched."[19]

Mayor de Blasio's plans to charge charter schools rent again ran into political opposition from Ms. Moskowitz, who led 10,000 people to the state capitol in Albany, to seek Governor Andrew Cuomo's help to stop Mayor de Blasio from charging rent. Mr. de Blasio also happened to be in Albany at the same time, addressing a crowd on different issues.

> Moskowitz's crowd dwarfed the mayor's. Suddenly the governor was bounding down the Capitol steps, bellowing to the parents and TV cameras: "You are not alone! We will save charter schools!"[20]

The governor and the state legislators were able to pass legislation preventing Mayor de Blasio from charging rent to charter schools. In fact, the legislation mandated that the city government help pay the rent for charter schools that are forced to rent space elsewhere, after being denied space in existing public school buildings.[21] The Success Academy won this particular battle, but the war against it and against other charter schools continued, on many fronts, not only in New York, but across the country.

The *New York Times* reported in 2019 that "political forces have turned decisively against charter schools over the last few years."[22] It was the same story as reported in the *Wall Street Journal*: "The school-reform movement is a victim of its own success as charters compete successfully with traditional public schools, prompting a political backlash from unions across the U.S."[23] *Philanthropy* magazine likewise reported similar trends and gave examples from around the country:

> In New York City, Boston, Los Angeles, and other areas where alternative schools have chalked up remarkable results, politicos are suddenly turning down applications for new charter academies, and blocking schools from procuring buildings.[24]

EDUCATION OFFICIALS' HOSTILITY

While there are many institutional arrangements— varying from state to state— for issuing and revoking the charters that authorize charter schools to operate and be financed as public schools, the dominant arrangement in most states is letting existing educational authorities set rules and policies for charter schools. This creates a situation in which existing officials representing the interests of existing traditional public schools, have both incentives and opportunities to impede the work of charter schools, in order to keep them from attracting many students out of traditional public schools. This can be done in a number of ways, including simply making it more difficult for charter schools to get sufficient classrooms to house all the students on their waiting lists.

One problem that charter schools across the country have had to contend with, which traditional public schools do not have to contend with, has been finding some physical space in which to hold classes. Schools are automatically built to provide classrooms for traditional public schools, but many charter schools are simply housed in whatever vacant space might happen to be available in existing public school buildings or to make whatever other kinds of arrangements they can. Those charter schools with access to outside money can rent space or buy space on the open market. But new, non-profit charter schools, without a track record that would attract outside money, may not have such options.

This situation has provided an opportunity for local school district officials to claim that there is no vacant space available in their traditional public schools— regardless of how many classrooms are in fact unused in existing school buildings, and regardless of how many school buildings have been completely vacant for years. Such tactics can block the creation of new charter schools or the expansion of existing charter schools that have a waiting list of students seeking admission.

In Detroit, where a drastic loss of population over the years has left a number of public school buildings entirely vacant, a public school district sold a vacant school building, with a proviso in the deed that the building could be used thereafter only for *residential* purposes.[25] Meanwhile, Detroit Prep— a charter elementary school— was holding classes in makeshift quarters in a church basement. A newly created school, its students had not yet reached the third grade, where they would begin to take statewide education tests. But there were other indications that they were meeting or exceeding educational norms for their grade levels.[26] Eventually, the Mackinac Center for Public Policy, an independent non-profit organization, reported on the controversy:

> Detroit Prep was growing and needed to move out from the church basement and into a new location. Luckily, a mile down the road sits the former Anna Joyce Elementary School. It was part of Detroit Public Schools until the downsizing district permanently closed its doors in 2009. Five years later, district leaders sold the building to a private developer. Today the building sits abandoned and in disrepair, but it's in a perfect location and is just the right size for an expanding Detroit Prep.[27]

Here the issue was not the Mayor Bill de Blasio argument against providing "free" classroom space to charter schools. Detroit Prep was prepared to *buy* the school building with its own money. But the local public school officials had already sold it to a developer, with the already noted restriction in the deed, which prevented the developer from selling it to the charter school. In this case, it took a combination of litigation, media exposure, public outcry and legislation to enable Detroit Prop to acquire that building.[28]

When questioned as to why he blocked the sale of the building to a charter school, the Detroit superintendent of schools asserted "the right of elected school boards to determine the future of their own assets."[29] But of course these buildings were *not* the school board members' own assets. They were taxpayer-provided assets, provided for the express purpose of educating *schoolchildren*— that often ignored group in controversies surrounding charter schools. A member of the Board of Education put it plainly, that "there is no way we should be sustaining our competition."[30]

It is not surprising that the traditional public school officials in Detroit feared the competition of charter schools, even though most Detroit charter schools were not comparable in quality to some highly successful charter schools elsewhere. However, even these less successful charter schools were an alternative to the traditional public schools in Detroit, whose student performance results were ranked the worst in the nation on National Assessment of Educational Progress tests in 2018.[31] The *Wall Street Journal* reported:

> Detroit charters are low performing— only 19% of students are proficient in English— but they're better than the alternative. Charter students in Detroit on average score 60% more proficient on state tests than kids attending the city's traditional public schools. Eighteen of the top 25 schools in Detroit are charters while 23 of the bottom 25 are traditional schools.[32]

The situation in Detroit is very relevant to arguments made by various critics of charter schools, who often argue that educational results in charter schools *as a whole* are no better than educational results in traditional public schools *as a whole*.[33]

This raises again the problem dealt with in Chapter 1, comparing apples and oranges. Gross comparisons are particularly irrelevant for parents in low-income minority communities, who face the *practical* problem of trying to find an available alternative when they want to take their children out of a failing traditional public school in their neighborhood. Their options seldom include traditional public schools *as a whole*.

The most obvious option— and perhaps the only one realistically available in many cases— can be some local neighborhood school, whose educational results are like those we have seen repeatedly in traditional public schools that are paired with charter schools in the same buildings in New York City's low-income minority neighborhoods. There may be some fine traditional public schools in more upscale communities. But that can be completely irrelevant, if not a mockery.

Tactics similar to those used in Detroit have been used in other places across the country, to block the ability of charter schools to acquire space in which to expand, even when there are many students on waiting lists to get into charter schools and much empty space in traditional public schools. Indeed, such practices have become sufficiently widespread, and sufficiently well known, that a number of states have passed laws aimed at requiring public school district officials to make vacant school buildings available for use by charter schools. Such laws have been met with various evasions. A newspaper account in the *Cleveland Plain Dealer*, for example, reported:

> A Cleveland School District plan for 30 closed buildings calls for slightly less than half to be torn down or used as storage. The rest would land in a classification that could be labeled "miscellaneous."
>
> By using vague designations or declaring that buildings are unusable, Cleveland can avoid Ohio's requirement that the schools be offered to charter-school operators at fair market value.[34]

In other words, some public school officials would rather *tear down* vacant school buildings than let them be used by charter schools. Protecting their turf from competition is more important to them than letting classrooms be available for the education of children on waiting lists to get into charter schools.

In Cincinnati as well, a school district there sold nine buildings, "stipulating that the structures not be used for schools."[35] In Tucson,

Arizona, in 2016 the Tucson Unified School District sold a building that had once been an elementary school to a developer for just under $1.5 million— after a charter school had offered $2.1 million.[36] In 2018, a newspaper account reported that a new state law in Arizona would go into effect on August 3rd of that year, declaring that school districts "cannot pull a school off the market solely because a private or charter school is the highest bidder." As a result:

> The Tucson Unified School District is racing to sell its long-vacant Corbett Elementary School, attempting to beat the deadline for a new state law that could force it to sell to a charter or private school.[37]

The school building in question was closed in 2013— five years earlier— and the district spent approximately $30,000 a year on its maintenance.[38]

It was much the same story in Milwaukee, where in 2014 the city owned at least 15 unused school buildings, costing the taxpayers more than $1.4 million a year for maintenance. When the president of the Milwaukee Public Schools Board was asked what he thought about a pending proposal to pass a law, forcing the traditional public school board to sell vacant school buildings, his reply was that this would be "like asking the Coca-Cola Company to turn over its facilities to Pepsi so Pepsi can expand and compete with the Coca-Cola Company."[39]

The analogy fails because the Coca-Cola Company bought and paid for its own assets, while the taxpayers bought and paid for the school buildings— for the purpose of educating children, *not* for the purpose of protecting incumbents in the education establishment from competition. Nevertheless, the school board president's candid statement tells us much about what the real issues are in the charter school controversies, and the tactics often used to keep children from being able to leave traditional public schools and go to charter schools.

As of 2014, this intent to prevent competition was spelled out in a proviso that vacant school buildings in Milwaukee could not be sold for "competing use." This included "use by any school operating under Wis. Stat 119.23"— Milwaukee's parent choice program— or any school that "could have the effect of 'diminishing Pupil Enrollment as compared to Pupil Enrollment in the immediately preceding School Year.'"[40]

A state law was passed in Wisconsin in 2015, mandating that school districts' vacant property be sold to charter schools or private schools. But, in 2018, the *Wall Street Journal* reported, "the district still hasn't sold a single vacant building to other schools despite 13 letters of interest from private and charter operators for 11 vacant buildings." The city had not classified many unused buildings as officially "vacant."[41]

It was a very similar story in Chicago. The *Chicago Sun-Times* reported:

> Hoping to earn some much-needed cash and sweep away the troubles of vacant property, Chicago Public Schools officials are putting 40 empty school buildings up for sale, still with a caveat that they cannot be used for charter schools.[42]

In this case, these 40 vacant schools— costing more than $2 million a year in expenses— were not to be sold to "any K-12 schools that don't charge tuition." In other words, these buildings could be sold to private schools that charge tuition, *but not to charter schools*. Local school district officials understand that charter schools are their real competitors, not expensive private schools that low-income parents cannot afford, so it is charter schools that must be prevented from getting classrooms in which to teach students who are on their waiting lists.

The nation's capital showed the same pattern of preventing charter schools from getting classrooms in which to teach more students. In school year 2015–2016, there were five public school buildings in Washington that were empty and six that were less than half full. School buildings that were no longer used as schools were used for administrative purposes, including being used by other government agencies and non-profit organizations.[43] A commentary in the *Washington Post* in 2018 said that "buildings that used to be schools" in the District of Columbia were being turned into "apartments, retail spaces, museums and restaurants" in mixed-use developments, despite legal obligations to "give charter schools the right of first offer."[44]

In Indiana, as in various other states, there is a law which requires public school districts with vacant buildings "to make those properties available to charter schools before selling to other buyers," according to the *Indianapolis Star*. But this newspaper also reported that Indianapolis Public Schools (IPS) was "refusing to engage in negotiations" with two charter schools that were trying to lease a building from them. The *Indianapolis Star* raised an issue that would apply in many other cities across the country:

> The cash-strapped school district's dismissal of millions of dollars in potential revenue, just months before it plans to ask voters for a property tax increase, raises questions for at least one city leader about whether IPS is more motivated to find the best real estate deal for Broad Ripple High School or to keep charter schools— potential competitors— out of the building.[45]

In New York City, Success Academy founder Eva Moskowitz encountered claims that there were no vacant spaces available in existing public school buildings, but she produced official data showing where there were in fact vacancies in schools. These included a school building where the traditional public school had only 99 students in a building with a capacity for more than a thousand students.[46] In 2015, the *New York Daily News* reported:

> Dozens of times now, de Blasio and Schools Chancellor Carmen Fariña have declared no room at the inn, and dozens of schools have filed appeals to Albany. In 44 out of 45 cases, the state Education Department has forced the city to pay rent to get space on the private market.[47]

The charter schools won this particular battle but the war goes on, not only in New York but across the country. Under a front-page headline, "A Tug of War Over Empty Classrooms," the *Los Angeles Times*, reported, "the district has gone so far as to demolish outdated and outlying buildings, which increases playground areas while also deterring charters from claiming available classroom space."[48]

In Los Altos, California, it took "nearly a decade of heated negotiations and millions of dollars spent on legal battles" before the Los Altos School District and a local charter school reached a tentative agreement in 2019 to let the charter school have its own facilities. The agreement required the charter school to limit its enrollment to 1,111 students, virtually the same as its projected enrollment of 1,105 students for school year 2019–2020. The president of the Los Altos school board called the charter school's growing enrollment an "existential threat to the district."[49] In other words, the legal right of parents to send their children to a charter school was capped, so that the local school district would not lose so many students, and the money those students represented.

Even when a state law authorizes the creation of charter schools, the existing educational establishment can delay all the myriad requirements for actually opening a charter school. For example, the Connecticut state government authorized the creation of charter schools in 1996. But, while charter schools have been created in various communities in that state— albeit with spending per student averaging a few thousand dollars a year less than for students in traditional public schools[50]— the city of Danbury, Connecticut, had still not allowed a single charter school to open, as late as 2018. As reported in a local newspaper:

> The four-year effort to open the first public charter school in the city's history has cleared a major hurdle— but still faces obstacles before it becomes a reality.
>
> Now that the Danbury Prospect Charter School received approval from the state Board of Education on Wednesday, its leaders must turn to their next and most difficult effort: Convincing state legislators to fund the new school next spring.[51]

When it can take *four years* just to get a decision that would allow a proposal for a new charter school to reach the preliminary stage of being able to begin trying to get that school funded, it is not at all clear how many people trying to establish such a school are going to persist in the effort that long— much less how many parents will remain interested in sending their children to that charter school when it finally opens, if ever. This is just one of the ways in which slow-walking the process can impede the creation, maintenance or expansion of charter schools.

Similar tactics were reported in San Jose, California.[52] After people trying to establish a charter school there were able to get adverse decisions by the local school board officials over-ruled by the state board of education and by a court, they were then offered space in a school some distance away from the building they wanted, and away from the community whose children they planned to enroll.[53] Not all communities either need or want charter schools, nor are all charter schools designed to serve all communities. Therefore simply changing the location where a school building will be made available to a charter school can stifle its chances, even after it has won the legal right to get classrooms.

An almost textbook example of the zeal to shut down successful charter schools was a decision of the Oakland, California, school board in March 2013 to revoke the charter of the American Indian Model Schools (AIMS) for alleged financial misdeeds of a *former* head of this network of schools, Ben Chavis. These charges had not been tried in a court of law. Indeed, *six years later*, after a federal investigation, the following outcome was reported in the *Wall Street Journal*:

> Last week the U.S. attorney's office in San Francisco quietly dropped all charges of financial impropriety against Mr. Chavis. He pleaded guilty to a technical violation unrelated to any of the initial allegations.[54]

Ben Chavis was sentenced to probation. But the schools had been scheduled to be shut down six years earlier, at the end of the school year in 2013.

A court injunction against the school board's order prevented that from happening. When the Oakland Unified School District appealed to a higher court, its appeal was rejected unanimously by the appellate judges. The court's ruling pointed out that the educational achievements of the students were "the most important factor in determining whether to revoke a charter."[55]

Clearly that was not the most important factor to the local school board. The *Oakland Tribune* reported that another court pointed out that "the American Indian middle school had the highest Academic Performance Index for all of Alameda County in 2012 and was the fourth-highest performing middle school in the state that year."[56] That same year *Newsweek* magazine listed an American Indian charter school among the top 100 public high schools in the nation.[57]

A study the previous year found the American Indian Model Schools to be "the highest-performing charter school network in the state, by a wide margin." Regardless of its name, the American Indian charter schools have served low-income minority students in general. A local newspaper reported: "Low-income black and Hispanic AIM students actually outperform the statewide averages for wealthier whites and Asians. AIM even outperforms Lowell, one of San Francisco's most respected and academically selective high schools."[58]

The haste to try to close down this charter school network, over legal issues not yet tried in court, and having nothing to do with the education of students, is another painful revelation of the mindset of those preoccupied with protecting their own turf from competition— and the loss of money when students transfer to charter schools. It also tells us something about how little the education of students weighs in the balance in their actions, as distinguished from their rhetoric. When a network of highly successful charter schools was threatened with extinction, based on unsubstantiated charges against a man who was already a *former* principal, that tells us more than any rhetoric.

Chapter 4

ACCOUNTABILITY

If we are serious about the education of children— and there are few things more important to be serious about— we need to pay far more attention to specific facts and far less attention to slippery words and phrases that obscure those facts. Surely this is an issue important enough for us to distinguish talking points from serious arguments, and to test fashionable beliefs against hard evidence.

One of the criticisms often made against charter schools is that they are not "accountable" the way traditional public schools are, because they are allowed more autonomy in their internal operations. But the word "accountability" has very different meanings in practice, and those who use it seldom bother to define what they mean. The most fundamental question is: Accountable to *whom* and for *what*?

Traditional public schools are accountable for following innumerable rules, regulations and teachers union contract provisions. In New York City, teachers union contracts have been a monument of micromanagement. As New York City's former Chancellor of Public Schools Joel Klein put it, the teachers union contract is "an extraordinary document, running for hundreds of pages, governing who can teach what and when, who can be assigned to hall-monitor or lunchroom duty and who can't, who has to be given time off to do union work during the school day, and so on."[1] The *California Education Code* has more than 2,500 pages.[2]

This is accountability for following *procedures*. It is not accountability for *end results*, such as the quality of educational outcomes for students. That is precisely what teachers, principals and administrators in many, if not most, traditional public schools do not have and apparently do not want, judging by their fierce attacks on what they call "high-stakes testing" being used to judge the success or failure of students, teachers and schools. These tests are part of the kind of accountability that can affect teachers' employment, pay and promotion in many charter schools. These charter schools typically do not have the kind of micromanaging procedural accountability. They have accountability for end results.

The difference is fundamental. It is the difference between putting the emphasis on inputs and procedures, rather than on outputs, in terms of educational results for students.

Nothing so highlights this fundamental difference as the traditional public school policies and practices as regards standards of accountability for teachers' job performances and personal conduct in unionized traditional public schools. What also needs scrutiny are the standards— or lack of standards— of accountability for administrators who have used the school buildings they control, paid for by taxpayers for educating students, to instead *prevent* students from being educated in those buildings, if the students seek to go to charter schools.

TEACHER ACCOUNTABILITY

In 2010 the *New York Times* reported that there were "about 550" New York City public school teachers in "rubber rooms," costing the city "$30 million a year."[3]

The more sedate official term for these places was "Temporary Reassignment Centers," but the bizarre circumstances involved have led, over the years, to use of the term "rubber rooms," which had previously been used to describe padded rooms for some patients in mental hospitals.

The teachers reporting to Temporary Reassignment Centers in various parts of New York City were teachers who did no teaching, nor anything else, because education officials did not want them in the classrooms for various reasons, ranging from incompetence to misconduct. And yet these teachers could not be simply fired, under the highly restrictive provisions of the schools' contracts with the teachers unions. To fire them could take years of minutely specified procedures, and they were not wanted in the classroom while this long process dragged on.

In 2009, a *New Yorker* magazine article estimated the number of teachers in the city's "rubber rooms" as more than six hundred, and described their routine:

> The teachers have been in the Rubber Room for an average of about three years, doing the same thing every day— which is pretty much nothing at all. Watched over by two private security guards and two city Department of Education supervisors, they punch a time clock for the same hours that they would have kept at school— typically, eight-fifteen to three-fifteen.[4]

During all the time spent in the "rubber room," teachers not only received their full salary but also continuing contributions to their retirement fund and continued accumulation of seniority.

One of the teachers in a "rubber room" was there because she had been found unconscious in a classroom with 34 students, and a fellow teacher who came near her smelled alcohol. After two years in the "rubber room," she and the school system reached a negotiated agreement. She would be allowed to return for one semester of teaching, and then be reassigned to non-teaching duties in a school office, where she would be retained as long as she submitted to random alcohol testing.

Eventually, however, she passed out in the office, and was unable even to blow into a breathalyzer to be tested for alcohol. But alcohol was found in her water bottle, so she was able to be fired, under the special terms of her special agreement.[5] But that such an arrangement had to be negotiated, after two years of her being paid for doing nothing in a "rubber room," was one sign of how much more costly it would have been to have tried to fire her outright, when she was first found passed out in a classroom and smelling of alcohol. This woman was *not* typical of teachers, nor is that the point. The point is to show to what extremes the tenure protections of unionized teachers can be carried.

By contrast, in many charter schools teachers can be fired just for being incompetent. They do not get second, third and fourth chances to ruin the education of second, third and fourth classes of students. But unionized teachers who are hard to fire, even for some egregious behavior, make the idea of firing traditional public school teachers merely for incompetence seem almost quixotic. Moreover, the teachers in traditional public schools who are *not* egregious do not face either penalties for poor teaching or rewards for outstanding teaching, as do teachers in successful charter schools that both reward and penalize on the basis of which teachers get better or worse results from students.

It should also be noted, as former chancellor of New York City's schools Joel Klein pointed out, that in addition to teachers in the "rubber rooms," costing the city tens of millions of dollars per year, there was also another category called the "absent teacher reserve." These were "more than 1,000 teachers who get full pay to perform substitute or administrative duties because no principal wants to hire them full-time."[6] These other teachers cost "more than $100 million annually," according to former chancellor Klein. He also mentioned still another category of teachers:

> Then there were the several teachers accused of sexual misconduct— at least one was found guilty— whom union-approved arbitrators refused to terminate. The city was required to put them back in the classroom, but we refused to do so. Of course, the union has never sued to have the teachers reinstated. It just makes sure these deadbeats stay on the payroll with full pay and a lifetime pension.[7]

As regards teachers in the "rubber room," the political embarrassment when they were revealed in the press led to different arrangements being made. The *New York Times* reported in June 2010: "Beginning in the fall, those teachers will perform administrative duties or, if they are deemed a threat to students, be sent home."[8] At the time, there were estimated to be "roughly 700 teachers and administrators spread among seven reassignment centers, where they were sent after being accused of transgressions as small as persistent tardiness and as serious as sexually harassing students."[9]

As for the "absent teacher reserve," in November 2017 *Education Week* reported, under the headline "'Absent Reserve' Teachers Heading Back to New York City Classrooms":

> Hundreds of New York City teachers who'd lost their full-time positions but stayed on the payroll are back in classrooms or headed that way.
>
> About a third of those teachers have faced legal or disciplinary charges, and 12 percent of teachers in the pool received a rating of "ineffective" or "unsatisfactory"— the two lowest.
>
> District officials announced this summer that schools that hadn't filled all their teaching positions by Oct. 15 would be assigned educators from the "absent-teacher-reserve" pool. The district has said it expects to fill 300 or 400 vacancies that way.
>
> The move has caused upheaval, with critics accusing the district of instituting "forced placement" of teachers and putting unfit people in front of students. The district disputes those claims.[10]

Note that this is not about a few isolated teachers, here and there, but *hundreds* of teachers in one city, whom principals can be forced to accept back into classrooms when vacancies remain unfilled in mid-October. While all these hundreds of teachers have not immediately found places in school classrooms, the fact that such a program exists may reduce a political problem for Mayor de Blasio, who can point to his efforts to reduce the problem, perhaps reducing the number of politically damaging stories in the media about hundreds of teachers getting full pay for performing substitute or administrative duties. What the educational consequences for the children they teach will be is another matter.

Extreme job protection under teachers union contracts is by no means confined to New York City. The Los Angeles Unified School District spent 3.5 million dollars trying to fire 7 teachers— that is, half a million dollars per teacher— and ended up able to fire only 4 of them.[11] In Woodside, California, it cost a school district $584,000 to try to fire just one teacher— unsuccessfully.[12] It is against such a background that it is possible to understand why mere incompetence is seldom enough to get a unionized teacher fired.

None of this is new or unusual. For decades, a common phrase, "the dance of the lemons,"[13] has been used in discussions of a widespread practice of transferring teachers out of schools where their behavior or lack of competence has become a local scandal, with potential repercussions for local officials. Because of the enormous investment of money and time required to try to fire them, under the terms of teachers union contracts, such teachers— the "lemons"— are simply passed from school to school.

The educational system has thus saved itself huge money costs. But an even more exorbitant cost may be paid— for a lifetime— by the students, when they are taught by teachers whose main reason for being in the classroom is that it is prohibitively expensive to try to get rid of them.

To Professor Diane Ravitch of New York University— long a critic of charter schools and defender of traditional public schools— "tenure means due process."[14] But if "due process" has any definable meaning, and hence boundaries, then there must also be *undue* process beyond those boundaries. It would be hard to find a clearer example of undue process than the bureaucratic labyrinth that schools are required to go through, in order to fire a unionized teacher with tenure. Data from the New York State School Boards Association, as reported in the *Wall Street Journal*, showed that "firing an incompetent teacher on average takes 830 days and costs $313,000."[15] That is more than two years, and even that does not guarantee that an incompetent teacher will be fired.

Professor Ravitch responds to critics who "say that the dismissal process is too cumbersome and too costly" by agreeing that "the issue should not take years to resolve," and saying: "It is the job of the state and the district to negotiate a fair and expeditious process to handle charges and hearings."[16] But are we now discussing tenure in the real world, in unionized public schools? And public officials elected with teachers union campaign contributions? The only schools that children can go to are schools in the real world, including unionized public schools that have failed— for generations— to produce the kinds of educational outcomes widely achieved today in New York City's low-income minority neighborhoods by the charter schools that Professor Ravitch attacks.

"Accountability," as applied to unionized teachers in traditional public schools, is accountability for having such *inputs* as academic credentials and seniority— but not accountability for such educational *end results* as how well their students learn the subjects taught. Whatever the merits or demerits of particular formulas, or practices, for linking teacher performance to rewards, the complete divorce of the two things is surely a sacrifice of children's education— and futures— to the organized and entrenched self-interests of adults in the education system.

ADMINISTRATIVE ACCOUNTABILITY

The accountability of educational administrators in traditional unionized public schools is, like the accountability of teachers, seldom an accountability for educational results. Indeed, as we have seen, they are not held accountable, even when they deliberately impede the education of children, by withholding classrooms from charter schools with thousands of children on waiting lists. Nor are administrators held accountable for failing their fiduciary responsibility, by not selling vacant school buildings to charter schools that may offer a higher price than developers who bid for the same buildings for residential or commercial uses.

Between micromanagement by school system rules and teachers union contracts, there is inherently less scope for managerial decisions in traditional public schools than in private industry or in charter schools. Public school administrators are responsible for following administrative procedures, enforcing current educational policies and responding to political pressures. But that is very different from being held accountable for the consequences, in terms of the education of students.

TEST ACCOUNTABILITY

The Role of Tests

In virtually every kind of organized endeavor— whether industrial, medical, musical, military, financial or innumerable other organized activities— there is usually some point where people are tested for the quality of what they are doing— usually with consequences when that quality is below what was expected or required. Only among defenders of traditional unionized public schools is it considered an unjustified imposition to judge students, teachers or schools by how much learning has actually taken place. But standardized tests seem especially appropriate in a subject like mathematics, where there is little room for subjective criteria.

Professor Diane Ravitch and others make a sharp distinction between *diagnostic* tests— used by teachers to track how well students are learning what is being taught, so as to make adjustments for teaching individual students or classes— as contrasted with *"high-stakes"* tests that lead to positive or negative consequences for students, teachers, or schools. According to Professor Ravitch, "testing should be used diagnostically, not to hand out rewards or punishments."[17] Consistent with that premise, she declares:

> Test scores should remain a private matter between parents and teachers, not shared with the district or the state for any individual student. The district or state may aggregate scores for entire schools but should not judge teachers or schools on the basis of these scores.[18]

There could hardly be a clearer repudiation of accountability for educational end results. Amid Professor Ravitch's many declarations of things *other than teachers and schools* that might be causes of low educational outcomes in low-income minority communities, it is hard to find anything that could test whether teachers or schools might have *any conceivable effect*, whether large or small, on educational achievement gaps. Her position is consistent, if nothing else: "The achievement gaps are rooted in social, political, and economic structures. If we are unwilling to change the root causes, we are unlikely ever to close the gaps. What we call achievement gaps are in fact opportunity gaps."[19]

The very consistency of this logic makes it vulnerable to refutation by facts. The educational achievement gap between students in low-income minority communities and those in the larger society that Professor Ravitch said was unlikely ever to close has in fact already been closed in New York City's charter schools— but not in the traditional unionized public schools in the same buildings with them. While Professor Ravitch is a prominent advocate for the argument she makes, such arguments are widespread, among intellectuals, politicians and— above all— teachers unions.

To the teachers unions, and those who march in lockstep with them, what is fundamentally wrong with annual standardized tests is that these are "high-stakes" tests— tests with consequences. But *life is high stakes*! Nowhere are the stakes higher than for children born into low-income minority families, with not only less money, but usually also less education and fewer contacts in the wider world that could help their children advance into a better life.

Test Score Evidence

Tests of mathematics and English are among the plainest and most direct forms of accountability for results— and they are widely condemned by critics of charter schools. These critics prefer input accountability, such as teachers' academic degrees and seniority. According to Diane Ravitch, high-stakes testing has led to "the harm it inflicted on children and public schools."[20] She asserts, without evidence, that tests "quash imagination, creativity, and divergent thinking."[21] But it is not obvious how these qualities— however desirable in some contexts— are essential for mathematics at the levels taught in the public schools.

Algebra is centuries old, geometry is thousands of years old, and arithmetic is even older. How are schoolchildren's "imagination, creativity, and divergent thinking" supposed to affect mathematics, even if these qualities were not "quashed"? And how are we to know that students even understand these subjects without testing them?

If students cannot master mathematics, there is a whole spectrum of professional occupations from which they will be automatically barred as adults. And if they have also not mastered the English language, there is yet another range of professional occupations that will be, for all practical purposes, off-limits to them.

That is the real meaning, and painful implications, of those schools where a majority of the children are scoring down at the bottom at Level 1 in mathematics. No rhetoric can change that. What Diane Ravitch refers to as the "harsh sanctions" of standardized testing[22] in the schools are as nothing compared to the bitter and lasting consequences that life has waiting for those who go out into the world as adults, with neither skills nor the educational foundation for acquiring skills that would give them a better life.

Curriculum

The effects of standardized tests on the kind of curriculum followed by schools has become a major point of contention by those opposed to both standardized tests and those charter schools whose students do exceptionally well on those tests. The argument is that an emphasis on such tests tends to narrow the curriculum to those things that are tested, at the expense of other important things that are not tested. Professor Daniel Koretz, of the Harvard Graduate School of Education, is one of those who have argued along these lines:

> We can't make the mistake again of settling on just a few goals that are uncontroversial— who can argue with more learning in math and reading?— and pretending that the other important stuff will come along of its own accord. It won't.[23]

A similar argument has been made by Professor Ravitch:

> What do the most demanding families seek in a school? Whether they are parents in an affluent suburb or parents whose children attend an expensive private school, they expect their children to have

much, much more than training in basic skills. They expect their
children to study history and literature, science and mathematics, the
arts and foreign languages.[24]

Whatever the merits, in the abstract, of some of these things that
are said by Professors Koretz and Ravitch, such arguments are like
something out of *Alice in Wonderland* when applied to children *unable
to do arithmetic* in their neighborhood public school, nor be fluent
in the language of the wider society beyond their neighborhood— a
society which they must ultimately deal with as adults. As the principal
of a Washington, D.C. school put it, "I'm not going to put my kids in
art when they can't read."[25]

For low-income minority students, a mastery of mathematics and
English is a ticket out of poverty, and a foundation for developing
skills in a wide range of professions. Without such skills, these children
will be lucky to find decent jobs when they reach adulthood, much
less fulfilling careers. To say, as Professor Koretz does, that there is
"other important stuff" in no way changes the need for trade-offs, or
even triage, in the education of some students from an educationally
impoverished background.

Wherever anyone wants to go— whether literally or figuratively—
they can get there only from where they are. And people from different
social backgrounds are in very different places educationally. There is
no need for a one-size-fits-all education, even if that presents a tableau
pleasing to adults with a particular social vision. In many contexts, it
is necessary to keep reminding ourselves of the fundamental fact that
schools exist to educate children— and that children differ greatly in
what they bring to school.

Mathematics and English may be depicted as narrow subjects, but
their applications in the real world are far from narrow. Moreover, the
bugaboo of "teaching to the test," as it applies to mathematics, seems
hard to distinguish in practice from simply teaching algebra, geometry
or arithmetic. If a mathematics test asks for the distance from home
plate to second base on a baseball diamond— a square, with 90 feet

on each side— you either know the Pythagorean theorem or you don't. It doesn't matter whether you learned it for a test or for its own sake.

As a practical matter, the ability to determine distances without physically measuring them can be important in many contexts. Optical rangefinders, based on mathematical principles, have been used from photography to naval warfare, where this can be a matter of life and death. Skills exist for a reason. They are not just an arbitrary obstacle course in schools.

It is hard to escape the conclusion that the real objection to standardized tests in a subject like mathematics is that the results cannot be evaded or concealed by rhetoric. Even the most talented dispensers of rhetoric cannot talk away the painful— and tragic— failures of too many schools in low-income minority neighborhoods to provide their students with a basic foundation in arithmetic for the higher mathematical skills required in a growing range of professions. These educational failures are harder to conceal when other children from the very same neighborhoods are mastering those same skills in the very same buildings.

The mastery of language, like the mastery of mathematics, is crucial. Not just "important stuff" but *crucial*. Language is the vehicle in which knowledge, skills and analysis are conveyed. The precision, complexity, subtlety and depth of what is conveyed by words can vary enormously— and consequentially— whether receiving or sending information, or when interacting with others in innumerable ways in a wide range of very different settings.

Understanding reasons why students from some social backgrounds may sometimes require different trade-offs in their education does not imply that all the charges made against charter schools by their critics are true, as regards regimenting students in test-preparation isolation. In fact, the longer school days and longer school years in many charter schools, such as the Success Academy and the KIPP schools, mean that there is more total time available in these schools for doing many things. Nor is the often-promoted "boot camp" image of education in charter schools, made by such people as Diane Ravitch,[26] consistent with what is known by those who have bothered to check out the facts.

An observer who had been a Senior Fellow of the Manhattan Institute visited a Success Academy charter school in Harlem and found a very different scene from that depicted in anti-charter-school rhetoric:

> In one room, the chess team prepared for the national tournament; in another, students worked on the school newspaper; down the hall, students rehearsed a musical; in other rooms, students worked on art projects or learned computer coding. Success's debate and chess teams have begun to win national awards.[27]

A Senior Director of the Center for Education at the Pacific Research Institute reported that the Success Academy was "arranging field trips for students to visit museums, theaters, circuses, and other notable venues"— these trips numbering "about twenty per year." A writer who spent a year observing a Success Academy charter school in the Bronx reported that Success Academy students "get science every day." They also take "art, music, dance, and chess."[28] The same writer reported: "More than their public school peers, Success Academy scholars spend a good deal of time out of the classroom on 'field studies.'"[29] Yet again, the world of facts differs greatly from the world of rhetoric by critics of charter schools.

FINANCIAL ACCOUNTABILITY

One of the most often used arguments against charter schools is that they "take money from the public schools," making it harder for the public schools to do their job. Often-repeated phrases about how charter schools "siphon"[30] money from traditional public schools or "drain"[31] money from traditional public schools insinuate a process very different from what happens in the real world. It is not charter schools that determine how many students transfer to them from traditional public schools. That initiative is in the hands of parents. And it is the transfer of students that causes money to be transferred with them, since these children cannot be educated without money to pay for the things that education requires, beginning with teachers and books.

The Division of Money

None of this is rocket science. Americans are a mobile people. At any given time, millions of American families are moving from one neighborhood to another, from one city to another and from one state to another. When families with children move from the east side of Manhattan to the west side of Manhattan, and the children go from one public school district to a different public school district, does anyone think it strange that the taxpayers' money— provided to educate those children— goes where the children go, rather than remaining back in the district they left? There is no public angst or outcry about the transfer of money to follow the children— *unless the children are going from a traditional public school to a public charter school.*

What is the money for, if not to educate children? Why are traditional public schools then less able to educate a *smaller* number of students with a correspondingly smaller amount of money? If 20 percent of the children in a traditional public school district leave to go to charter schools, and 20 percent of the money is transferred with them, the amount of money *per pupil* has not gone down in the school district they left.

Critics of charter schools who express great concern about the money "lost" by traditional public schools seldom mention that per-pupil expenditures provided by local, state and federal government sources for children in charter schools are, on average, *less* than per-pupil expenditures on traditional public schools nearby.[32] That difference has been an average of 28 percent less for charter school students nationwide. For an average-sized charter school, that difference has been estimated as being enough to pay the salaries and benefits for at least 20 teachers.[33]

Some critics of charter schools argue that there are some fixed costs in the traditional public schools that may not go down when students depart. But the magnitude of these fixed costs is seldom— if ever— quantified, much less compared to the financial disadvantages of charter schools which get less taxpayer money per student, or compared to the tens of millions of dollars paid annually to unionized teachers in New York City's "rubber rooms" who were doing no teaching. Moreover, fixed costs seem to attract no attention at all when students transfer from one traditional public school to another.

Nevertheless, fixed costs are a talking point, and apparently that is sufficient for those trying to block charter schools from being able to receive students from their waiting lists.

Money is sometimes discussed in another context by critics of charter schools— namely, that many successful charter schools receive, in addition to the taxpayers' money, donations from wealthy individuals and foundations. Here, yet again, we must go back to basics and put this issue in the context of schools as a place for educating children, rather than a place for preserving the vested interests of adults. How are any children, in any kind of school, made worse off when voluntary donations are added to the taxpayers' money for some charter schools?

It should also be noted that voluntary donations to charter schools are not automatic. Educational achievements can attract money and sustain a continued inflow of money, but that does not mean that big money is what creates the achievements in the first place. Although the KIPP network of charter schools is today the largest network of non-profit charter schools in the country, the first KIPP school had very financially shaky beginnings.

The idea of starting this charter school originated with two young men in their twenties— Michael Feinberg and David Levin— who had finished college and volunteered for the Teach for America program, which sent recent college graduates to teach in low-income minority neighborhoods. Based on their own experiences, and some ideas from a more experienced black teacher colleague, they decided to create their own school. In seeking money to finance the first KIPP school in Houston, Michael Feinberg sent out letters to more than a hundred corporations and foundations, asking for an appointment to discuss the financing of their project. None of those he wrote to gave him an appointment, much less money, and most did not even reply.[34] The joint money-raising efforts of these two young men produced a total of $4,000.

Eventually, however, they encountered a local furniture store owner, known as "Mattress Mack," who decided to help them financially to get started, with a few dozen students educated in makeshift quarters. Statewide tests later "showed that almost every KIPP student had moved up two grade levels in just one year."[35] Such results helped put them on the map, and media attention— notably on network television's "60 Minutes"— helped attract money. But it was not big money that created the educational results.

Conversely, even extravagant spending does not guarantee educational benefits. As a result of a lawsuit over the racial composition of students in a Kansas City, Missouri, school district, a federal district judge in 1987 ordered a massive increase in spending on such things as an Olympic-sized swimming pool, a planetarium, a 25-acre wildlife sanctuary and classes with a teacher:student ratio of 1:13. In 1992, the *Wall Street Journal* reported: "Construction alone has cost $500 million and counting."[36] The total spending ended up exceeding a billion dollars.[37]

All of this was done to counteract the effects of "white flight," which had left no-longer-officially-segregated schools almost as overwhelmingly black as they had been during the era of legal segregation. These amenities were intended to lure white students back to these schools, and that in turn was intended to raise the educational level of the black students, in accordance with prevailing views in the courts and beyond. As the *St. Louis Post-Dispatch* reported, years later:

> What has been the effect? More failure. The students who were supposed to profit aren't doing better, but worse. High school dropout rates... have soared and now exceed 60 percent— more than double the national rate. Black grade-school students score lower on reading and math tests than they did when the experiment began.[38]

At one time, statistics in various communities often showed that per-pupil spending on the education of minority youngsters was significantly lower than per-pupil spending on white youngsters. Yet, long after that situation began changing, and in some cases reversed, the argument that more money was the key to better education continued unabated, despite a failure of changed spending patterns to produce corresponding changes in educational outcomes.[39]

The Effectiveness of Money

Of course it takes money to run a school. But the great emphasis on money differences as an explanation— or excuse— for differences in educational outcomes ignores the plain fact that the most fundamental things are among the least expensive to teach. Mathematics has been taught for centuries, requiring nothing more expensive than a book, pencil and paper for students, and chalk and a blackboard for teachers. Many "innovative" and "exciting" new gimmicks on tangential projects in schools are likely to be far more expensive.

Nevertheless, it remains a common defense of substandard educational outcomes in the traditional unionized public schools to claim that money is the reason— that the schools have "inadequate funding" and that poverty is the reason minority students cannot learn. Such explanations are presented as if they were unchallenged, axiomatic truths. But, in fact, such explanations have been challenged over the years, not only by scholars who have analyzed empirical data,[40] but also by some government officials in both political parties. Back in 1967, Democratic Senator Robert F. Kennedy of New York, in an exchange with Commissioner of Education Harold Howe, said:

> I wonder if you would make a comment. . .as to whether we are, in fact, doing more than just putting money in the hands of the authorities and whether we are just continuing practices that have been in existence for decades and which have not, in my judgment, achieved the education of the deprived child.[41]

Senator Kennedy clearly did not regard the spending of more money as the answer:

> I think what we do is appropriate sums of money and, in many of these communities and cities and areas of the system, the money goes into the educational system and they continue exactly what they have been doing for the last several decades, which means

not educating the child properly and means turning out children undertrained to meet this world's needs.[42]

Years later, Secretary of Education Roderick R. Paige, in a Republican administration, likewise said:

> After spending $125 billion of Title I money over 25 years, we have virtually nothing to show for it.[43]

More recently, Professor Walter E. Williams of George Mason University reported:

> In 2016, in 13 of Baltimore's 39 high schools, not a single student scored proficient on the state's mathematics exam. In six other high schools, only 1% tested proficient in math. In raw numbers, 3,804 Baltimore students took the state's math test and 14 tested proficient. Citywide, only 15% of Baltimore students passed the state's English test. Money is not the problem. Of the nation's 100 largest school systems, Baltimore schools rank third in spending per pupil.[44]

In most endeavors, spending substantially more money usually has some tangible effect. Expensive clothes, cars or cameras are usually better in some noticeable way. This is also true in *private* schools, where those schools with outstanding reputations for educational quality can charge higher tuition and still have an ample supply of students. But, in traditional public schools, an ample supply of students is assured by compulsory attendance laws, regardless of the quality— or lack of quality— of their education. This is especially so in low-income neighborhoods, where parents are unable to send their children to expensive private schools when they are dissatisfied with the local public school.

In these circumstances, the assignment of particular students to particular schools, based on where those students live, has long virtually guaranteed district school monopolies within each geographic area, regardless of whether the education in one public school district was better or worse than the education in another public school district. Special exceptions may allow some students to escape their local district schools[45] but mass escapes are very unlikely unless there is some free alternative, such as public charter schools or inexpensive alternatives such as some low-cost Catholic parochial schools.

Local monopolies of schoolchildren living in a given district do not make public school officials or teachers union officials indifferent to money. Their jobs, their pay, promotions, and power all depend on how much money comes into the system for them to dispense. That in turn depends on how many students are in the system— but it does *not* depend on whether those students are adequately educated. It is the physical presence of these students that is financially crucial, because that is what brings the taxpayers' money into the system. But once that money is in the system, there is nothing to guarantee that it will be spent to improve the education of students.

Perennial complaints about "inadequate funding" of public schools, sometimes accompanied with accounts of a shortage of school supplies, and particular teachers who have spent their own money to buy some of those supplies for use by their own students, are by no means proof that there is insufficient money in the system. How the money is spent is a crucial question seldom asked.

Before Eva Moskowitz became founder and head of the Success Academy charter schools, she was an elected official who headed a committee of the New York City Council with oversight of the city's public schools. Among the things she discovered was that there were public schools where the bathrooms had no toilet paper.[46] But the tens of millions of dollars spent annually on teachers in the "rubber rooms," who were doing no teaching, would probably have bought a lot of toilet paper and other needed supplies.

Public charter schools do *not* automatically get students from compulsory attendance laws. Children come to charter schools because their parents choose to have them apply, and the luck of a lottery usually determines who becomes eligible. Like private schools, public charter schools must offer an education that attracts students and their parents. While charter schools do not charge tuition, the quality of their education can attract voluntary donations from wealthy individuals and foundations.

The net result is that all three of these different kinds of schools— traditional public schools, private schools and public charter schools— tend to have policies and practices consistent with the incentives and constraints that each kind of school faces.

Students' Family Incomes

Sometimes money is said to be a major factor in educational outcomes in a very different sense. Professor Diane Ravitch is one of many to cite poverty as one of the "root causes" of substandard educational outcomes in low-income communities.[47] Correlations can be cited in support of this view but, as statisticians have often warned, correlation is not causation. Professor Ravitch herself recognizes that, on other issues.[48]

Even where there is causation, that by itself tells us nothing about the *direction* of causation. Poverty might cause low educational outcomes— or parents' low educational outcomes might be a cause of family poverty, when a lack of basic skills prevents parents from getting well-paying jobs. In such cases, their children's low educational outcomes could be a result of behavior patterns similar to that of their parents. It could be possible to devise empirical tests to determine which of the various explanations fit the facts. But those who are content to have a talking point need not trouble themselves to find out.

One set of relevant evidence is that there have been vast differences in educational outcomes between charter schools and the traditional public schools housed in the same buildings with them, even though most of the data in Appendix III show no comparable socioeconomic magnitudes of differences between students in these two kinds of schools.

Conversely, large socioeconomic differences do not predestine correspondingly large educational outcomes. In 2019 the Success Academy charter school network as a whole had a slightly higher percentage of its students reach the "proficient" level and above— in both mathematics and English— than did any of the three New

York State public school districts with the highest percentages of their students scoring at the "proficient" level and above. The average family income of children in the Success Academy charter schools was $49,800. The average family income of children in the three highest scoring public school districts in New York State ranged from $153,369 to $291,542.[49]

Chapter 5

STUDENT DIFFERENCES

The most fundamental fact about traditional public schools is that compulsory attendance laws guarantee that children of all sorts of dispositions and capabilities must attend. To assume that they all want to be there, and are all striving to achieve success there, is to ignore the most blatant realities. There is no reason to have expected any such thing, and such expectations defy painfully large amounts of evidence to the contrary, not only in the United States but in other countries as well.

Whatever the intellectual or other potential that human beings may have at the moment of conception, that is no measure of what developed capabilities they will have when they enter schools. Nor is their intellectual potential at the moment of conception even a measure of their "native intelligence," because research has shown that nutritional differences among pregnant women have produced IQ differences when their children were old enough to be tested.[1] *There is no equality of circumstances*, even in the womb. Newborn babies do not enter the world with equal chances, even in a society with equal opportunity for people who have equally developed capabilities.

Where one might expect to find the greatest equality— among children born to the same parents and raised in the same home— there are nevertheless striking inequalities, not only in the United States but also in countries on the other side of the Atlantic, as shown by studies going back as far as the nineteenth century.[2] A specific example of a general pattern was shown by a study of National Merit Scholarship finalists. More than half the finalists were the first-born child in their family, whether in two-child, three-child, four-child or five-child families. Even in five-child families, the first-born was the National Merit Scholarship finalist more often than the four other siblings combined.[3]

Other studies have shown that first-born children tend to average higher IQs than their siblings, and to be over-represented in various kinds of achievements, ranging from leading composers of classical music to astronauts.[4] Children who were an only child had similar above-average achievements.[5] This suggests that undivided parental attention in early childhood has long-run benefits. This conclusion is also consistent with the fact that twins tend to have slightly lower average IQs than people born singly[6]— but not by as much if one twin is still-born or dies early.[7] Lesser parental attention is also received by children raised by a single parent— and such children have, on average, far more problems when growing up and in adulthood— again, not just in the United States but also on the other side of the Atlantic.[8]

Even among people whose IQs are all in the top one percent, there have been large disparities in their educational and other outcomes, differing with the kinds of families in which they were raised.[9] When we add socioeconomic differences, the probabilities of equally developed capabilities among children become even less likely— not just from differences in money, but from very different child-rearing practices in different socioeconomic classes.

Children of parents with professional occupations hear nearly twice as many words per hour as children of parents with working class occupations, and more than three times as many words per hour as children in families on welfare.[10] Moreover, the *kinds* of words are also different— overwhelmingly more positive and encouraging words than negative or discouraging words in families where the parents have professional occupations, and more negative and discouraging words than positive and encouraging words in families on welfare.[11] Can anyone believe that such different treatment throughout children's formative years makes no difference in how they develop?

There is no point arguing as if there is some "natural" or probable equality of developed capabilities, so that unequal outcomes are evidence or proof of some malign intervention that has thwarted this "natural" or statistically probable outcome which has been assumed. Even if we assume a natural equality at the moment of conception, that does not imply a natural equality of development in different circumstances.

The implicit assumption of a natural equality of capabilities is at the heart of social visions that attribute differences in outcomes to some malign external factor which has prevented that supposedly natural equality from being found in educational, economic or other outcomes. None of this denies that there has also been malign treatment of individuals and groups— on every continent inhabited by human beings, and over thousands of years of recorded history. Inhumanity to fellow human beings has long been a painful reality. But it has no monopoly as a cause of differences in outcomes. There are too many other factors— many of them beyond any individual or social control— making equal capabilities, or even equal striving for the same things, very unlikely.

Fierce controversies as to whether differences in educational, economic and other outcomes are due to genetic differences or to social injustices often ignore the possibility that there are many other causes of disparate outcomes, including differences in what people *want* to do, and are prepared to invest their time and efforts in trying to do.

If Asian Americans are greatly under-represented in professional basketball, for example, that is not necessarily because they are innately incapable of playing the game or because there are evil people determined to keep them out. We should at least not dismiss the possibility that many Asian Americans may be culturally oriented toward putting their aspirations and efforts in other directions— where they tend to be quite successful. Other groups as well have particular endeavors in which they excel and other endeavors where they are either unsuccessful or virtually non-existent. Even groups whose educational or socioeconomic outcomes in general are substandard tend nevertheless to have some particular endeavors in which they not only hold their own but excel.[12]

Given the many factors operating against an equal development of capabilities among individuals and groups— including demography[13] and geography,[14] each of which can have huge consequences for individuals, groups and nations— we may never have a definitive answer to the question as to why some individuals and groups do better in some things than do other individuals and groups. However, we live with less than definitive answers to many questions, and even make progress nevertheless. But dogmatic certainty is a greater threat, when it narrows the many causes of inequalities to whatever fits a particular social vision. That is a danger all too often found in the field of education, as regards the education of schoolchildren.

Differences in capabilities and outcomes are not *automatically* anybody's fault. Whose fault is it that someone was the last child born in a family, rather than the first? That their parents had little education, while other parents had much education? Or that they were raised in a culture that exalts other things more so than education? These are facts of life, and they cannot all be dealt with by social crusades against villains. Nor can these problems be solved by the make-believe equality of "inclusion" rather than by the harder task of creating genuine equality of educational achievement.

CULTURAL DIFFERENCES

Because differences between different groups of American schoolchildren have so often been discussed in a context of race— a subject often generating more heat than light— it may be helpful to begin by discussing some of these educational issues in a different society, with different demographics and a different social history. Both the similarities and the differences may offer a new perspective on some important issues.

Attitudes Toward Education

In his deeply perceptive book *Life at the Bottom*, Theodore Dalrymple reported on his first-hand experiences as a physician in a hospital located in a low-income, predominantly white underclass neighborhood in England— where many students had negative attitudes toward school and hostile attitudes toward those of their classmates who wanted to learn:

> If you don't mend your ways and join us, they were saying, we'll beat you up. This was no idle threat: I often meet people in their

twenties and thirties in my hospital practice who gave up at school under such duress and subsequently realize that they have missed an opportunity which, had it been taken, would have changed the whole course of their lives much for the better.[15]

The beatings meted out have included some that required medical attention in a hospital emergency room, where the victims were treated by Dr. Dalrymple. Others have ended up in the emergency room after having deliberately taken overdoses to avoid the prospect of such beatings.[16] In England, as in the United States, there have long been people promoting the idea that low incomes are automatically due to social injustices— class injustices there to a predominantly white underclass— and that class solidarity in opposition to the larger society is the remedy. Some young people in low-income communities take this to mean opposition to the school system, and resent students in their community who strive for success within that system.

Even aside from such incidents of violence, the whole atmosphere in schools in such neighborhoods is often antithetical to education. In *Life at the Bottom*, Dr. Dalrymple said, "I cannot recall meeting a sixteen-year-old white from the public housing estates that are near my hospital who could multiply nine by seven (I do not exaggerate). Even three by seven often defeats them."[17] The distinguished British magazine *The Economist* reported that white 16-year-olds in the borough of Knowsley had worse test results "than do black 16-year-olds in any London borough."[18] Among students from families with incomes low enough to make the students eligible for free school meals, black African pupils were among those who scored higher on standardized tests than white British pupils, according to a 2016 report from a British research group.[19]

If this racial disparity in British education seems strange, compared to racial disparities in the United States, a major difference between the two countries is that most blacks in Britain are *not* descended from African slaves in Britain— but are immigrants, or offspring of immigrants, from Africa or the Caribbean. Many other non-whites in Britain are immigrants or the offspring of immigrants, largely of Asian ancestry. In general, this non-white population of Britain, which has largely immigrated there, is often successful, both educationally and economically,[20] as such groups as African and Asian immigrants often are in the United States as well.[21]

On both sides of the Atlantic, these non-white immigrants have been spared generations of indoctrination in the ideology of victimhood, grievance and entitlement— which is the legacy of England's white underclass instead. Sending young people out into the world without basic skills, but well supplied with resentments and rhetoric, is not doing them any favor, on either side of the Atlantic, and regardless of the color of their skin.

One significant difference between the two countries is that, with most of the underclass in England being of the same race as the majority population, such things can be discussed more openly there, without fear of being accused of racism. There has even been a popular song in England with the title "Poor, White, and Stupid."[22]

The same educational phenomenon occurs in both countries, despite racial differences in their respective underclasses. Moreover, 16.6 percent of the students are classified as functionally illiterate in both countries,[23] and there are schools in England which have been described as being "on the knife-edge of anarchy"[24]— a situation not uncommon in some American schools. Moreover, negative reactions by some youngsters in school to positive educational efforts and educational achievements among their peers have also been found among Maoris in New Zealand and Burakumin in Japan.[25]

The taboo against discussing such things openly in the United States works to the disadvantage of the very people that taboo is supposedly protecting. Those black or Hispanic youngsters who are motivated to learn can pay a social penalty, at least, from classmates of their own ethnic background in some schools. An empirical study of more than 90,000 black, white and Hispanic students in grades 7 through 12 found that, among black and Hispanic students whose grade-point averages are above some level— 2.5 among Hispanics and 3.5 among blacks— they have fewer friends of their own ethnicity.[26]

Hispanic students with a grade point average of 4.0 were found to average three fewer fellow Hispanic friends, unlike white students with the same grade point average, who suffered no such loss of fellow white friends.[27] Reduced numbers of friends of the same ethnicity by black students with high grade-point averages has likewise been part of a pattern of negative responses by their peers to black students perceived as "acting white." An empirical study of the "acting white" phenomenon by Professor Roland G. Fryer of Harvard concluded that this pattern "is most prevalent in racially integrated public schools" and is "less of a problem in the private sector and in predominantly black public schools."[28]

In other words, what critics call "segregated" charter schools are schools in predominantly minority communities, where motivated minority students are educated among other motivated minority students. In these settings, such students can freely pursue academic achievement without the negative social pressures that can be acute in some racially integrated schools where minority students with behavior patterns and academic achievements similar to those of white students in those schools can be seen as traitors to their race who are "acting white." In England, the parallel phrase is "class treachery."[29]

This is not to say that racially homogeneous schools should be sought as a goal. But it does suggest that, where charter schools are located in predominantly black and/or Hispanic neighborhoods, the reality of educational success should not be sacrificed for the rhetoric of "integration" or "diversity." The successful educational track record of these charter schools, and the contrasting educational futility of racial "integration" crusades, both demonstrate that white classmates are neither necessary nor sufficient for non-white students to achieve educational success.

"Segregation," "Integration" and "Diversity"
For many generations, black schoolchildren were, by law, educated in schools separate from those in which white schoolchildren were educated— universally throughout the South, and at various times also in Northern communities, either by law or *de facto* by gerrymandered

attendance zones or in other ways. Back in 1896 the Supreme Court of the United States ruled that racial segregation was not in violation of the Fourteenth Amendment's guarantee of equal protection of the laws, if segregated facilities for blacks were "separate but equal." For more than half a century this "separate but equal" doctrine prevailed, despite numerous and blatant indications that the separate schools for black children were by no means equal in resources or otherwise.

The historic 1954 Supreme Court decision in *Brown v. Board of Education* repudiated the "separate but equal" doctrine, with Chief Justice Earl Warren declaring that separate schools were "inherently unequal." In the atmosphere of acclaim for this overdue landmark decision, few questioned the implications of the rationale that schools whose students were all black were inherently unequal.

Nevertheless, only about a mile from the Supreme Court building where this pronouncement was made, was an all-black school— Dunbar High School— which sent a higher percentage of its graduates off to college than any white public high school in Washington.[30] As far back as 1899, when there were four academic public high schools in Washington, students from this all-black public high school* scored higher on tests than two of the three white public high schools.[31] Over the next half-century, alumni of this all-black high school went to some of the most elite colleges in the country, graduating Phi Beta Kappa from Harvard, Yale, Amherst and other top-tier academic institutions.[32]

The first three black women to receive a Ph.D. in America were all from this high school— two as students and one as a teacher.[33] Other alumni of this school included the first black federal judge,[34] the first black general,[35] the first black Cabinet member[36] and the first black tenured professor at a major national university[37]— as well as Dr. Charles Drew, who became internationally recognized for his pioneering work on the use of blood plasma.[38] Separate schools were *not* "inherently unequal." As happens all too often in the history of

---

*   The name "Dunbar High School" was used, beginning in 1916, for a new building in which this school was housed. Before, the same institution was called the "M Street School." But it was continuously the same school, referred to here as "Dunbar High School" to avoid confusion.

ideas, even the correction of a demonstrably false idea can go too far in the other direction, and introduce another false idea.

The Jim Crow laws in the South, like the apartheid laws in South Africa, did not simply separate blacks from whites, but deliberately discriminated against blacks in innumerable ways. The separation facilitated the discrimination. Major League Baseball did not admit black players until 1947. But that did not make black ballplayers inferior, even though they played in a separate league of their own. After black players entered Major League Baseball, there were seven consecutive years when no white player won the National League's Most Valuable Player award.[39]

The logical corollary of Chief Justice Warren's pronouncement was that black students needed to be educated in the same schools with white students, for the education to be equal. Even though the 1954 decision did *not* say that, this logic took over, and years were spent busing black children to white schools in search of higher educational results that were expected to close the racial educational achievement gap— but which it failed to do. Closing the racial gap in educational achievement began to happen on a large scale long after the busing crusade was over, and it happened largely in overwhelmingly non-white charter schools, of which the Success Academy charter schools in Harlem and other low-income minority neighborhoods are a classic example.

Social crusades, however, have their own momentum, and mere facts are often unable to stop them. The slipperiness of words has allowed critics of charter schools to condemn them for being "segregated." Anti-charter-school intellectuals, politicians and organizations have repeatedly raised the cry of "segregation" against charter schools located in low-income minority communities such as Harlem, Bedford-Stuyvesant and the South Bronx.[40]

To Professor Diane Ravitch, for example, substandard educational levels in traditional public schools in such communities are not the problem, and charter schools are not the answer, because "charters will not end the poverty at the root of low academic performance."[41] Instead, what she sees as needed are broader social policies:

> We should set national goals to reduce segregation and poverty.
> In combination, these are the root causes of the achievement gaps
> between economic and racial groups.[42]

In short, Professor Ravitch sees the problem as not being in the educational system, but in a failure of the larger society to deal with poverty and a lack of racial integration. But, in terms of hard evidence, New York City charter schools that have had no capacity to end either poverty or racial concentrations of minority students have nevertheless closed the racial achievement gap in education.

Another prominent intellectual opposed to charter schools— Jonathan Kozol, whose book *The Shame of the Nation* has the subtitle *The Restoration of Apartheid Schooling in America*— argues that the way to counter negative peer pressure against minority students seeking educational excellence "is to change the *make-up* of their peers by letting them go to schools where all their classmates are not black and brown and poor."[43] But the research by Professor Roland G. Fryer of Harvard showed that it is in the very kinds of schools recommended by Mr. Kozol that the "acting white" hostility to black students seeking educational achievement is strongest.[44]

Some people have made a plausible-sounding argument that black students need not only educational skills but also a social familiarity with the culture of the larger white society around them. A statement quoted approvingly by Jonathan Kozol is that the historic *Brown v. Board of Education* decision "was not about raising scores" for non-white students "but about giving black children access to majority culture, so they could negotiate it more confidently." The same source quoted approvingly by Mr. Kozol also declared: "It is foolhardy to think black children can be taught, no matter how well, in isolation and then have the skills and confidence as adults to succeed in a white world where they have no experience."[45]

Plausible as this argument might seem, what was dismissed as "foolhardy" is precisely what Dunbar High School graduates succeeded in doing, for generations, as they went on to become "the first black who" had various educational and professional achievements, paving the way for other blacks to follow. The fact that an idea sounds plausible, and is consistent with the prevailing social vision, does not exempt it from the test of empirical evidence.

The school system and the city in which Dunbar students lived were by no stretch of the imagination racially integrated. Not only were the schools racially segregated by law in Washington, prior to the *Brown v. Board of Education* decision, as late as 1950 there were movie theaters, restaurants, and hotels in Washington where blacks were simply not admitted as customers, as well as a taxi company that carried no black passengers, except at the train station, where it was required to accept all travelers. A suburban amusement park in nearby Glen Echo, Maryland, refused to admit black children. This of course in no way justifies racial segregation and discrimination. But it does justify basing conclusions on facts rather than rhetoric.

Professor Gary Orfield of UCLA is one of the leading figures among those who are still fighting the educational battles of the past, on the assumptions of the past, that racial "integration" is imperative for improving educational outcomes for minority students.

Professor Orfield has condemned "the rapid growth of charter schools" which "has been expanding a sector that is even more segregated than the public schools." Charter schools are themselves public schools, but Professor Orfield found it "particularly distressing that charter schools enroll a disproportionate share of black students and expose them to the highest level of segregation." He has called charter schools "apartheid schools with zero to one percent white classmates, the very kind of schools that decades of civil rights struggles fought to abolish in the South."[46]

Here, yet again, the central function of a school— to educate students— receives remarkably little attention, compared to other things that preoccupy some adults. Unlike other public schools, charter schools can receive only children who voluntarily apply. Therefore charter schools are in no position to mix and match racial or ethnic groups for "diversity," in order to create a tableau to fit the preconceptions of Professor Orfield, Jonathan Kozol or other adults. Professor Orfield may choose to call this "shoddy educational and civil rights policy"[47] but hard data on educational outcomes tell a very different story.

What seems truly questionable is the use of words like "segregation" and "apartheid" to describe statistics. A dictionary definition of the verb "segregate" reads: "to separate or set apart from others."[48] It is something imposed by someone on someone else. That is why racial segregation in the United States and apartheid in South Africa were abhorred. But is opening a school in a community whose population is already heavily of one racial or ethnic background *segregating* that population? In most cases, whatever caused that racial or ethnic concentration existed before the first charter school existed.

If a charter school opens in New York City's Chinatown, and all the children who enroll are Chinese, is that segregation? Should we have expected Irish or Jewish children in Chinatown? Neither racial segregation in the United States nor apartheid in South Africa were just statistical conditions. Nor would people have fought, and even put their lives on the line, if segregation and apartheid were just statistical conditions.

Even using the redefined definition of "segregation," a nationwide empirical study of 4,574 school districts found very little difference in the proportion of racial minority students in charter schools, compared to traditional public schools in the same districts. For example, "if the average district in the sample shut down all of its charter schools, we would expect its overall segregation of black and Hispanic students to decline from 15.0 to 14.2 percent."[49] Is this what all the sound and fury is about— a difference of less than one percentage point?

The use of the words "segregation" and "apartheid" in situations where there are racial concentrations *not* imposed by a particular institution, in charter schools or elsewhere, is by no means confined to Gary Orfield. The same ambiguous words have been used by Jonathan Kozol, Diane Ravitch and others.[50] A large feature article in the *New York Times* in 2019 was titled "Then as Now, a Fight over School Segregation."[51] It was about the fact that highly selective New York City public high schools, such as Stuyvesant High School, have students whose ethnic backgrounds are very different from the ethnic backgrounds of the New York City population as a whole.

It was not even claimed that these schools chose students on the basis of race or ethnicity, since students were selected by admission test scores. Moreover, the racial or ethnic proportions of students are not fixed over time. While Asian students vastly outnumber black students admitted to Stuyvesant High School today, back in 1971 black students outnumbered Asian students at Stuyvesant.[52] At one time, critics called Stuyvesant a "free prep school for Jews."[53] Depicting a pattern as proof of an intention or a policy is the seemingly invincible fallacy of presuming that order implies design, so that statistical differences in outcomes imply that somebody prevented the less fortunate from succeeding.

We have already seen just some of the many reasons for statistical differences in outcomes for individuals, groups and nations— even among children born to the same parents and raised in the same homes, as well as major differences in educational and other achievements among people who were all in the top one percent in IQ.[54]

Scholars who have studied the facts about social differences in many countries have often reached conclusions similar to that of eminent French historian Fernand Braudel: "In no society have all regions and all parts of the population developed equally."[55] By contrast, the proportional representation— used as a norm by social theorists who regard disproportionalities as automatically evidence of discrimination— has not been shown by those theorists to have existed in any nation, anywhere in the world, or any time over thousands of years of recorded history.

It is a painful irony that people who are promoting the make-believe equality of "inclusion" and "diversity" in schools are attacking charter schools that are producing the real equality of educational achievement.

Sorting and Unsorting Students

Although cultural differences have often been discussed in the context of differences between ethnic or socioeconomic groups, such differences are both present and consequential *within* the same ethnic or socioeconomic groups. Differences in student attitudes toward education within both black and Hispanic populations, for example, have already been noted. There have been similar internal cultural differences within innumerable other ethnic groups in countries around the world. One consequence is that they tend to sort themselves out internally, as well as being sorted out by others.[56]

When there is a charter school in a Harlem neighborhood, for example, there is no need to assume that parents who try to get their children into that charter school have the same cultural values and personal priorities as parents who do not. While some critics of charter schools may depict these schools as cherry-picking the students they admit[57]— despite the widespread use of lotteries for admissions purposes— there is no need to overlook the possibility that highly motivated parents may be more common among the parents of children in charter schools.

The importance of self-motivation, by both parents and students, in the educational process has been used by critics of charter schools, and defenders of traditional public schools, as an "unfair" advantage that charter schools have, because traditional public schools have to accept all students, motivated or not. As Diane Ravitch put it: "Our schools cannot improve if charter schools siphon away the most motivated students and their families in the poorest communities from the regular public schools."[58] But the issue is not so simple as that.

While those parents who enter their children's names in the lotteries for admission to charter schools may well be more motivated to promote their children's education, and to cooperate with schools in doing so, those who *win* in these lotteries are greatly outnumbered by those who *do not win*— as in other lotteries in general. In 2017, for example, there were 17,000 applicants for 3,000 places available in the Success Academy charter schools.[59] When charter schools take a *fraction* of the children from motivated families, why does that prevent the traditional public schools from comparably educating the remaining *majority* of children from those motivated families?

A survey of empirical studies in various cities indicates that students who were motivated to enter lotteries for admission to charter schools— but who *did not win* in these lotteries— did not subsequently do as well in the traditional public schools as those who happened to be lucky enough to win and enter charter schools. For example, the *Wall Street Journal* reported:

> In New York City, Stanford economist Caroline Hoxby found that students accepted by lottery to charter schools were significantly outpacing the academic progress of their peers who lost the lottery and were forced to return to district schools.
>
> Florida State economist Tim Sass and colleagues found that middle-school students at charters in Florida and Chicago who continued into charter high schools were significantly more likely to graduate and go on to college than their peers who returned to district high schools because charter high schools were not available.
>
> The most telling study is by Harvard economist Tom Kane about charter schools in Boston. It found that students accepted by lottery at independently operated charter schools significantly outperformed students who lost the lottery and returned to district schools.[60]

A study published in a scholarly journal at the University of Chicago in 2015 found that, among students who entered a lottery for admission to a charter school in Harlem, those who were admitted subsequently scored "higher on academic achievement outcomes" than those who did not win admission. Moreover, the proportion of girls who subsequently became pregnant was less among the girls admitted to the charter school, and the boys were "less likely to be incarcerated."[61] Apparently charter schools do make a difference, and it is not just a matter of who was motivated to enter the lottery.

The often-repeated argument that traditional public schools must take *all* the students who show up does not mean that they must lump them all together when teaching them. If some successful charter schools today benefit from having many highly-motivated students, as critics claim, there is nothing to prevent traditional public schools from having the same beneficial effects from the even larger number of highly-motivated students who entered the lottery for a charter school but *did not win*. If officials who decide policies for traditional public schools prefer instead policies based on such concepts as "inclusion" or "diversity," then responsibility for the educational consequences that follow is theirs, and are not the fault of charter schools.

If some parents decide not to enroll their child in a charter school when confronted with academic or behavioral standards they are not used to, or if they withdraw their children later after discovering that they find the standards too hard, that is not simply the charter school expelling students in order to maintain a good record. How critics could possibly know how many of these internal decisions were made for what particular reason is one of many mysteries about how some charter school critics reach their conclusions.

A leading charter school critic, Professor Diane Ravitch of New York University, has based a sweeping conclusion on her interpretation of charter schools' educational results:

> Charter schools are a failed experiment. Study after study has shown that they do not get better test scores than public schools unless they screen out English-language learners and students with profound disabilities. [62]

There have been studies that reached opposite conclusions as to whether charter schools get better test scores than traditional public schools,[63] and if Professor Ravitch chooses to believe those studies that fit her assumptions, so be it. But as to her accusation that charter schools "do not get better test scores than public schools unless they screen out English-language learners and students with profound disabilities," that is something that can be tested empirically.

A nationwide study comparing the proportion of students with disabilities in both charter schools and traditional public schools, found that the average difference between the proportion of students with disabilities in traditional public schools was higher by about *two percentage points*.[64] Statistics cited by Professor Ravitch herself, in her book *Reign of Error*, showed that "while 11 percent of students in the nation have disabilities, charter schools enroll only 8 percent."[65] In 2019, the *New York Post* reported that "20,847 students with disabilities make up 18.5 percent of total charter enrollment, vs. 19.4 percent in the rest of the public system."[66] In other words, the difference was just under *one* percentage point.

Are differences of these magnitudes— from one to three percentage points— supposed to explain away charter school students' better educational outcomes than the outcomes in traditional public schools in the same communities? Such differences may provide talking points, but are such talking points the way to evaluate the education of children for whom education is one of their few hopes for a better life?

STUDENT DISCIPLINE DIFFERENCES

Despite the plain fact that students come from many very different backgrounds— on both sides of the Atlantic— and exhibit very different behavior patterns, the prevailing preconception and policy in many public schools is that statistical disparities in the disciplining of students from different racial, ethnic or other social backgrounds must be due to biased treatment of those students, rather than to any possible differences in student behavior.

The illogic of this was pointed out, years ago, in a landmark study titled *No Excuses* by Abigail Thernstrom and Stephan Thernstrom. They cited data showing that black students "are two-and-half times as likely to be disciplined as whites and five times as likely as Asians." But, as they also pointed out, from the same data, whites were disciplined at a rate twice that of Asians. Was that racism against whites? If not, then why was it automatically racism when blacks were disciplined two and a half times as often as whites?[67]

The Thernstroms also showed that the differing rates of school discipline were highly correlated with differing proportions of children raised in single-parent homes in these three groups. But the rate of disciplining of black students was *not* correlated with whether their teachers were predominantly white or included a substantial proportion of teachers who were black. In fact, one study indicated that, when teachers were asked to characterize which of their students were disruptive, black teachers named black students more often than did white teachers.[68]

The seemingly invincible fallacy that differences in outcomes between groups can only be due to other people's biases against particular groups, not to any differences in the behavior of the groups themselves, has led to school policies directed at reducing statistical disparities between groups in such disciplinary actions as suspensions or expulsions for disorderly or violent conduct. Here, as in other contexts, school officials' "accountability" has meant accountability for carrying out specified policies and procedures— *not* accountability for the educational consequences of those policies and procedures.

The consequences of reducing statistical disparities in rates of punishment have included imperatives to reduce the statistical rate of punishments in general. Since one cannot *increase* the rate of punishment for groups with low levels of disruptions and violence, the only viable alternative for reducing statistical disparities is to reduce the rate of punishment of students in groups with higher levels of disruptions and violence. Moreover, students themselves become quite aware when there is little or nothing that teachers can do to them when they misbehave.

Just how far the degeneration of school discipline can go was illustrated by incidents when David Levin, a co-founder of the KIPP schools, was a beginning teacher in a traditional public school in Houston, under the Teach for America program:

> One of the older children walked across the room during class, zipped down his fly, pulled out his penis, and asked a girl for oral sex. Levin sent him to the principal. He was sent back in thirty minutes. Another student threw a book at Levin's head. The office kept him an hour before sending him back, sucking on a Tootsie Pop.[69]

The point here is *not* to claim that these are typical offenses, but to demonstrate how egregious student behavior can become and still be tolerated under existing policies and practices in some traditional public schools.

Later, when Levin and Michael Feinberg founded the first KIPP school, their policy was "instant and overwhelming response to any violation of the rules."[70] This is what led some critics of KIPP school discipline to give the schools' initials the meaning "Kids In Prison Program."[71] The analogy fails, however, because students in KIPP charter schools— as in other charter schools— are there by choice and are free to leave. Instead, KIPP charter schools have grown over the years, to become the nation's largest non-profit charter school network. An observer of a KIPP charter school in the Bronx, where its students were housed in the same building with a traditional public school, found this scene at lunchtime:

> At lunch on any given day, children from the same neighborhood, eating the same food, at the same time, in the same room are a portrait in contrast. On one side of the room the KIPP students, all but two in attendance, are seated in order and eat while they talk in quiet, conversational tones. On the other side of the room, chaos is breaking out. Although a full third of the local school students are missing, lunch monitors scream at the children through bull horns, desperately trying to maintain control.[72]

An account by another observer of a Success Academy class of second-graders, riding the subway on a field trip to the Brooklyn Bridge, seems similar to the account of KIPP school students:

> Few things will empty a subway car of cranky commuters more quickly than rambunctious school groups. But their fellow riders seem either indifferent or charmed by the well-behaved second graders.[73]

Though neither behavioral standards nor any other single factor is likely to explain why some schools do much better than others, it is hard to imagine how educational quality can be maintained amid bedlam. Yet the behavioral standards in charter schools have repeatedly come under fire from critics, and the ability of charter schools to maintain such standards have been restricted by law in California's 2019 educational "reforms."[74]

Unsubstantiated accusations of excessive harshness in student discipline are in keeping with a more general notion that unjustified punishment against minority students is the beginning of a "school to prison pipeline." The opposite possibility— that lax discipline in school can lead to habits of lawless behavior by young people, increasing their chances of ending up in prison as adults— is seldom mentioned, much less tested empirically.

Reports of disruptions and violence— against both fellow students and teachers— have become common around the country. The *Minneapolis Star Tribune*, for example, reported that a St. Paul high school teacher was "choked and body-slammed by a student and hospitalized with a traumatic brain injury." It added:

> Though many— including St. Paul school officials— seem reluctant to acknowledge it, the escalating violence and disorder follow a major change in school disciplinary policies. In recent years, district leaders have increasingly removed consequences for misbehavior, and led kids to believe they can wreak havoc with impunity.[75]

According to *Education Week*, when a New Jersey teacher leaned over to talk to a disruptive student, "the student struck her in the face, causing Andrews' neck to snap backwards." This "caused permanent nerve damage." The result:

> The student was suspended for a week for disrespect toward a teacher— not for assault— and then returned to Andrews' classroom in Bridgeton, N.J.
> When Andrews asked her principal to permanently remove the student from her classroom, she says the principal told her to "put on her big girl panties and deal with it."[76]

In this case, the teacher was able to successfully sue the school board. But it can be difficult even to get accurate statistics on assaults against either teachers or other students when both the data and the definitions are controlled by the very authorities who promote lax discipline policies— and who are "accountable" for reducing suspension rates, but *not* "accountable" for the educational consequences.

In New York City, for example, after Mayor Bill de Blasio's administration reduced suspensions, "the de Blasio administration removed the vast majority of school-order-related questions on the NYC School Survey." Nevertheless, in this case, teachers and students indicated that the school climate "deteriorated dramatically when de Blasio's reform was implemented (i.e., from 2013–14 to 2015–16)."[77] Students reported more physical fighting and gang activity.[78]

At the federal government level, there was a further major restriction of disciplinary actions against disruptive and violent students. On January 8, 2014, a joint declaration by the U.S. Department of Education and the U.S. Department of Justice, in a "Dear Colleague" letter to school officials, declared that "Federal law prohibits public school districts from discriminating in the administration of student discipline based on certain personal characteristics."

Statistical disparities were now being equated with discrimination, with the full power of the federal government behind that interpretation. Although this policy was presented as an effort to prevent discrimination, the lower standards of discipline it promoted would in practice apply to students in general, since other students could hardly be punished for things for which students from racial or ethnic minorities were not being punished.

A later study in the wake of the 2014 "Dear Colleague" letter found that the percentage of public school teachers who reported that they had been attacked by a student from their school in school year 2015–2016 was "higher than in all previous survey years."[79] In St. Paul, Minnesota, "the number of assaults against teachers doubled from 2014 to 2015."[80] In Indianapolis, a teacher told the school board: "At the beginning of the year, a student assaulted a teacher in broad daylight in a hallway of our school. . . . He was back the next day."[81]

One of the painful problems in disciplinary policies is that this issue has gotten tangled up with racial issues. But the very same kinds of policies produce the same kinds of results in England, where the underclass is predominantly white. British victims of violent students include a pregnant teacher who had a miscarriage after being physically attacked by a student,[82] and another teacher who was stabbed to death in the classroom, in front of her other students.[83] It has long been recognized that teenagers especially tend to test the limits of what they can get away with. The question for adults is not simply where to draw the line but *whether* to draw the line.

Too often, hazy and lofty rhetoric— "restorative justice" being a phrase and a process currently in vogue— uses talk as a substitute for drawing a line with consequences.

Incidentally, the student attack on a pregnant teacher in England had its counterpart in New York City:

> At Norman Thomas High School, a student had punched a pregnant teacher in the stomach and said, "I'm going to kick the baby out of you. I'm going to make you have that baby." Instead of immediately suspending the student, DOE[84] had allowed him to return to school until his suspension hearing took place.[85]

Many people with a particular social vision regard punishment as something that can be replaced by other ways of changing people's conduct. In other words, they are ideologically opposed to punishment in general. Others have reasons to be opposed to punishment for reasons of their own self-interest. In the United States, teachers unions have supported policies reducing student suspensions and expulsions, despite the fact that teachers have often been targets of student violence.[86]

The cost to other students of having their education— and their chances in life as adults— ruined by chronic troublemakers in the schools is seldom even considered in such arguments. Keeping the troublemakers in school may not mean that they are actually learning anything, except how to be troublemakers. But some people may think that, if troublemakers are no longer in school, they are likely to drift into a life of crime on the streets. However, if instead of stealing from stores or homes when they are out of school, the troublemakers ruin the education— and the futures— of the students around them, the damage may be far worse.

Even if lax discipline policies produce no real benefits in the long run to either troublemakers or other students, there are benefits for adults who run the schools. From the standpoint of officials in the public school system, and officials in the teachers unions, the worst hoodlum in a school and the most conscientious and intelligent student in that same school bring exactly the same amount of taxpayer money into the system. There is the same financial incentive to keep hoodlums in the system as there is to prevent conscientious and successful students from transferring to charter schools.

Every student who leaves the traditional unionized public school system— whether by expulsion, dropping out or transferring to a charter school— causes the system to lose money that is based on how many students are enrolled. In a city the size of New York, this can add up to millions of dollars a year. That is incentive enough to try to keep as many students as possible in the system as long as possible, whether they are learning anything or not, and even if some of them ruin the education— and with it the futures— of other students.

People who are opposed to firm discipline, whether for ideological or financial reasons, often criticize charter schools, whose discipline policies and practices tend to be stricter than in traditional public schools. But charter schools face an inherently different set of incentives and constraints.

Unlike traditional public schools, which automatically receive students, due to compulsory attendance laws, charter schools receive only those students whose parents voluntarily choose to apply for their admission. Letting some disruptive and violent students ruin the education of a much larger number of other students who are in school to learn would be counterproductive for the charter schools themselves.

Parents seek admission of their children to charter schools not only for a better education but also for better safety than in schools where disruptive and violent students are allowed far more latitude. Therefore charter schools would lose more than they would gain by following the same lax discipline policies as traditional public schools. Moreover, anti-charter-school "reforms" that force the charter schools to accept more disruptive and violent student behavior reduce the charter schools' attraction for parents seeking both safety and better education for their children.

Like most such "reforms," the real beneficiaries are adults with vested interests in traditional unionized public schools, when the competitive attractions of charter schools are reduced.

Chapter 6

DANGERS

> Charter schools are like many education reforms: They have broad but shallow support among a majority of the population and intense but narrow opposition from teachers unions and their allies.
>
> David Osborne[1]

Against a background of decades of widespread angst about how, when or whether non-white youngsters could close the test score gap between themselves and their white counterparts, the fact that this gap has already been closed by non-white youngsters in New York City charter schools as a whole[2] is a landmark achievement. It is also an achievement that has received relatively little public recognition, in proportion to the magnitude of that achievement and in proportion to the number of educational doctrines which that achievement has exposed as fallacies.

The educational success of these charter schools undermines theories of genetic determinism, claims of cultural bias in the tests, assertions that racial "integration" is necessary for blacks to reach educational parity and presumptions that income differences are among the "root causes" of educational differences.[3] This last claim has been used for decades to absolve traditional public schools of any responsibility for educational failures in low-income minority communities. The supposed imperative for smaller class sizes is also called into question when the most successful of the charter school networks— the Success Academy charter schools— have average class sizes of thirty or more students.[4]

What happened in New York City's charter schools is no guarantee of the same things happening in other communities, though in fact somewhat similar results have been found elsewhere.[5] Nor are outstanding charter school results a guarantee that charter schools are *categorically* superior to all traditional public schools, even in New York City, or that the methods used by many charter schools are best for children from all socioeconomic backgrounds. But, whatever the limitations of the social range of what charter schools have achieved thus far, the implications of their existing achievements can nevertheless be a game-changer in the field of education— to the extent that facts are known and heeded.

As an analogy, the initial flight of the Wright brothers' plane was shorter than the wingspan of a Boeing 747, but *the implications of what it proved*— on however small a scale— reverberated around the world, and changed that world forever. Once it was proved that a machine could lift itself into the air, and move forward through the air under its own power, even for a distance not quite as far as from home plate to second base on a baseball diamond,[6] that was decisive. How much the scope of that machine could be expanded was an engineering question that only the future could answer. But the scientific question was already answered by that first flight.

The educational achievements of charter schools may be little known to the general public, and either denied or downplayed by critics. But officials of the traditional public schools with whom they compete show by their actions that they see charter school achievements as a very real danger. So do teachers unions. And both actively make themselves dangers to charter schools.

From the standpoint of children's education— and especially the education of children for whom education is their one best chance for a better life— the dangers that matter most are not dangers to the survival of existing charter schools as institutions, or to those who wish to create additional charter schools. The biggest danger is that a new wave of anti-charter-school "reforms," which have already become law in California in 2019, can so increase the external impediments to charter schools and so stifle their internal operations as to lower their quality— and make them no longer such a threat to attract students from traditional public schools.

California's incoming Governor Gavin Newsom, elected in 2018, began in early 2019 to support a series of sweeping legislative "reforms" of charter schools. These "reforms" aimed at both restricting charter schools externally and changing them internally. The legislation he signed into law in 2019 closely follows patterns that have long been part of teachers union agendas, and similar policies are being urged in other states. So an examination of the California legislation has implications that extend far beyond that state.

ANTI-CHARTER-SCHOOL "REFORMS"

While it might be assumed that educational reforms would be focused on dealing with things affecting children's education, what is remarkable about the kind of legislation affecting charter schools that was passed in California in 2019, and is being proposed elsewhere, is that it has seldom made even a plausible case that it will improve the quality of children's education. But its protection of adult vested interests in traditional unionized public schools is far more apparent.

The kinds of "reforms" being proposed and enacted into law are both external and internal. That is, they include new powers in regulatory institutions external to the charter schools and new powers to prescribe what happens inside charter schools, eroding the autonomy that was a central reason for creating such schools in the first place.

External Restrictions

Existing examples of external restrictions include laws specifying in advance a numerical limit on the number of charter schools allowed in a given jurisdiction— *independently of whether the quality of education in those charter schools is good, bad, or indifferent.* These numbers are also independent of whether the quality of the education in the traditional public schools in the same communities is good, bad or indifferent. Whatever the rhetoric that may be deployed to justify such laws, these laws are not about improving the quality of education in either charter schools or traditional public schools. They are about limiting an exodus of students from traditional public schools to public charter schools.

An estimated one million students are on waiting lists for charter schools nationwide. This means billions of dollars that would move from traditional public schools to public charter schools, if there were enough charter schools with enough capacity to absorb all these students. That is ample incentive for both traditional public school officials and officials of teachers unions to make sure that no such thing happens. We have seen to what lengths school district officials have gone to prevent vacant school buildings from being used by charter schools. New anti-charter-school "reforms" in California expand the scope of local school district officials' powers to block the creation or expansion of charter schools.

New laws passed in California in 2019 empower local education officials to deny applications for establishing a charter school if the charter school "is demonstrably unlikely to serve the interests of the entire community in which the school is proposing to locate," or if the "school district is not positioned to absorb the fiscal impact of the proposed charter school."[7] In short, incumbents are empowered to determine if "the entire community" really *needs* their potential competitors, or if the competition of newcomers would inconvenience existing institutions. Absurd as it might seem to let incumbents decide whether new competitors are needed, doing so has a long history of political success in many other fields— holding back progress in those fields, sometimes for years and sometimes for decades.

Among the fields in which incumbents, or officials representing incumbents' interests, have delayed progress include airlines, freight transportation and both radio and television broadcasting. In fields where government regulation required newcomers seeking entrance into those fields to show where there was a public "necessity" or "convenience" for their services, that was obviously a subjective decision as to whether existing incumbents were already adequately serving the public. Even during many years of rapidly increasing airline travel, for example, there was apparently no need for corresponding increases in the number of airlines— as judged by those concerned about the impact of new competition on incumbent airlines.[8]

Once "deregulation" of the airline industry put an end to these restrictions, however, numerous new airlines were created, and various old and historic airlines went out of business in a more competitive industry, as air travel prices fell and far more flights went to far more places than before.[9] Apparently the public "necessity" and "convenience" were better served by competition than by leaving the determination of such things in the hands of those preoccupied with protecting incumbents.

For a very long time after railroads were established, they were the dominant way of transporting freight long distances over land. Eventually, however, the rising automobile industry began creating trucks that could also carry freight long distances over land, in competition with railroads— and, in particular cases, do so better and cheaper than railroads. Here, as well, government regulators, concerned for the economic survival of railroad incumbents, required interstate trucking companies to get federal authorization, based on showing a public "necessity" and "convenience" for authorization to carry freight between particular points only, leaving other places for the railroads.[10]

Decades later, after this industry was deregulated, freer competition both enabled and required greater efficiency. The price of shipping freight by truck fell, and customers reported that the service also improved as well.[11] In broadcasting, AM radio came first and, after FM radio was technologically available, regulatory protection of the AM incumbents delayed its introduction and spread.[12] Similarly, television broadcasting through the air came first and the availability of cable television was delayed by the same preoccupation with protecting incumbents from competition.[13]

The same preoccupation with protecting incumbents from the competition of newcomers— in the name of protecting the public— has already been demonstrated in public school education. Increasing the power of incumbent officials to stifle the growth of charter schools has nothing to do with improving the education of children and everything to do with protecting the vested interests of adults in traditional unionized public schools.

Internal Restrictions

External institutional restrictions on charter schools, such as numerical limits on the number of charter schools permitted or restrictions on their use of existing public school buildings, have been supplemented in the new anti-charter-school agenda by internal restrictions on charter schools' autonomy in making decisions about standards for student behavior and choices in the courses they teach.

One of the few things on which both critics and supporters of charter schools agree is that the level of discipline in the charter schools is significantly more strict than in traditional public schools. In general, students can be far more readily punished, suspended or expelled from charter schools. With recent political trends favoring opponents of charter schools, there have been calls for restricting charter schools' ability to impose what critics call "harsh" discipline. In 2019, the California Education Code was amended by Section 48901.1:

> (a) A pupil enrolled in a charter school in kindergarten or any of grades 1 to 5, inclusive, shall not be suspended on the basis of having disrupted school activities or otherwise willfully defied the valid authority of supervisors, teachers, administrators, school officials, or other school personnel engaged in the performance of their duties, and those acts shall not constitute grounds for a pupil enrolled in a charter school in kindergarten or any of grades 1 to 12, inclusive, to be recommended for expulsion.
> (b) a pupil enrolled in a charter school in any of grades 6 to 8, inclusive, shall not be suspended on the basis of having disrupted school activities or otherwise willfully defied the valid authority of supervisors, teachers, administrators, school officials, or other school personnel engaged in the performance of their duties.[14]

These restrictions are not peculiar to charter schools. They are lax discipline policies already imposed on traditional public schools that are now being imposed on charter schools.

With the strongest restrictions on suspensions being imposed in the earliest grades, this means that children entering the school system are allowed years to get used to violating rules with impunity before being confronted with consequences for violating rules. And of course rules without consequences for violations are not really rules, but suggestions. California has created the nearest thing to tenure for troublemakers among students.

Opposite policies in the Success Academy charter schools in New York are directed toward getting kindergarten students used to following rules from the first day— when showing up wearing the wrong socks with the school's uniform is enough to get the child turned away at the door.[15] It is not that socks are so important, but that rules are important, if time, energy and morale are not to be dissipated in simply trying to maintain order and keep students focused on the central task of getting an education.

Just a small number of students, allowed to disrupt classes and defy teachers with impunity, can ruin the education of many other students who are trying to learn. But this is just one of many ways in which the education of students plays no such important role in educational policy as in educational rhetoric.

If the purpose of restricting charter schools' ability to impose firm discipline is to reduce an "unfair" advantage in the competition with traditional public schools, then such lax discipline policies may make some sense from a purely political perspective. But imposing the handicaps of less successful institutions on more successful institutions is— once again— sacrificing the education of children for the sake of serving the vested interests of adults.

Another area in which the internal autonomy of charter schools has come under threat is in deciding what courses to teach. The curriculum in many traditional public schools has long included various kinds of ideological indoctrination courses.[16] Some adults see schools as a golden opportunity to indoctrinate a captive audience of children, and see themselves as crusading "agents of social change."

Charter schools, with their intense focus on educational fundamentals, may not be nearly so receptive to spending their students' time on these adult ideological interests and adventures.

Neither was Dunbar High School, back during its era of academic achievement.[17] Ideological agendas in public schools absorb time, energy and resources that are especially needed in the education of young people from a cultural background often lacking in many of the things that youngsters in more fortunate circumstances can take for granted— such as highly educated parents, books in the home and a whole way of life that prepares them in childhood for achievements as adults.

Propagandists in the classroom are a luxury that the poor can afford least of all. While a mastery of mathematics and English can be a ticket out of poverty, a highly cultivated sense of grievance and resentment is not. The merits or demerits of a particular ideology are irrelevant to the urgent task of educating young people in the skills that will determine what kind of future they will have available as adults. Replacing the beliefs of the political left by the beliefs of the political right would make no difference whatever in the tragedy of wasting opportunities for preparing the young for a better life as adults— opportunities they will get just one time in their lives, and whose good or bad consequences can dominate the rest of their lives as adults.

The process of forcing indoctrination courses into charter schools has already begun in California. Legislation forcing charter schools to teach what is called "sex education" has already been passed, and proposed legislation would also force them to teach what is called "ethnic studies." Similar ideological indoctrination courses have long been promoted in traditional public schools across the country.[18]

Among the reasons for creating charter schools in the first place was to see if an institution operating with more autonomy could develop some alternative ways of educating children— with whatever more successful practices might come out of that process providing examples that could be used to improve education in traditional public schools. In practice, however, factors enabling charter schools to get better educational results have been treated as "unfair" advantages to be countered, in the interest of preserving existing traditional schools for the adults they benefit.

Another "reform" that the teachers unions and their allies want imposed on charter schools is legislation requiring them to hold their meetings in public and open their internal records to public scrutiny.

In 2019, California's incoming Governor Gavin Newsom signed such legislation— Senate Bill 126— into law, in the name of "transparency." According to one of the proponents of this legislation: "Charter schools receive quite a few taxpayer dollars. There needs to be sunshine in all public schools and their governing bodies, and this is what this bill stands for."[19]

The most important information about a charter school was already available— how well its students are educated. Here, yet again, "transparency" has *nothing to do with the quality of education*. Open meetings and publicizing personal information about people who run a charter school, or who serve on its governing boards, are an open invitation for reprisals, threats or worse. During the mid-twentieth century struggles for civil rights in the South, a number of Southern states passed similar laws, requiring the NAACP to release such information about its members and donors. In striking down such laws, the Supreme Court of the United States said:

> Petitioner has made an uncontroverted showing that on past occasions revelation of the identity of its rank-and-file members has exposed these members to economic reprisal, loss of employment, threat of physical coercion, and other manifestations of public hostility. Under these circumstances, we think it apparent that compelled disclosure of petitioner's Alabama membership is likely to affect adversely the ability of petitioner and its members to pursue their collective effort to foster beliefs which they admittedly have the right to advocate, in that it may induce members to withdraw from the Association and dissuade others from joining it because of fear of exposure of their beliefs shown through their associations and of the consequences of this exposure.[20]

Given the manifest hostility to charter schools in various quarters today, the same grounds cited by the Supreme Court apply. It is necessary to cut through the rhetoric of such nice-sounding words as "sunshine" and "transparency" to the ugly realities behind such words. People who are willing to donate money to charter schools, or to serve on their governing boards, or in other capacities, may not be willing to see their businesses suffer reprisals or their homes vandalized and their families harassed or threatened. Nor is there any *educational* purpose served by imposing such requirements. Nor is it even alleged that some educational problem in charter schools would be solved by such requirements.

When Success Academy founder and leader Eva Moskowitz was questioned by a New York City Council committee, her testimony that she lived in Harlem was challenged by a committee member who demanded to know on what street. She declined to say, citing safety concerns for her children.[21] If "transparency" laws— being advocated by teachers unions and others— were to be imposed in New York, forcing her to either give up her job or jeopardize her family's security, should that be done for the sake of a nice-sounding word like "transparency" that conceals some very ugly realities?

The painful irony is that today's NAACP officials have come out in favor of "transparency" requirements for charter schools,[22] despite the history of similar tactics having been used across the South to try to destroy their own organization, during the civil rights struggles of the 1950s and 1960s. Then and now, such tactics amount to using the law to facilitate reprisals outside the law.

Then and now, the appearance of even-handedness has been used by advocates of such laws, by saying that other organizations were covered by the same laws. But a district court, back in 1958, saw through this theoretical equality to the real world differences:

> Registration of persons engaged in a popular cause imposes no hardship while, as the evidence in this case shows, registration of names of persons who resist the popular will would lead not only to expressions of ill will and hostility but to the loss of members by the plaintiff Association.[23]

In California, a group called the Charter Task Force was formed— and, ironically, held *private* meetings in a public institution, with neither "sunshine" nor "transparency"— to determine the fate of California's charter schools. A local newspaper reported:

Each Thursday, a group of educators and representatives of labor unions meets— out of the public eye— for several hours at the California Department of Education building in Sacramento to take on arguably the most contentious current issue on California's education reform landscape: charter school reform.[24]

However inconsistent this may be as a matter of principle, it is not at all hard to understand as a matter of politics. As a matter of principle, one might ask what possible benefit to *the education of children* could be expected from insistence on "transparency." But no such question is necessary, unless one takes seriously the often-repeated claims of teachers unions and politicians that what they are doing is "for the sake of the children."

What has happened in California is not unique. As *Philanthropy* magazine has reported:

Charitable donors who want to decide for themselves whether to be public or private in their giving have had a lot to be disheartened by in recent years. Bills have been filed in many state legislatures to limit the right of givers to stay out of the public eye.

For example, a bill was introduced in Maine's legislature during its 2019 session that would have required every nonprofit in the state to disclose all of its donors. . . .

There are also efforts that blatantly target specific groups, such as legislation in Connecticut aimed at forcing nonprofit charter-school operators to disclose major contributors.[25]

Even the advocates of new anti-charter-school laws and policies are hard-pressed to come up with any *educational* rationale for essentially forcing charter schools to follow the kinds of "reforms" imposed. The old saying, "If it ain't broke, don't fix it" has not been applied to charter schools. For the teachers unions, and those who support their agenda, the principle seems to be: "If it ain't broke, then break it!" That is what most of the proposed and enacted "reforms" of charter schools seem to amount to.

Legislative "reforms" such as those in California are not the only new initiatives that threaten the *educational* success of charter schools, even if they do not threaten the physical survival of charter schools as institutions. One particularly striking— and perhaps dangerous— institutional change has apparently already taken place in New York City.

In 2019 the *New York Times* reported that a former Deputy Mayor in Mayor Bill de Blasio's administration— Richard Buery— "took over last year as the head of policy at KIPP" after "KIPP executives' relationships with elected officials were fraying."[26] This was not an isolated appointment, but apparently part of a shift in institutional orientation:

> Mr. Buery is part of a push to reverse the norm of mostly black and Hispanic charters in New York being staffed mainly by white teachers. . . KIPP hired a chief diversity officer to promote "anti-racist practices."[27]

Here, as with the anti-charter-school legislation in California, these are not like the more or less *ad hoc* obstructions or harassments of local school district officials, such as blocking charter schools from getting vacant school buildings or slow-walking applications to set up charter schools. These new developments in New York City are *institutionalized* interventions within the charter schools themselves. They are part of the anti-charter-school backlash already noted by various observers, and exemplified by New York City Mayor Bill de Blasio's 2019 address to the National Education Association, the nation's largest teachers union.

Mayor de Blasio proclaimed his own feelings toward charter school founders and supporters, whom he called "the privatizers": "I hate the privatizers and I want to stop them." He added: "Get away from high-stakes testing, get away from charter schools. No federal funding for charter schools." He told the NEA gathering that no political candidate should ask for their support "unless they're willing to stand up to Wall Street and the rich people behind the charter school movement once and for all."[28] That Mayor de Blasio's former Deputy Mayor is now an official inside the KIPP charter school network in New York City is one sign of the times.

Some charter schools, and some organizations representing charter schools, seem reluctant to sound a general alarm about what is being done by anti-charter-school officials. After all, these government officials have the power to retaliate in various ways against charter schools that fight back. But Eva Moskowitz, who had political experience before becoming head of Success Academy charter schools, has followed opposite policies of public protests, and has in some cases forced Mayor Bill de Blasio to back down. Nevertheless, the anti-charter-school forces have also had their victories against Success Academy schools.

During one of these political clashes, New York State Governor Andrew Cuomo cautioned Ms. Moskowitz "that if I didn't compromise, I might lose and walk away with nothing," she recalled. Her response may be very relevant to issues involved in current anti-charter-school "reforms" elsewhere:

> I responded that I did understand this but was not willing to give up on opening our schools. What I didn't say was that I regarded defeat as preferable to surrender. A compromise with de Blasio would be an implicit endorsement of the outcome. If de Blasio was going to kill these schools, to take away these educational opportunities parents wanted for their children, I wanted the world to know that he'd done it. This was the best way to ensure that de Blasio didn't do to other charter schools what he'd done to us. Then, at least, our loss would serve some purpose.[29]

By contrast, organizations representing charter schools in California seem to have been far more circumspect in their opposition to the 2019 anti-charter-school "reforms"— thereby allowing Governor Gavin Newsom to represent those "reforms" as jointly negotiated agreements involving all parties concerned. In circumstances where the general public has no such hostility to charter schools as teachers unions and other vested interests have— but also not much knowledge of what is going on— even vast expenditures of money for television ads opposing anti-charter-school legislation are no substitute for the kind of clear and timely expressions of outrage used by Eva Moskowitz in New York.

Since the KIPP charter schools in New York City seem to have taken the opposite approach from that of Ms. Moskowitz, by taking one of Mayor de Blasio's officials into their own organization, time may tell which approach produces what results. Meanwhile, Eva Moskowitz has remained unabashedly outspoken. When the U.S. Department of Education awarded nearly ten million dollars to the Success Academy schools in 2019, to expand their operations, the *New York Post* reported:

> "Success is ready to open more great schools, and the city has become painfully aware of the lack of access children of color have to high-quality education," said Success CEO Eva Moskowitz.
>
> "But these schools can't open because the city is refusing to provide space in one of the 212 half-empty school buildings," she said. "The only thing standing between New York City children and a good education is Mayor de Blasio."[30]

THE CURRENT CRISIS

Over the years, the political pendulum has sometimes swung in favor of charter schools, and more recently has swung against them. A *New York Times* report, for example, said in 2019: "The city and state's political forces have turned decisively against charter schools over the last few years."[31] There were similar signs on the national political scene as well, as some leading candidates for their party's presidential nomination announced policy positions in opposition to charter schools.[32] A similar assessment was made by the *Wall Street Journal*: "The school-reform movement is a victim of its own success as charters compete successfully with traditional public schools, prompting a political backlash from unions across the U.S."[33]

The political pendulum may swing back the other way yet again sometime. But this process is not symmetrical. Progress is far more fragile than destruction. People who would like to see the opportunities that charter schools represent for children in low-income minority communities continue cannot simply wait and hope for the next swing of the pendulum. Once the educational quality of charter schools has been fundamentally reduced or destroyed, there is no guarantee that it can be revived if and when political trends turn favorable.

The fate of Dunbar High School in Washington, with its impressive record of educational achievements for black youngsters over an 85-year period, is a case in point. As of 1953, 81 percent of Dunbar High School graduates went on to college.[34] But, after a reorganization of Washington public schools, following the 1954 Supreme Court decision outlawing racial segregation, the city's public schools were made neighborhood schools. Dunbar could no longer accept black students from all over Washington, as before, but only students from its own local ghetto neighborhood district. By 1960, only 20 percent of Dunbar students went on to college. The trigonometry and three-dimensional geometry previously taught at Dunbar were replaced by arithmetic.[35]

In 2014, Dunbar was one of the lowest scoring high schools in Washington's Ward 5, on the mathematics test. A KIPP charter high school in that ward had three times as high a proportion of its students passing the mathematics test as did the students in Dunbar High School.[36] More than a century earlier, in 1903, a French educator visiting what was then called the "M Street School" described its students as "pursuing the same studies as our average college students."[37] A student from this high school in that era took the entrance examination for Amherst College— and, as a result of his performance on that exam, he was given credit for first year college mathematics, on the basis of what he had learned in the high school that was later named Dunbar.[38] He graduated from Amherst in three years, class of 1905, Phi Beta Kappa.[39]

Nor was he unique. Over a period of 62 years, ending in 1954, 34 graduates of Dunbar High School (and the "M Street School," as it was known before it was renamed in 1916), were admitted to Amherst

College. Of these, 74 percent graduated from Amherst, and of these graduates, more than one-fourth were Phi Beta Kappas.[40] Dunbar graduates also became Phi Beta Kappas at Harvard, Yale, Williams, Cornell, Dartmouth, and other elite institutions during that era.[41]

Dunbar's abrupt destruction as a quality educational institution in the 1950s was not done deliberately or maliciously. It was simply an imposed institutional change in just one aspect of its circumstances— a different source of students, who were black students both before and after the change. The school continues to exist today as an institution with students, staff and physical accommodations. Indeed, it now has an impressive new building, costing more than $100 million, and surpassing anything that Dunbar ever had when it was a high-quality educational institution. But Dunbar students' math test scores are now among the lowest in its ward.[42]

If the more numerous and intrusive "reforms" of charter schools being proposed and enacted today, closely following the agenda of the teachers unions, are successfully carried out, the consequences may not be so much a reduction in the number of charter schools as the undermining of the qualities that have enabled many of these schools to so outperform traditional public schools in their communities as to pose an existential danger to those unionized schools. Charter schools may well continue to exist as institutions, just as Dunbar High School does, after the heart of their educational success has been diminished or destroyed. Even if political trends later became more favorable to charter schools, restoring that success can be very unlikely.

A sharp distinction must always be made between the physical survival of particular schools and the survival of educational quality in those schools. The former may be important to adult incumbents in charge of those schools, but the latter is crucial to the fate of children— especially those children who have few other favorable options in life. For denatured charter schools to survive as institutions, in the same sense in which Dunbar High School today survives as an institution, would be only a painful mockery.

A much more optimistic view of the situation has been taken by the editor of the quarterly publication *Philanthropy*:

Even amidst today's pushback, there's another reality that should prevent ed reformers from becoming gloomy. The hard-won accomplishments of the last two decades are not going to go away. There are now tens of thousands of schools of choice across the country, enrolling more than 10 million children. Entire states like Florida, Arizona, Indiana, and Pennsylvania, and dozens of cities like New York, Washington, Boston, New Orleans, and Los Angeles have become wholly different ecosystems, educationally, than they were 20 years earlier.

...Over the next few difficult years, school improvers may not be able to move the ball much further down the field. But they're not going to surrender the yardage already gained. That's because, beneath the carping of apologists for failed schools, the classroom innovations of the last generation have produced concrete results in volume.[43]

We may hope that this optimistic view is vindicated by events, but that is a question which only the future can answer. Unfortunately, some of the yardage gained by charter schools seems already to have begun being lost in California and in New York City. As for the successful charter school "innovations of the last generation," it is not at all clear how much of that story has reached the general public through the filter of the media and the distortions of hostile politicians, teachers unions and other adults with their own agendas.

Destruction is often easier, faster and more permanent than creation. The stakes are very high, especially for those children who have few other opportunities for a better life. But this is ultimately not a question of choosing between charter schools as a whole and other public schools as a whole. The issue is *not* whether one kind of school is *categorically* superior to another in all kinds of communities and among children raised in all kinds of different social circumstances.

THE FUTURE

As Edmund Burke warned, more than two centuries ago, "we are too exquisite in our conjectures of the future."[44] We cannot simply compile a wish list of things we would like to see happen in the future. Trying to micromanage the future has a very poor track record— and so does simply letting things drift. What we can do is consider in advance what kind of general principles and specific institutions seem promising.

Perhaps the most important of these general principles is that schools exist for *the education of children*. Schools do not exist to provide iron-clad jobs for teachers, billions of dollars in union dues for teachers unions, monopolies for educational bureaucracies, a guaranteed market for teachers college degrees or a captive audience for indoctrinators. Those who want to see quality education remain available to youngsters in low-income minority neighborhoods must raise the question, again and again, when various policies and practices are proposed: "How is this going to affect *the education of children*?" A surprisingly large proportion of policies and practices cannot answer that question.

Institutional arrangements are especially in need of careful scrutiny, because so much of what institutions do is little known to the general public, despite having major effects on educational outcomes. How many members of the general public know that there are a million students on charter school waiting lists, while local district officials prevent charter schools from acquiring vacant school buildings in which to educate them? Given the small likelihood of a general public that can stay abreast of on-going institutional decisions, there is a special need for scrutiny of what particular institutions are being empowered to do, and what that is likely to lead to.

One current institutional arrangement that is long overdue for change is in the oversight of charter schools, which need oversight like all other institutions. But the crucial question is *what kind* of oversight. To have created an institutional situation where officials in the traditional and unionized public school system are in charge of providing classrooms and other services to charter schools reflects either a remarkable degree of naiveté or a remarkable degree of cynicism. This is an institutional situation very much in need of fundamental change, so that charter schools are not continually forced to dissipate time and resources fighting off harassments and obstructions— time and resources that could be far better used for the education of their students.

The recent California legislation empowering officials representing incumbent traditional unionized public schools to decide if new charter schools are *needed* by the public or *convenient* for existing schools is an institutional issue with a long track record of obstructing progress in other fields. If it is too late to reverse that legislation in California, it is not too late for other people in other places to understand why such institutional arrangements virtually guarantee that incumbents' vested interests are going to prevail over the interests of schoolchildren's education.

Possible ways of having charter schools independently overseen could include a separate chain of command for charter schools and/or an ombudsman— appointed not by politicians dependent on teachers union money, but by some independent authority, such as a court. A court of law could have a major deterrent effect on the widespread practice of traditional education officials pretending that there are no empty classrooms available in existing school buildings, and no vacant school buildings available, that could be used by charter schools with long waiting lists of applicants. Perjury laws and laws against violating fiduciary responsibilities have teeth.

Important as it is to try to get rid of institutionalized practices that cannot even plausibly claim to be about improving educational quality, at the present juncture it may be an even more urgent priority to prevent still more such institutionalized handicaps to *educating children* from being imposed in the future. Amid a swirl of slippery words such as "transparency," "accountability," and "due process," the plain and direct question that must be asked, again and again, is: "How, specifically, is this going to make *the education of children* better?"

This is especially important when considering children from a cultural background lacking the advantages that are common among children born into more fortunate circumstances. Children who have not received at home the educational, behavioral or other foundations for making the most of their natural abilities, must get those things in schools. These are the plain and harsh realities of circumstances.

The stakes are huge— not only for children whose education can be their one clear chance for a better life, but also for a whole society that needs productive members, fulfilling themselves while contributing their talents to the progress of the community at large. Students who emerge from their education with a mastery of mathematics, the English language and other fundamentals are ready to be those kinds of people, regardless of what color or class they come from. No narrow vested interests of adults— whether financial, political or ideological— should be allowed to block that.

APPENDIX

* Co-located schools are schools where public charter schools and traditional public schools are located together in the same school buildings. The data shown are for only those grade levels that the co-located schools have in common.

133

TEST SCORES, NEW YORK CITY, 2017–2018 SCHOOL YEAR: PUBLIC CHARTER SCHOOLS AND TRADITIONAL PUBLIC SCHOOLS, LOCATED IN THE SAME BUILDINGS

In the tables that follow, schools in a public charter school network are listed alphabetically by the name of their respective networks, and independent public charter schools are listed by their own individual school names.

Readers who wish to see data for particular traditional public schools can find the pages on which these schools' data appear by consulting the listings shown on the pages immediately preceding this one.

ACADEMIC LEADERSHIP CHARTER SCHOOL   New York State English Language Arts Test Results, 2017–2018

SCHOOLS HOUSED TOGETHER	CLASS GRADE LEVEL	LEVEL 1 RESULTS (Percent)	LEVEL 2 RESULTS (Percent)	LEVEL 3 RESULTS (Percent)	LEVEL 4 RESULTS (Percent)
ACADEMIC LEADERSHIP CHARTER SCHOOL	3rd grade	2	6	56	36
Mother Hale Academy	3rd grade	24	48	22	5
ACADEMIC LEADERSHIP CHARTER SCHOOL	4th grade	7	24	44	24
Mother Hale Academy	4th grade	17	40	36	6

Performance Levels: Level 1: Well Below Proficient   Level 2: Below Proficient   Level 3: Proficient   Level 4: Above Proficient
SOURCE: New York State Education Department

ACADEMIC LEADERSHIP CHARTER SCHOOL   New York State Mathematics Test Results, 2017–2018

SCHOOLS HOUSED TOGETHER	CLASS GRADE LEVEL	LEVEL 1 RESULTS (Percent)	LEVEL 2 RESULTS (Percent)	LEVEL 3 RESULTS (Percent)	LEVEL 4 RESULTS (Percent)
ACADEMIC LEADERSHIP CHARTER SCHOOL	3rd grade	2	10	32	56
Mother Hale Academy	3rd grade	33	38	26	3
ACADEMIC LEADERSHIP CHARTER SCHOOL	4th grade	4	27	22	47
Mother Hale Academy	4th grade	19	43	30	9

Performance Levels: Level 1: Well Below Proficient   Level 2: Below Proficient   Level 3: Proficient   Level 4: Above Proficient
SOURCE: New York State Education Department

ACHIEVEMENT FIRST CHARTER SCHOOLS New York State English Language Arts Test Results, 2017–2018

SCHOOLS HOUSED TOGETHER	CLASS GRADE LEVEL	LEVEL 1 RESULTS (Percent)	LEVEL 2 RESULTS (Percent)	LEVEL 3 RESULTS (Percent)	LEVEL 4 RESULTS (Percent)
ACHIEVEMENT FIRST CHARTER SCHOOL	5th grade	39	35	18	8
Adrian Hegeman School	5th grade	49	22	21	8
ACHIEVEMENT FIRST CHARTER SCHOOL	3rd grade	12	24	51	13
Alejandrina B. De Gautier School	3rd grade	19	63	19	0
ACHIEVEMENT FIRST CHARTER SCHOOL	4th grade	3	19	55	23
Alejandrina B. De Gautier School	4th grade	46	34	17	3
ACHIEVEMENT FIRST CHARTER SCHOOL	3rd grade	9	24	58	9
Ernest S. Jenkyns School	3rd grade	36	35	26	3
ACHIEVEMENT FIRST CHARTER SCHOOL	4th grade	4	33	43	20
Ernest S. Jenkyns School	4th grade	28	51	18	4
ACHIEVEMENT FIRST CHARTER SCHOOL	5th grade	13	28	36	23
Ernest S. Jenkyns School	5th grade	74	21	4	1
ACHIEVEMENT FIRST CHARTER SCHOOL	6th grade	3	21	39	36
Margaret S. Douglas Junior High School	6th grade	45	23	13	19
ACHIEVEMENT FIRST CHARTER SCHOOL	7th grade	5	27	58	10
Margaret S. Douglas Junior High School	7th grade	50	29	11	10
ACHIEVEMENT FIRST CHARTER SCHOOL	8th grade	0	11	45	45
Margaret S. Douglas Junior High School	8th grade	17	34	24	25

Performance Levels: Level 1: Well Below Proficient Level 2: Below Proficient Level 3: Proficient Level 4: Above Proficient
SOURCE: New York State Education Department

ACHIEVEMENT FIRST CHARTER SCHOOLS   New York State English Language Arts Test Results, 2017–2018
(Continued)

SCHOOLS HOUSED TOGETHER	CLASS GRADE LEVEL	LEVEL 1 RESULTS (Percent)	LEVEL 2 RESULTS (Percent)	LEVEL 3 RESULTS (Percent)	LEVEL 4 RESULTS (Percent)
ACHIEVEMENT FIRST CHARTER SCHOOL	6th grade	6	24	35	34
New Heights Middle School	6th grade	46	29	13	12
ACHIEVEMENT FIRST CHARTER SCHOOL	7th grade	10	34	52	4
New Heights Middle School	7th grade	44	33	19	5
ACHIEVEMENT FIRST CHARTER SCHOOL	8th grade	4	26	35	35
New Heights Middle School	8th grade	28	52	11	8
ACHIEVEMENT FIRST CHARTER SCHOOL	5th grade	8	34	38	20
Philippa Schuyler Junior High School	5th grade	16	21	39	24
ACHIEVEMENT FIRST CHARTER SCHOOL	6th grade	6	18	24	52
Philippa Schuyler Junior High School	6th grade	11	17	34	38
ACHIEVEMENT FIRST CHARTER SCHOOL	7th grade	0	19	58	23
Philippa Schuyler Junior High School	7th grade	12	33	45	9
ACHIEVEMENT FIRST CHARTER SCHOOL	8th grade	0	8	47	46
Philippa Schuyler Junior High School	8th grade	5	23	41	30
ACHIEVEMENT FIRST CHARTER SCHOOL	3rd grade	2	17	58	23
Roberto Clemente School	3rd grade	43	28	28	1
ACHIEVEMENT FIRST CHARTER SCHOOL	4th grade	2	22	41	34
Roberto Clemente School	4th grade	26	38	20	16

Performance Levels: Level 1: Well Below Proficient   Level 2: Below Proficient   Level 3: Proficient   Level 4: Above Proficient
SOURCE: New York State Education Department

ACHIEVEMENT FIRST CHARTER SCHOOLS   New York State Mathematics Test Results, 2017–2018

SCHOOLS HOUSED TOGETHER	CLASS GRADE LEVEL	LEVEL 1 RESULTS (Percent)	LEVEL 2 RESULTS (Percent)	LEVEL 3 RESULTS (Percent)	LEVEL 4 RESULTS (Percent)
ACHIEVEMENT FIRST CHARTER SCHOOL	5th grade	48	26	18	7
Adrian Hegeman School	5th grade	59	22	15	4
ACHIEVEMENT FIRST CHARTER SCHOOL	3rd grade	3	17	29	50
Alejandrina B. De Gautier School	3rd grade	25	31	44	0
ACHIEVEMENT FIRST CHARTER SCHOOL	4th grade	2	10	19	68
Alejandrina B. De Gautier School	4th grade	47	36	8	8
ACHIEVEMENT FIRST CHARTER SCHOOL	3rd grade	6	12	36	47
Ernest S. Jenkyns School	3rd grade	46	27	23	4
ACHIEVEMENT FIRST CHARTER SCHOOL	4th grade	4	30	35	31
Ernest S. Jenkyns School	4th grade	41	37	17	5
ACHIEVEMENT FIRST CHARTER SCHOOL	5th grade	12	23	33	32
Ernest S. Jenkyns School	5th grade	74	22	4	0
ACHIEVEMENT FIRST CHARTER SCHOOL	6th grade	2	19	49	30
Margaret S. Douglas Junior High School	6th grade	46	26	16	11
ACHIEVEMENT FIRST CHARTER SCHOOL	7th grade	2	8	26	64
Margaret S. Douglas Junior High School	7th grade	61	18	10	11
ACHIEVEMENT FIRST CHARTER SCHOOL	8th grade	0	4	41	55
Margaret S. Douglas Junior High School	8th grade	28	30	17	25

Performance Levels: Level 1: Well Below Proficient   Level 2: Below Proficient   Level 3: Proficient   Level 4: Above Proficient
SOURCE: New York State Education Department

ACHIEVEMENT FIRST CHARTER SCHOOLS   New York State Mathematics Test Results, 2017–2018 (Continued)

SCHOOLS HOUSED TOGETHER	CLASS GRADE LEVEL	LEVEL 1 RESULTS (Percent)	LEVEL 2 RESULTS (Percent)	LEVEL 3 RESULTS (Percent)	LEVEL 4 RESULTS (Percent)
ACHIEVEMENT FIRST CHARTER SCHOOL	6th grade	18	31	34	17
New Heights Middle School	6th grade	54	30	11	5
ACHIEVEMENT FIRST CHARTER SCHOOL	7th grade	5	23	39	33
New Heights Middle School	7th grade	60	24	16	0
ACHIEVEMENT FIRST CHARTER SCHOOL	8th grade	8	20	29	44
New Heights Middle School	8th grade	59	29	13	0
ACHIEVEMENT FIRST CHARTER SCHOOL	5th grade	0	12	41	47
Philippa Schuyler Junior High School	5th grade	0	24	42	34
ACHIEVEMENT FIRST CHARTER SCHOOL	6th grade	6	20	37	36
Philippa Schuyler Junior High School	6th grade	20	30	37	12
ACHIEVEMENT FIRST CHARTER SCHOOL	7th grade	1	3	21	74
Philippa Schuyler Junior High School	7th grade	22	34	32	12
ACHIEVEMENT FIRST CHARTER SCHOOL	8th grade	0	2	17	80
Philippa Schuyler Junior High School	8th grade	27	34	25	14
ACHIEVEMENT FIRST CHARTER SCHOOL	3rd grade	0	1	26	73
Roberto Clemente School	3rd grade	57	16	19	7
ACHIEVEMENT FIRST CHARTER SCHOOL	4th grade	1	27	28	44
Roberto Clemente School	4th grade	38	16	23	23

Performance Levels: Level 1: Well Below Proficient   Level 2: Below Proficient   Level 3: Proficient   Level 4: Above Proficient
SOURCE: New York State Education Department

BRONX CHARTER SCHOOL FOR BETTER LEARNING   New York State English Language Arts Test Results, 2017–2018

SCHOOLS HOUSED TOGETHER	CLASS GRADE LEVEL	LEVEL 1 RESULTS (Percent)	LEVEL 2 RESULTS (Percent)	LEVEL 3 RESULTS (Percent)	LEVEL 4 RESULTS (Percent)
BRONX CHARTER SCHOOL FOR BETTER LEARNING	3rd grade	3	31	56	10
Seton Falls School	3rd grade	27	43	28	1
BRONX CHARTER SCHOOL FOR BETTER LEARNING	4th grade	4	37	31	28
Seton Falls School	4th grade	28	37	28	7
BRONX CHARTER SCHOOL FOR BETTER LEARNING	5th grade	23	34	31	11
Seton Falls School	5th grade	46	30	19	5

Performance Levels: Level 1: Well Below Proficient   Level 2: Below Proficient   Level 3: Proficient   Level 4: Above Proficient
SOURCE: New York State Education Department

BRONX CHARTER SCHOOL FOR BETTER LEARNING   New York State Mathematics Test Results, 2017–2018

SCHOOLS HOUSED TOGETHER	CLASS GRADE LEVEL	LEVEL 1 RESULTS (Percent)	LEVEL 2 RESULTS (Percent)	LEVEL 3 RESULTS (Percent)	LEVEL 4 RESULTS (Percent)
BRONX CHARTER SCHOOL FOR BETTER LEARNING	3rd grade	9	16	32	43
Seton Falls School	3rd grade	33	26	32	10
BRONX CHARTER SCHOOL FOR BETTER LEARNING	4th grade	4	21	33	41
Seton Falls School	4th grade	39	35	26	0
BRONX CHARTER SCHOOL FOR BETTER LEARNING	5th grade	13	21	39	26
Seton Falls School	5th grade	58	20	19	3

Performance Levels: Level 1: Well Below Proficient   Level 2: Below Proficient   Level 3: Proficient   Level 4: Above Proficient
SOURCE: New York State Education Department

BRONX GLOBAL LEARNING INSTITUTE FOR GIRLS CHARTER SCHOOL
(THE SHIRLEY RODRIGUEZ-REMENESKI SCHOOL) New York State English Language Arts Test Results,
2017–2018

SCHOOLS HOUSED TOGETHER	CLASS GRADE LEVEL	LEVEL 1 RESULTS (Percent)	LEVEL 2 RESULTS (Percent)	LEVEL 3 RESULTS (Percent)	LEVEL 4 RESULTS (Percent)
BRONX GLOBAL LEARNING INSTITUTE FOR GIRLS CHARTER SCHOOL (THE SHIRLEY RODRIGUEZ-REMENESKI SCHOOL)	3rd grade	17	46	35	2
Concourse Village Elementary School	3rd grade	0	4	77	20
BRONX GLOBAL LEARNING INSTITUTE FOR GIRLS CHARTER SCHOOL (THE SHIRLEY RODRIGUEZ-REMENESKI SCHOOL)	4th grade	16	50	24	10
Concourse Village Elementary School	4th grade	0	16	43	41
BRONX GLOBAL LEARNING INSTITUTE FOR GIRLS CHARTER SCHOOL (THE SHIRLEY RODRIGUEZ-REMENESKI SCHOOL)	5th grade	22	45	22	10
Concourse Village Elementary School	5th grade	8	15	44	33

Performance Levels: Level 1: Well Below Proficient   Level 2: Below Proficient   Level 3: Proficient   Level 4: Above Proficient
SOURCE: New York State Education Department

BRONX GLOBAL LEARNING INSTITUTE FOR GIRLS CHARTER SCHOOL (THE SHIRLEY RODRIGUEZ-REMENESKI SCHOOL) New York State Mathematics Test Results, 2017–2018

SCHOOLS HOUSED TOGETHER	CLASS GRADE LEVEL	LEVEL 1 RESULTS (Percent)	LEVEL 2 RESULTS (Percent)	LEVEL 3 RESULTS (Percent)	LEVEL 4 RESULTS (Percent)
BRONX GLOBAL LEARNING INSTITUTE FOR GIRLS CHARTER SCHOOL (THE SHIRLEY RODRIGUEZ-REMENESKI SCHOOL)	3rd grade	29	40	31	0
Concourse Village Elementary School	3rd grade	0	0	24	76
BRONX GLOBAL LEARNING INSTITUTE FOR GIRLS CHARTER SCHOOL (THE SHIRLEY RODRIGUEZ-REMENESKI SCHOOL)	4th grade	36	38	22	4
Concourse Village Elementary School	4th grade	0	13	31	56
BRONX GLOBAL LEARNING INSTITUTE FOR GIRLS CHARTER SCHOOL (THE SHIRLEY RODRIGUEZ-REMENESKI SCHOOL)	5th grade	37	29	24	10
Concourse Village Elementary School	5th grade	5	24	50	21

Performance Levels: Level 1: Well Below Proficient   Level 2: Below Proficient   Level 3: Proficient   Level 4: Above Proficient
SOURCE: New York State Education Department

BROOKLYN CHARTER SCHOOL New York State English Language Arts Test Results, 2017–2018

SCHOOLS HOUSED TOGETHER	CLASS GRADE LEVEL	LEVEL 1 RESULTS (Percent)	LEVEL 2 RESULTS (Percent)	LEVEL 3 RESULTS (Percent)	LEVEL 4 RESULTS (Percent)
BROOKLYN CHARTER SCHOOL	3rd grade	6	34	47	13
Carter G. Woodson School	3rd grade	22	36	42	0
BROOKLYN CHARTER SCHOOL	4th grade	10	35	39	16
Carter G. Woodson School	4th grade	36	44	12	8
BROOKLYN CHARTER SCHOOL	5th grade	31	41	28	0
Carter G. Woodson School	5th grade	30	36	30	3

Performance Levels: Level 1: Well Below Proficient   Level 2: Below Proficient   Level 3: Proficient   Level 4: Above Proficient
SOURCE: New York State Education Department

BROOKLYN CHARTER SCHOOL New York State Mathematics Test Results, 2017–2018

SCHOOLS HOUSED TOGETHER	CLASS GRADE LEVEL	LEVEL 1 RESULTS (Percent)	LEVEL 2 RESULTS (Percent)	LEVEL 3 RESULTS (Percent)	LEVEL 4 RESULTS (Percent)
BROOKLYN CHARTER SCHOOL	3rd grade	13	16	28	44
Carter G. Woodson School	3rd grade	28	17	28	28
BROOKLYN CHARTER SCHOOL	4th grade	6	29	29	35
Carter G. Woodson School	4th grade	58	23	19	0
BROOKLYN CHARTER SCHOOL	5th grade	13	22	28	38
Carter G. Woodson School	5th grade	45	27	27	0

Performance Levels: Level 1: Well Below Proficient   Level 2: Below Proficient   Level 3: Proficient   Level 4: Above Proficient
SOURCE: New York State Education Department

BROOKLYN URBAN GARDEN CHARTER SCHOOL New York State English Language Arts Test Results, 2017–2018

SCHOOLS HOUSED TOGETHER	CLASS GRADE LEVEL	LEVEL 1 RESULTS (Percent)	LEVEL 2 RESULTS (Percent)	LEVEL 3 RESULTS (Percent)	LEVEL 4 RESULTS (Percent)
BROOKLYN URBAN GARDEN CHARTER SCHOOL	6th grade	16	28	30	26
Carroll Gardens School for Innovation	6th grade	18	26	27	30
BROOKLYN URBAN GARDEN CHARTER SCHOOL	7th grade	22	44	28	6
Carroll Gardens School for Innovation	7th grade	21	26	37	16
BROOKLYN URBAN GARDEN CHARTER SCHOOL	8th grade	8	35	40	17
Carroll Gardens School for Innovation	8th grade	14	31	33	22

Performance Levels: Level 1: Well Below Proficient   Level 2: Below Proficient   Level 3: Proficient   Level 4: Above Proficient
SOURCE: New York State Education Department

BROOKLYN URBAN GARDEN CHARTER SCHOOL New York State Mathematics Test Results, 2017–2018

SCHOOLS HOUSED TOGETHER	CLASS GRADE LEVEL	LEVEL 1 RESULTS (Percent)	LEVEL 2 RESULTS (Percent)	LEVEL 3 RESULTS (Percent)	LEVEL 4 RESULTS (Percent)
BROOKLYN URBAN GARDEN CHARTER SCHOOL	6th grade	19	28	31	22
Carroll Gardens School for Innovation	6th grade	15	25	35	25
BROOKLYN URBAN GARDEN CHARTER SCHOOL	7th grade	35	29	27	8
Carroll Gardens School for Innovation	7th grade	27	21	27	25
BROOKLYN URBAN GARDEN CHARTER SCHOOL	8th grade	30	60	11	0
Carroll Gardens School for Innovation	8th grade	43	53	3	0

Performance Levels: Level 1: Well Below Proficient   Level 2: Below Proficient   Level 3: Proficient   Level 4: Above Proficient
SOURCE: New York State Education Department

CHILDREN'S AID COLLEGE PREP CHARTER SCHOOL   New York State English Language Arts Test Results, 2017–2018

SCHOOLS HOUSED TOGETHER	CLASS GRADE LEVEL	LEVEL 1 RESULTS (Percent)	LEVEL 2 RESULTS (Percent)	LEVEL 3 RESULTS (Percent)	LEVEL 4 RESULTS (Percent)
CHILDREN'S AID COLLEGE PREP CHARTER SCHOOL	5th grade	27	37	27	8
PS 211 Bronx	5th grade	49	31	16	4
CHILDREN'S AID COLLEGE PREP CHARTER SCHOOL	6th grade	27	24	24	25
PS 211 Bronx	6th grade	65	12	10	13
Math, Science & Technology Through Arts	6th grade	67	19	7	7

Performance Levels: Level 1: Well Below Proficient   Level 2: Below Proficient   Level 3: Proficient   Level 4: Above Proficient
SOURCE: New York State Education Department

CHILDREN'S AID COLLEGE PREP CHARTER SCHOOL New York State Mathematics Test Results, 2017–2018

SCHOOLS HOUSED TOGETHER	CLASS GRADE LEVEL	LEVEL 1 RESULTS (Percent)	LEVEL 2 RESULTS (Percent)	LEVEL 3 RESULTS (Percent)	LEVEL 4 RESULTS (Percent)
CHILDREN'S AID COLLEGE PREP CHARTER SCHOOL	5th grade	40	33	18	8
PS 211 Bronx	5th grade	59	27	12	2
CHILDREN'S AID COLLEGE PREP CHARTER SCHOOL	6th grade	31	35	21	13
PS 211 Bronx	6th grade	43	34	18	5
Math, Science & Technology Through Arts	6th grade	73	21	5	2

Performance Levels: Level 1: Well Below Proficient   Level 2: Below Proficient   Level 3: Proficient   Level 4: Above Proficient
SOURCE: New York State Education Department

COMMUNITY PARTNERSHIP CHARTER SCHOOLS   New York State English Language Arts Test Results, 2017–2018

SCHOOLS HOUSED TOGETHER	CLASS GRADE LEVEL	LEVEL 1 RESULTS (Percent)	LEVEL 2 RESULTS (Percent)	LEVEL 3 RESULTS (Percent)	LEVEL 4 RESULTS (Percent)
COMMUNITY PARTNERSHIP CHARTER SCHOOL	5th grade	38	42	18	2
Benjamin Banneker School	5th grade	41	26	26	7
COMMUNITY PARTNERSHIP CHARTER SCHOOL	3rd grade	21	33	41	5
Johann DeKalb School	3rd grade	14	36	50	0
COMMUNITY PARTNERSHIP CHARTER SCHOOL	4th grade	21	42	32	5
Johann DeKalb School	4th grade	20	70	10	0

Performance Levels: Level 1: Well Below Proficient   Level 2: Below Proficient   Level 3: Proficient   Level 4: Above Proficient
SOURCE: New York State Education Department

COMMUNITY PARTNERSHIP CHARTER SCHOOLS   New York State Mathematics Test Results, 2017–2018

SCHOOLS HOUSED TOGETHER	CLASS GRADE LEVEL	LEVEL 1 RESULTS (Percent)	LEVEL 2 RESULTS (Percent)	LEVEL 3 RESULTS (Percent)	LEVEL 4 RESULTS (Percent)
COMMUNITY PARTNERSHIP CHARTER SCHOOL	5th grade	49	23	19	9
Benjamin Banneker School	5th grade	44	19	30	7
COMMUNITY PARTNERSHIP CHARTER SCHOOL	3rd grade	21	37	24	18
Johann DeKalb School	3rd grade	43	21	14	21
COMMUNITY PARTNERSHIP CHARTER SCHOOL	4th grade	53	18	18	11
Johann DeKalb School	4th grade	70	20	10	0

Performance Levels: Level 1: Well Below Proficient   Level 2: Below Proficient   Level 3: Proficient   Level 4: Above Proficient
SOURCE: New York State Education Department

DR. RICHARD IZQUIERDO HEALTH AND SCIENCE CHARTER SCHOOL New York State English Language Arts Test Results, 2017–2018

SCHOOLS HOUSED TOGETHER	CLASS GRADE LEVEL	LEVEL 1 RESULTS (Percent)	LEVEL 2 RESULTS (Percent)	LEVEL 3 RESULTS (Percent)	LEVEL 4 RESULTS (Percent)
DR. RICHARD IZQUIERDO HEALTH AND SCIENCE CHARTER SCHOOL	6th grade	42	33	18	7
Bronx Latin School	6th grade	43	31	11	14
DR. RICHARD IZQUIERDO HEALTH AND SCIENCE CHARTER SCHOOL	7th grade	31	42	25	3
Bronx Latin School	7th grade	35	40	21	5
DR. RICHARD IZQUIERDO HEALTH AND SCIENCE CHARTER SCHOOL	8th grade	16	44	33	6
Bronx Latin School	8th grade	31	41	15	13

Performance Levels: Level 1: Well Below Proficient   Level 2: Below Proficient   Level 3: Proficient   Level 4: Above Proficient
SOURCE: New York State Education Department

DR. RICHARD IZQUIERDO HEALTH AND SCIENCE CHARTER SCHOOL New York State Mathematics Test Results, 2017–2018

SCHOOLS HOUSED TOGETHER	CLASS GRADE LEVEL	LEVEL 1 RESULTS (Percent)	LEVEL 2 RESULTS (Percent)	LEVEL 3 RESULTS (Percent)	LEVEL 4 RESULTS (Percent)
DR. RICHARD IZQUIERDO HEALTH AND SCIENCE CHARTER SCHOOL	6th grade	56	19	17	8
Bronx Latin School	6th grade	54	20	16	10
DR. RICHARD IZQUIERDO HEALTH AND SCIENCE CHARTER SCHOOL	7th grade	37	36	22	5
Bronx Latin School	7th grade	51	28	16	5

Performance Levels: Level 1: Well Below Proficient   Level 2: Below Proficient   Level 3: Proficient   Level 4: Above Proficient
SOURCE: New York State Education Department

EAST HARLEM SCHOLARS ACADEMY II CHARTER SCHOOL, New York State English Language Arts Test Results, 2017–2018

SCHOOLS HOUSED TOGETHER	CLASS GRADE LEVEL	LEVEL 1 RESULTS (Percent)	LEVEL 2 RESULTS (Percent)	LEVEL 3 RESULTS (Percent)	LEVEL 4 RESULTS (Percent)
EAST HARLEM SCHOLARS ACADEMY II CHARTER SCHOOL	3rd grade	22	50	26	2
Central Park East I School	3rd grade	30	20	50	0
EAST HARLEM SCHOLARS ACADEMY II CHARTER SCHOOL	4th grade	11	55	18	16
Central Park East I School	4th grade	17	17	33	33
EAST HARLEM SCHOLARS ACADEMY II CHARTER SCHOOL	5th grade	40	37	13	10
Central Park East I School	5th grade	25	38	13	25

Performance Levels: Level 1: Well Below Proficient   Level 2: Below Proficient   Level 3: Proficient   Level 4: Above Proficient
SOURCE: New York State Education Department

EAST HARLEM SCHOLARS ACADEMY II CHARTER SCHOOL   New York State Mathematics Test Results, 2017–2018

SCHOOLS HOUSED TOGETHER	CLASS GRADE LEVEL	LEVEL 1 RESULTS (Percent)	LEVEL 2 RESULTS (Percent)	LEVEL 3 RESULTS (Percent)	LEVEL 4 RESULTS (Percent)
EAST HARLEM SCHOLARS ACADEMY II CHARTER SCHOOL	3rd grade	28	28	34	9
Central Park East I School	3rd grade	38	38	13	13
EAST HARLEM SCHOLARS ACADEMY II CHARTER SCHOOL	5th grade	40	28	19	13
Central Park East I School	5th grade	40	20	0	40

Performance Levels: Level 1: Well Below Proficient   Level 2: Below Proficient   Level 3: Proficient   Level 4: Above Proficient
SOURCE: New York State Education Department

EMBER CHARTER SCHOOL   New York State English Language Arts Test Results, 2017–2018

SCHOOLS HOUSED TOGETHER	CLASS GRADE LEVEL	LEVEL 1 RESULTS (Percent)	LEVEL 2 RESULTS (Percent)	LEVEL 3 RESULTS (Percent)	LEVEL 4 RESULTS (Percent)
EMBER CHARTER SCHOOL	3rd grade	11	34	53	2
Clara Cardwell School	3rd grade	48	40	12	0
EMBER CHARTER SCHOOL	4th grade	9	47	26	18
Clara Cardwell School	4th grade	56	17	17	11
EMBER CHARTER SCHOOL	5th grade	34	39	19	8
Clara Cardwell School	5th grade	53	21	21	5

Performance Levels: Level 1: Well Below Proficient   Level 2: Below Proficient   Level 3: Proficient   Level 4: Above Proficient
SOURCE: New York State Education Department

EMBER CHARTER SCHOOL   New York State Mathematics Test Results, 2017–2018

SCHOOLS HOUSED TOGETHER	CLASS GRADE LEVEL	LEVEL 1 RESULTS (Percent)	LEVEL 2 RESULTS (Percent)	LEVEL 3 RESULTS (Percent)	LEVEL 4 RESULTS (Percent)
EMBER CHARTER SCHOOL	3rd grade	33	34	25	8
Clara Cardwell School	3rd grade	76	12	12	0
EMBER CHARTER SCHOOL	4th grade	40	40	18	2
Clara Cardwell School	4th grade	50	33	6	11
EMBER CHARTER SCHOOL	5th grade	56	30	10	5
Clara Cardwell School	5th grade	53	32	16	0

Performance Levels: Level 1: Well Below Proficient   Level 2: Below Proficient   Level 3: Proficient   Level 4: Above Proficient
SOURCE: New York State Education Department

EXPLORE SCHOOLS CHARTER SCHOOLS   New York State English Language Arts Test Results, 2017–2018

SCHOOLS HOUSED TOGETHER	CLASS GRADE LEVEL	LEVEL 1 RESULTS (Percent)	LEVEL 2 RESULTS (Percent)	LEVEL 3 RESULTS (Percent)	LEVEL 4 RESULTS (Percent)
EXPLORE SCHOOLS CHARTER SCHOOL	3rd grade	26	26	44	4
Brooklyn Arts and Science Elementary School	3rd grade	15	54	28	2
EXPLORE SCHOOLS CHARTER SCHOOL	4th grade	31	39	20	9
Brooklyn Arts and Science Elementary School	4th grade	40	30	18	12
EXPLORE SCHOOLS CHARTER SCHOOL	5th grade	43	21	20	16
Brooklyn Arts and Science Elementary School	5th grade	62	23	15	0
EXPLORE SCHOOLS CHARTER SCHOOL	6th grade	38	44	10	8
Ebbets Field Middle School	6th grade	77	10	10	3
EXPLORE SCHOOLS CHARTER SCHOOL	7th grade	22	36	38	4
Ebbets Field Middle School	7th grade	48	27	20	5
EXPLORE SCHOOLS CHARTER SCHOOL	8th grade	2	43	40	15
Ebbets Field Middle School	8th grade	35	33	23	9
EXPLORE SCHOOLS CHARTER SCHOOL	6th grade	33	21	20	26
Isaac Bildersee Junior High School	6th grade	52	28	12	8
EXPLORE SCHOOLS CHARTER SCHOOL	7th grade	22	49	22	7
Isaac Bildersee Junior High School	7th grade	45	36	16	3
EXPLORE SCHOOLS CHARTER SCHOOL	8th grade	12	41	36	12
Isaac Bildersee Junior High School	8th grade	24	57	12	7

Performance Levels: Level 1: Well Below Proficient   Level 2: Below Proficient   Level 3: Proficient   Level 4: Above Proficient
SOURCE: New York State Education Department

EXPLORE SCHOOLS CHARTER SCHOOLS   New York State English Language Arts Test Results, 2017–2018 (Continued)

SCHOOLS HOUSED TOGETHER	CLASS GRADE LEVEL	LEVEL 1 RESULTS (Percent)	LEVEL 2 RESULTS (Percent)	LEVEL 3 RESULTS (Percent)	LEVEL 4 RESULTS (Percent)
EXPLORE SCHOOLS CHARTER SCHOOL	3rd grade	21	39	37	4
MS 394 Brooklyn	3rd grade	13	58	29	0
EXPLORE SCHOOLS CHARTER SCHOOL	4th grade	15	36	40	9
MS 394 Brooklyn	4th grade	35	29	21	15
EXPLORE SCHOOLS CHARTER SCHOOL	5th grade	23	42	22	13
MS 394 Brooklyn	5th grade	34	45	15	6
EXPLORE SCHOOLS CHARTER SCHOOL	6th grade	31	29	19	21
MS 394 Brooklyn	6th grade	48	22	12	18
EXPLORE SCHOOLS CHARTER SCHOOL	7th grade	27	43	25	4
MS 394 Brooklyn	7th grade	22	30	40	8
EXPLORE SCHOOLS CHARTER SCHOOL	8th grade	15	37	41	7
MS 394 Brooklyn	8th grade	14	42	22	22
EXPLORE SCHOOLS CHARTER SCHOOL	6th grade	28	30	25	18
Parkside Preparatory Academy	6th grade	42	20	25	13
EXPLORE SCHOOLS CHARTER SCHOOL	7th grade	24	35	33	7
Parkside Preparatory Academy	7th grade	26	34	27	13
EXPLORE SCHOOLS CHARTER SCHOOL	8th grade	2	39	46	14
Parkside Preparatory Academy	8th grade	13	31	33	24
EXPLORE SCHOOLS CHARTER SCHOOL	3rd grade	3	36	50	10
Ryder Elementary School	3rd grade	21	37	43	0
EXPLORE SCHOOLS CHARTER SCHOOL	4th grade	5	33	36	26
Ryder Elementary School	4th grade	3	39	34	23

EXPLORE SCHOOLS CHARTER SCHOOLS   New York State Mathematics Test Results, 2017–2018

SCHOOLS HOUSED TOGETHER	CLASS GRADE LEVEL	LEVEL 1 RESULTS (Percent)	LEVEL 2 RESULTS (Percent)	LEVEL 3 RESULTS (Percent)	LEVEL 4 RESULTS (Percent)
EXPLORE SCHOOLS CHARTER SCHOOL	3rd grade	33	17	35	15
Brooklyn Arts and Science Elementary School	3rd grade	55	23	15	6
EXPLORE SCHOOLS CHARTER SCHOOL	4th grade	33	26	19	22
Brooklyn Arts and Science Elementary School	4th grade	66	22	10	2
EXPLORE SCHOOLS CHARTER SCHOOL	5th grade	48	21	18	13
Brooklyn Arts and Science Elementary School	5th grade	68	27	2	2
EXPLORE SCHOOLS CHARTER SCHOOL	6th grade	24	44	22	9
Ebbets Field Middle School	6th grade	63	15	17	5
EXPLORE SCHOOLS CHARTER SCHOOL	7th grade	18	32	36	14
Ebbets Field Middle School	7th grade	57	28	13	2
EXPLORE SCHOOLS CHARTER SCHOOL	8th grade	13	27	48	12
Ebbets Field Middle School	8th grade	44	16	23	16
EXPLORE SCHOOLS CHARTER SCHOOL	6th grade	55	17	20	9
Isaac Bildersee Junior High School	6th grade	60	19	15	6
EXPLORE SCHOOLS CHARTER SCHOOL	7th grade	37	28	28	7
Isaac Bildersee Junior High School	7th grade	49	32	17	3
EXPLORE SCHOOLS CHARTER SCHOOL	8th grade	46	32	17	5
Isaac Bildersee Junior High School	8th grade	45	42	10	3

Performance Levels: Level 1: Well Below Proficient   Level 2: Below Proficient   Level 3: Proficient   Level 4: Above Proficient
SOURCE: New York State Education Department

EXPLORE SCHOOLS CHARTER SCHOOLS New York State Mathematics Test Results, 2017–2018 (Continued)

SCHOOLS HOUSED TOGETHER	CLASS GRADE LEVEL	LEVEL 1 RESULTS (Percent)	LEVEL 2 RESULTS (Percent)	LEVEL 3 RESULTS (Percent)	LEVEL 4 RESULTS (Percent)
EXPLORE SCHOOLS CHARTER SCHOOL	3rd grade	26	23	37	14
MS 394 Brooklyn	3rd grade	36	36	24	3
EXPLORE SCHOOLS CHARTER SCHOOL	4th grade	32	34	19	15
MS 394 Brooklyn	4th grade	44	26	18	12
EXPLORE SCHOOLS CHARTER SCHOOL	5th grade	46	24	19	12
MS 394 Brooklyn	5th grade	57	32	8	4
EXPLORE SCHOOLS CHARTER SCHOOL	6th grade	35	33	15	17
MS 394 Brooklyn	6th grade	67	24	4	6
EXPLORE SCHOOLS CHARTER SCHOOL	7th grade	27	31	18	24
MS 394 Brooklyn	7th grade	59	24	14	2
EXPLORE SCHOOLS CHARTER SCHOOL	8th grade	28	33	20	19
MS 394 Brooklyn	8th grade	33	35	15	17
EXPLORE SCHOOLS CHARTER SCHOOL	6th grade	14	25	39	23
Parkside Preparatory Academy	6th grade	45	35	12	7
EXPLORE SCHOOLS CHARTER SCHOOL	7th grade	17	35	24	24
Parkside Preparatory Academy	7th grade	53	26	16	4
EXPLORE SCHOOLS CHARTER SCHOOL	8th grade	7	33	30	30
Parkside Preparatory Academy	8th grade	46	28	21	5
EXPLORE SCHOOLS CHARTER SCHOOL	3rd grade	3	10	37	49
Ryder Elementary School	3rd grade	49	34	16	0
EXPLORE SCHOOLS CHARTER SCHOOL	4th grade	9	22	22	47
Ryder Elementary School	4th grade	23	39	17	21

FUTURE LEADERS INSTITUTE CHARTER SCHOOL   New York State English Language Arts Test Results, 2017–2018

SCHOOLS HOUSED TOGETHER	CLASS GRADE LEVEL	LEVEL 1 RESULTS (Percent)	LEVEL 2 RESULTS (Percent)	LEVEL 3 RESULTS (Percent)	LEVEL 4 RESULTS (Percent)
FUTURE LEADERS INSTITUTE CHARTER SCHOOL	3rd grade	13	37	45	5
Young Diplomats Magnet Academy	3rd grade	17	65	13	4
FUTURE LEADERS INSTITUTE CHARTER SCHOOL	4th grade	30	32	30	9
Young Diplomats Magnet Academy	4th grade	40	40	15	5
FUTURE LEADERS INSTITUTE CHARTER SCHOOL	5th grade	21	34	34	11
Young Diplomats Magnet Academy	5th grade	27	23	19	31

Performance Levels: Level 1: Well Below Proficient   Level 2: Below Proficient   Level 3: Proficient   Level 4: Above Proficient
SOURCE: New York State Education Department

FUTURE LEADERS INSTITUTE CHARTER SCHOOL   New York State Mathematics Test Results, 2017–2018

SCHOOLS HOUSED TOGETHER	CLASS GRADE LEVEL	LEVEL 1 RESULTS (Percent)	LEVEL 2 RESULTS (Percent)	LEVEL 3 RESULTS (Percent)	LEVEL 4 RESULTS (Percent)
FUTURE LEADERS INSTITUTE CHARTER SCHOOL	3rd grade	42	24	29	5
Young Diplomats Magnet Academy	3rd grade	48	35	13	4
FUTURE LEADERS INSTITUTE CHARTER SCHOOL	4th grade	21	30	30	19
Young Diplomats Magnet Academy	4th grade	50	41	9	0
FUTURE LEADERS INSTITUTE CHARTER SCHOOL	5th grade	25	48	15	13
Young Diplomats Magnet Academy	5th grade	41	22	22	15

Performance Levels: Level 1: Well Below Proficient   Level 2: Below Proficient   Level 3: Proficient   Level 4: Above Proficient
SOURCE: New York State Education Department

GIRLS PREP CHARTER SCHOOLS New York State English Language Arts Test Results, 2017–2018

SCHOOLS HOUSED TOGETHER	CLASS GRADE LEVEL	LEVEL 1 RESULTS (Percent)	LEVEL 2 RESULTS (Percent)	LEVEL 3 RESULTS (Percent)	LEVEL 4 RESULTS (Percent)
GIRLS PREP CHARTER SCHOOL	6th grade	9	21	33	37
East Side Community School	6th grade	18	26	28	28
GIRLS PREP CHARTER SCHOOL	7th grade	6	25	49	20
East Side Community School	7th grade	17	44	30	9
GIRLS PREP CHARTER SCHOOL	8th grade	2	19	43	37
East Side Community School	8th grade	8	26	37	29
GIRLS PREP CHARTER SCHOOL	3rd grade	9	27	51	12
Island School	3rd grade	10	35	50	5
GIRLS PREP CHARTER SCHOOL	4th grade	4	34	44	17
Island School	4th grade	12	46	37	5
GIRLS PREP CHARTER SCHOOL	6th grade	15	30	32	23
Paul L. Dunbar Middle School	6th grade	48	38	14	0
GIRLS PREP CHARTER SCHOOL	7th grade	21	34	36	10
Paul L. Dunbar Middle School	7th grade	59	27	11	4
GIRLS PREP CHARTER SCHOOL	8th grade	3	26	47	24
Paul L. Dunbar Middle School	8th grade	41	43	16	0

Performance Levels: Level 1: Well Below Proficient   Level 2: Below Proficient   Level 3: Proficient   Level 4: Above Proficient
SOURCE: New York State Education Department

GIRLS PREP CHARTER SCHOOLS   New York State Mathematics Test Results, 2017–2018

SCHOOLS HOUSED TOGETHER	CLASS GRADE LEVEL	LEVEL 1 RESULTS (Percent)	LEVEL 2 RESULTS (Percent)	LEVEL 3 RESULTS (Percent)	LEVEL 4 RESULTS (Percent)
GIRLS PREP CHARTER SCHOOL	6th grade	21	37	29	13
East Side Community School	6th grade	19	26	33	23
GIRLS PREP CHARTER SCHOOL	7th grade	13	15	43	29
East Side Community School	7th grade	25	34	32	8
GIRLS PREP CHARTER SCHOOL	8th grade	4	28	38	30
East Side Community School	8th grade	13	33	37	17
GIRLS PREP CHARTER SCHOOL	3rd grade	4	11	45	40
Island School	3rd grade	31	33	33	3
GIRLS PREP CHARTER SCHOOL	4th grade	14	26	30	30
Island School	4th grade	21	57	19	2
GIRLS PREP CHARTER SCHOOL	6th grade	39	29	19	13
Paul L. Dunbar Middle School	6th grade	58	33	7	1
GIRLS PREP CHARTER SCHOOL	7th grade	17	29	29	25
Paul L. Dunbar Middle School	7th grade	64	24	9	3
GIRLS PREP CHARTER SCHOOL	8th grade	18	14	30	38
Paul L. Dunbar Middle School	8th grade	67	23	10	0

Performance Levels: Level 1: Well Below Proficient   Level 2: Below Proficient   Level 3: Proficient   Level 4: Above Proficient
SOURCE: New York State Education Department

HYDE LEADERSHIP CHARTER SCHOOLS   New York State English Language Arts Test Results, 2017–2018

SCHOOLS HOUSED TOGETHER	CLASS GRADE LEVEL	LEVEL 1 RESULTS (Percent)	LEVEL 2 RESULTS (Percent)	LEVEL 3 RESULTS (Percent)	LEVEL 4 RESULTS (Percent)
HYDE LEADERSHIP CHARTER SCHOOL	6th grade	24	29	24	24
Hunts Point School	6th grade	58	23	14	5
HYDE LEADERSHIP CHARTER SCHOOL	7th grade	27	31	40	3
Hunts Point School	7th grade	72	24	3	0
HYDE LEADERSHIP CHARTER SCHOOL	8th grade	6	25	51	18
Hunts Point School	8th grade	43	45	11	0
HYDE LEADERSHIP CHARTER SCHOOL	3rd grade	12	38	43	7
Phyllis Wheatley School	3rd grade	21	59	21	0
HYDE LEADERSHIP CHARTER SCHOOL	4th grade	24	36	32	8
Phyllis Wheatley School	4th grade	25	39	25	11
HYDE LEADERSHIP CHARTER SCHOOL	5th grade	26	42	28	4
Phyllis Wheatley School	5th grade	61	30	6	3

Performance Levels: Level 1: Well Below Proficient   Level 2: Below Proficient   Level 3: Proficient   Level 4: Above Proficient
SOURCE: New York State Education Department

HYDE LEADERSHIP CHARTER SCHOOLS New York State Mathematics Test Results, 2017–2018

SCHOOLS HOUSED TOGETHER	CLASS GRADE LEVEL	LEVEL 1 RESULTS (Percent)	LEVEL 2 RESULTS (Percent)	LEVEL 3 RESULTS (Percent)	LEVEL 4 RESULTS (Percent)
HYDE LEADERSHIP CHARTER SCHOOL	6th grade	22	29	36	13
Hunts Point School	6th grade	76	18	4	2
HYDE LEADERSHIP CHARTER SCHOOL	7th grade	16	41	26	18
Hunts Point School	7th grade	72	23	5	0
HYDE LEADERSHIP CHARTER SCHOOL	3rd grade	18	26	30	26
Phyllis Wheatley School	3rd grade	77	17	3	3
HYDE LEADERSHIP CHARTER SCHOOL	4th grade	28	24	24	24
Phyllis Wheatley School	4th grade	30	34	16	20
HYDE LEADERSHIP CHARTER SCHOOL	5th grade	18	49	27	6
Phyllis Wheatley School	5th grade	67	12	15	6

Performance Levels: Level 1: Well Below Proficient   Level 2: Below Proficient   Level 3: Proficient   Level 4: Above Proficient
SOURCE: New York State Education Department

ICAHN CHARTER SCHOOLS   New York State English Language Arts Test Results, 2017–2018

SCHOOLS HOUSED TOGETHER	CLASS GRADE LEVEL	LEVEL 1 RESULTS (Percent)	LEVEL 2 RESULTS (Percent)	LEVEL 3 RESULTS (Percent)	LEVEL 4 RESULTS (Percent)
ICAHN CHARTER SCHOOL	3rd grade	0	34	54	11
Albert G. Oliver School	3rd grade	26	46	26	3
ICAHN CHARTER SCHOOL	4th grade	8	38	33	21
Albert G. Oliver School	4th grade	29	44	20	7
ICAHN CHARTER SCHOOL	5th grade	15	32	41	12
Albert G. Oliver School	5th grade	45	35	12	8
ICAHN CHARTER SCHOOL	3rd grade	5	18	72	5
Crotona Park West School	3rd grade	34	41	22	3
ICAHN CHARTER SCHOOL	4th grade	14	33	45	7
Crotona Park West School	4th grade	44	37	16	2
ICAHN CHARTER SCHOOL	3rd grade	0	16	74	11
Van Nest Academy	3rd grade	11	35	47	7
ICAHN CHARTER SCHOOL	4th grade	0	4	43	54
Van Nest Academy	4th grade	13	48	29	10
ICAHN CHARTER SCHOOL	5th grade	0	19	44	36
Van Nest Academy	5th grade	32	37	18	13
ICAHN CHARTER SCHOOL	6th grade	8	6	33	53
Van Nest Academy	6th grade	15	27	30	28
ICAHN CHARTER SCHOOL	7th grade	0	47	47	6
Van Nest Academy	7th grade	12	38	40	9
ICAHN CHARTER SCHOOL	8th grade	6	15	45	33
Van Nest Academy	8th grade	2	39	30	30

Performance Levels: Level 1: Well Below Proficient   Level 2: Below Proficient   Level 3: Proficient   Level 4: Above Proficient
SOURCE: New York State Education Department

ICAHN CHARTER SCHOOLS   New York State Mathematics Test Results, 2017–2018

SCHOOLS HOUSED TOGETHER	CLASS GRADE LEVEL	LEVEL 1 RESULTS (Percent)	LEVEL 2 RESULTS (Percent)	LEVEL 3 RESULTS (Percent)	LEVEL 4 RESULTS (Percent)
ICAHN CHARTER SCHOOL	3rd grade	9	26	37	29
Albert G. Oliver School	3rd grade	38	36	21	5
ICAHN CHARTER SCHOOL	4th grade	10	23	36	31
Albert G. Oliver School	4th grade	39	37	17	7
ICAHN CHARTER SCHOOL	5th grade	9	24	45	21
Albert G. Oliver School	5th grade	46	25	19	10
ICAHN CHARTER SCHOOL	3rd grade	5	8	46	41
Crotona Park West School	3rd grade	25	37	28	10
ICAHN CHARTER SCHOOL	4th grade	17	24	17	43
Crotona Park West School	4th grade	40	35	21	5
ICAHN CHARTER SCHOOL	3rd grade	3	8	34	55
Van Nest Academy	3rd grade	7	25	43	25
ICAHN CHARTER SCHOOL	4th grade	0	0	18	82
Van Nest Academy	4th grade	6	27	44	22
ICAHN CHARTER SCHOOL	5th grade	5	5	22	68
Van Nest Academy	5th grade	23	37	20	20
ICAHN CHARTER SCHOOL	6th grade	3	14	33	50
Van Nest Academy	6th grade	19	40	29	13
ICAHN CHARTER SCHOOL	7th grade	3	14	39	44
Van Nest Academy	7th grade	12	38	31	19
ICAHN CHARTER SCHOOL	8th grade	6	21	24	48
Van Nest Academy	8th grade	22	30	31	18

Performance Levels: Level 1: Well Below Proficient   Level 2: Below Proficient   Level 3: Proficient   Level 4: Above Proficient
SOURCE: New York State Education Department

KIPP CHARTER SCHOOLS   New York State English Language Arts Test Results, 2017–2018

SCHOOLS HOUSED TOGETHER	CLASS GRADE LEVEL	LEVEL 1 RESULTS (Percent)	LEVEL 2 RESULTS (Percent)	LEVEL 3 RESULTS (Percent)	LEVEL 4 RESULTS (Percent)
KIPP CHARTER SCHOOL	3rd grade	7	19	68	7
Alexander Humboldt School	3rd grade	28	37	33	1
KIPP CHARTER SCHOOL	6th grade	3	17	37	42
Maria Teresa School	6th grade	52	24	19	5
Patria Mirabal School	6th grade	42	37	13	7
KIPP CHARTER SCHOOL	7th grade	11	42	35	12
Maria Teresa School	7th grade	44	36	17	3
Patria Mirabal School	7th grade	37	41	19	3
KIPP CHARTER SCHOOL	8th grade	0	30	44	26
Maria Teresa School	8th grade	13	40	28	19
Patria Mirabal School	8th grade	23	37	30	10
KIPP CHARTER SCHOOL	6th grade	14	29	28	29
New Design Middle School	6th grade	56	33	11	0
KIPP CHARTER SCHOOL	7th grade	14	37	42	7
New Design Middle School	7th grade	57	26	15	2
KIPP CHARTER SCHOOL	8th grade	2	26	35	36
New Design Middle School	8th grade	18	55	18	8

Performance Levels: Level 1: Well Below Proficient   Level 2: Below Proficient   Level 3: Proficient   Level 4: Above Proficient
SOURCE: New York State Education Department

KIPP CHARTER SCHOOLS   New York State English Language Arts Test Results, 2017–2018 (Continued)

SCHOOLS HOUSED TOGETHER	CLASS GRADE LEVEL	LEVEL 1 RESULTS (Percent)	LEVEL 2 RESULTS (Percent)	LEVEL 3 RESULTS (Percent)	LEVEL 4 RESULTS (Percent)
KIPP CHARTER SCHOOL	6th grade	19	24	32	25
School of Integrated Learning	6th grade	14	24	22	39
KIPP CHARTER SCHOOL	7th grade	25	38	26	11
School of Integrated Learning	7th grade	22	31	35	12
KIPP CHARTER SCHOOL	8th grade	13	26	37	24
School of Integrated Learning	8th grade	18	41	23	18
KIPP CHARTER SCHOOL	5th grade	25	31	27	17
William Lloyd Garrison School	5th grade	51	32	10	7
KIPP CHARTER SCHOOL	6th grade	9	20	23	48
William Lloyd Garrison School	6th grade	53	29	10	7
Lou Gehrig School	6th grade	48	28	23	1
KIPP CHARTER SCHOOL	7th grade	10	35	46	9
William Lloyd Garrison School	7th grade	54	28	14	4
Lou Gehrig School	7th grade	58	34	8	0
KIPP CHARTER SCHOOL	8th grade	8	15	42	35
William Lloyd Garrison School	8th grade	24	57	13	6
Lou Gehrig School	8th grade	51	39	8	3

Performance Levels: Level 1: Well Below Proficient   Level 2: Below Proficient   Level 3: Proficient   Level 4: Above Proficient
SOURCE: New York State Education Department

KIPP CHARTER SCHOOLS   New York State Mathematics Test Results, 2017–2018

SCHOOLS HOUSED TOGETHER	CLASS GRADE LEVEL	LEVEL 1 RESULTS (Percent)	LEVEL 2 RESULTS (Percent)	LEVEL 3 RESULTS (Percent)	LEVEL 4 RESULTS (Percent)
KIPP CHARTER SCHOOL	3rd grade	7	15	41	37
Alexander Humboldt School	3rd grade	25	31	30	14
KIPP CHARTER SCHOOL	6th grade	6	10	49	35
Maria Teresa School	6th grade	50	29	18	4
Patria Mirabal School	6th grade	41	25	22	13
KIPP CHARTER SCHOOL	7th grade	16	21	31	31
Maria Teresa School	7th grade	35	35	19	11
Patria Mirabal School	7th grade	37	35	20	8
KIPP CHARTER SCHOOL	8th grade	6	23	29	41
Maria Teresa School	8th grade	23	38	18	22
Patria Mirabal School	8th grade	37	48	13	1
KIPP CHARTER SCHOOL	6th grade	4	21	34	41
New Design Middle School	6th grade	85	5	10	0
KIPP CHARTER SCHOOL	7th grade	6	13	13	68
New Design Middle School	7th grade	71	22	7	0
KIPP CHARTER SCHOOL	8th grade	4	12	16	68
New Design Middle School	8th grade	61	24	12	3

Performance Levels: Level 1: Well Below Proficient   Level 2: Below Proficient   Level 3: Proficient   Level 4: Above Proficient
SOURCE: New York State Education Department

KIPP CHARTER SCHOOLS   New York State Mathematics Test Results, 2017–2018 (Continued)

SCHOOLS HOUSED TOGETHER	CLASS GRADE LEVEL	LEVEL 1 RESULTS (Percent)	LEVEL 2 RESULTS (Percent)	LEVEL 3 RESULTS (Percent)	LEVEL 4 RESULTS (Percent)
KIPP CHARTER SCHOOL	6th grade	23	28	32	17
School of Integrated Learning	6th grade	18	27	39	16
KIPP CHARTER SCHOOL	7th grade	28	22	30	20
School of Integrated Learning	7th grade	43	30	16	11
KIPP CHARTER SCHOOL	8th grade	14	24	22	40
School of Integrated Learning	8th grade	8	45	27	20
KIPP CHARTER SCHOOL	5th grade	20	26	33	20
William Lloyd Garrison School	5th grade	70	16	10	5
KIPP CHARTER SCHOOL	6th grade	15	14	34	37
William Lloyd Garrison School	6th grade	52	31	13	3
Lou Gehrig School	6th grade	72	21	7	0
KIPP CHARTER SCHOOL	7th grade	15	10	37	37
William Lloyd Garrison School	7th grade	69	24	5	1
Lou Gehrig School	7th grade	85	10	5	0
KIPP CHARTER SCHOOL	8th grade	10	17	32	40
William Lloyd Garrison School	8th grade	44	43	10	3
Lou Gehrig School	8th grade	77	19	3	1

Performance Levels: Level 1: Well Below Proficient   Level 2: Below Proficient   Level 3: Proficient   Level 4: Above Proficient
SOURCE: New York State Education Department

MANHATTAN CHARTER SCHOOL   New York State English Language Arts Test Results, 2017–2018

SCHOOLS HOUSED TOGETHER	CLASS GRADE LEVEL	LEVEL 1 RESULTS (Percent)	LEVEL 2 RESULTS (Percent)	LEVEL 3 RESULTS (Percent)	LEVEL 4 RESULTS (Percent)
MANHATTAN CHARTER SCHOOL	3rd grade	16	44	29	11
Amalia Castro School	3rd grade	10	31	59	0
MANHATTAN CHARTER SCHOOL	4th grade	3	31	44	22
Amalia Castro School	4th grade	14	46	34	6
MANHATTAN CHARTER SCHOOL	5th grade	18	35	29	18
Amalia Castro School	5th grade	46	34	11	9

Performance Levels: Level 1: Well Below Proficient   Level 2: Below Proficient   Level 3: Proficient   Level 4: Above Proficient
SOURCE: New York State Education Department

MANHATTAN CHARTER SCHOOL   New York State Mathematics Test Results, 2017–2018

SCHOOLS HOUSED TOGETHER	CLASS GRADE LEVEL	LEVEL 1 RESULTS (Percent)	LEVEL 2 RESULTS (Percent)	LEVEL 3 RESULTS (Percent)	LEVEL 4 RESULTS (Percent)
MANHATTAN CHARTER SCHOOL	3rd grade	42	27	20	11
Amalia Castro School	3rd grade	21	32	39	7
MANHATTAN CHARTER SCHOOL	4th grade	6	13	25	56
Amalia Castro School	4th grade	50	32	15	3
MANHATTAN CHARTER SCHOOL	5th grade	24	24	29	24
Amalia Castro School	5th grade	38	29	29	3

Performance Levels: Level 1: Well Below Proficient   Level 2: Below Proficient   Level 3: Proficient   Level 4: Above Proficient
SOURCE: New York State Education Department

NEW AMERICAN ACADEMY CHARTER SCHOOL   New York State English Language Arts Test Results, 2017–2018

SCHOOLS HOUSED TOGETHER	CLASS GRADE LEVEL	LEVEL 1 RESULTS (Percent)	LEVEL 2 RESULTS (Percent)	LEVEL 3 RESULTS (Percent)	LEVEL 4 RESULTS (Percent)
NEW AMERICAN ACADEMY CHARTER SCHOOL	3rd grade	12	38	43	7
Langston Hughes School	3rd grade	11	37	50	2
NEW AMERICAN ACADEMY CHARTER SCHOOL	4th grade	12	38	38	11
Langston Hughes School	4th grade	21	42	27	10
NEW AMERICAN ACADEMY CHARTER SCHOOL	5th grade	22	46	22	10
Langston Hughes School	5th grade	35	38	22	5

Performance Levels: Level 1: Well Below Proficient   Level 2: Below Proficient   Level 3: Proficient   Level 4: Above Proficient
SOURCE: New York State Education Department

NEW AMERICAN ACADEMY CHARTER SCHOOL   New York State Mathematics Test Results, 2017–2018

SCHOOLS HOUSED TOGETHER	CLASS GRADE LEVEL	LEVEL 1 RESULTS (Percent)	LEVEL 2 RESULTS (Percent)	LEVEL 3 RESULTS (Percent)	LEVEL 4 RESULTS (Percent)
NEW AMERICAN ACADEMY CHARTER SCHOOL	3rd grade	22	23	42	13
Langston Hughes School	3rd grade	20	15	46	20
NEW AMERICAN ACADEMY CHARTER SCHOOL	4th grade	38	29	11	22
Langston Hughes School	4th grade	43	42	14	1
NEW AMERICAN ACADEMY CHARTER SCHOOL	5th grade	35	35	23	8
Langston Hughes School	5th grade	52	31	12	4

Performance Levels: Level 1: Well Below Proficient   Level 2: Below Proficient   Level 3: Proficient   Level 4: Above Proficient
SOURCE: New York State Education Department

SOUTH BRONX CLASSICAL CHARTER SCHOOLS   New York State English Language Arts Test Results, 2017–2018

SCHOOLS HOUSED TOGETHER	CLASS GRADE LEVEL	LEVEL 1 RESULTS (Percent)	LEVEL 2 RESULTS (Percent)	LEVEL 3 RESULTS (Percent)	LEVEL 4 RESULTS (Percent)
SOUTH BRONX CLASSICAL CHARTER SCHOOL	6th grade	0	10	29	61
Entrada Academy	6th grade	56	25	12	7
School of Performing Arts Middle School	6th grade	61	25	11	4
SOUTH BRONX CLASSICAL CHARTER SCHOOL	7th grade	0	21	50	29
Entrada Academy	7th grade	54	38	7	0
School of Performing Arts Middle School	7th grade	39	39	23	0
SOUTH BRONX CLASSICAL CHARTER SCHOOL	8th grade	0	3	36	61
Entrada Academy	8th grade	44	31	15	10
School of Performing Arts Middle School	8th grade	28	48	16	7
SOUTH BRONX CLASSICAL CHARTER SCHOOL	3rd grade	0	0	64	36
Jonathan D. Hyatt School	3rd grade	8	28	56	8
SOUTH BRONX CLASSICAL CHARTER SCHOOL	4th grade	2	9	49	40
Jonathan D. Hyatt School	4th grade	19	37	33	11
SOUTH BRONX CLASSICAL CHARTER SCHOOL	5th grade	0	4	48	48
Jonathan D. Hyatt School	5th grade	36	38	21	5

Performance Levels: Level 1: Well Below Proficient   Level 2: Below Proficient   Level 3: Proficient   Level 4: Above Proficient
SOURCE: New York State Education Department

SOUTH BRONX CLASSICAL CHARTER SCHOOLS   New York State Mathematics Test Results, 2017–2018

SCHOOLS HOUSED TOGETHER	CLASS GRADE LEVEL	LEVEL 1 RESULTS (Percent)	LEVEL 2 RESULTS (Percent)	LEVEL 3 RESULTS (Percent)	LEVEL 4 RESULTS (Percent)
SOUTH BRONX CLASSICAL CHARTER SCHOOL	6th grade	0	3	44	53
Entrada Academy	6th grade	60	27	11	2
School of Performing Arts Middle School	6th grade	69	23	6	2
SOUTH BRONX CLASSICAL CHARTER SCHOOL	7th grade	0	7	32	61
Entrada Academy	7th grade	61	35	4	0
School of Performing Arts Middle School	7th grade	61	18	18	4
SOUTH BRONX CLASSICAL CHARTER SCHOOL	8th grade	0	6	30	64
Entrada Academy	8th grade	61	28	9	2
School of Performing Arts Middle School	8th grade	58	28	11	2
SOUTH BRONX CLASSICAL CHARTER SCHOOL	3rd grade	0	0	19	81
Jonathan D. Hyatt School	3rd grade	14	30	46	10
SOUTH BRONX CLASSICAL CHARTER SCHOOL	4th grade	0	5	21	74
Jonathan D. Hyatt School	4th grade	40	33	19	7
SOUTH BRONX CLASSICAL CHARTER SCHOOL	5th grade	0	13	35	52
Jonathan D. Hyatt School	5th grade	41	25	21	13

Performance Levels: Level 1: Well Below Proficient   Level 2: Below Proficient   Level 3: Proficient   Level 4: Above Proficient
SOURCE: New York State Education Department

SUCCESS ACADEMY CHARTER SCHOOLS　　New York State English Language Arts Test Results, 2017–2018

SCHOOLS HOUSED TOGETHER	CLASS GRADE LEVEL	LEVEL 1 RESULTS (Percent)	LEVEL 2 RESULTS (Percent)	LEVEL 3 RESULTS (Percent)	LEVEL 4 RESULTS (Percent)
SUCCESS ACADEMY CHARTER SCHOOL	3rd grade	1	12	77	11
Benjamin Franklin School	3rd grade	18	34	45	3
SUCCESS ACADEMY CHARTER SCHOOL	4th grade	0	7	39	54
Benjamin Franklin School	4th grade	24	43	26	7
SUCCESS ACADEMY CHARTER SCHOOL	6th grade	0	0	15	85
Bronx Writing Academy	6th grade	43	20	17	21
Jordan L. Mott Junior High School	6th grade	39	32	22	7
SUCCESS ACADEMY CHARTER SCHOOL	7th grade	0	3	58	38
Bronx Writing Academy	7th grade	44	33	21	2
Jordan L. Mott Junior High School	7th grade	50	39	12	0
SUCCESS ACADEMY CHARTER SCHOOL	8th grade	0	0	33	67
Bronx Writing Academy	8th grade	35	40	19	6
Jordan L. Mott Junior High School	8th grade	40	43	13	4
SUCCESS ACADEMY CHARTER SCHOOL	3rd grade	0	3	75	21
Crown Elementary School	3rd grade	22	32	42	4
SUCCESS ACADEMY CHARTER SCHOOL	4th grade	0	5	58	37
Crown Elementary School	4th grade	26	48	21	5

Performance Levels:　Level 1: Well Below Proficient　Level 2: Below Proficient　Level 3: Proficient　Level 4: Above Proficient
SOURCE: New York State Education Department

SUCCESS ACADEMY CHARTER SCHOOLS   New York State English Language Arts Test Results, 2017–2018 (Continued)

SCHOOLS HOUSED TOGETHER	CLASS GRADE LEVEL	LEVEL 1 RESULTS (Percent)	LEVEL 2 RESULTS (Percent)	LEVEL 3 RESULTS (Percent)	LEVEL 4 RESULTS (Percent)
SUCCESS ACADEMY CHARTER SCHOOL	6th grade	0	14	44	42
Frederick Douglass Academy II	6th grade	36	36	27	0
Wadleigh Performing and Visual Arts	6th grade	36	32	20	12
SUCCESS ACADEMY CHARTER SCHOOL	7th grade	5	14	62	20
Frederick Douglass Academy II	7th grade	31	38	25	6
Wadleigh Performing and Visual Arts	7th grade	35	40	25	0
SUCCESS ACADEMY CHARTER SCHOOL	8th grade	0	1	49	50
Frederick Douglass Academy II	8th grade	29	43	14	14
Wadleigh Performing and Visual Arts	8th grade	25	42	33	0
SUCCESS ACADEMY CHARTER SCHOOL	5th grade	0	9	41	50
Henry H. Garnet School	5th grade	46	34	16	4
SUCCESS ACADEMY CHARTER SCHOOL	3rd grade	1	9	61	29
Hernandez/Hughes School	3rd grade	24	32	41	3
SUCCESS ACADEMY CHARTER SCHOOL	4th grade	0	12	53	35
Hernandez/Hughes School	4th grade	13	39	39	10
SUCCESS ACADEMY CHARTER SCHOOL	3rd grade	0	8	81	12
Mahalia Jackson School	3rd grade	52	36	12	0
SUCCESS ACADEMY CHARTER SCHOOL	4th grade	0	14	53	33
Mahalia Jackson School	4th grade	34	40	19	6
SUCCESS ACADEMY CHARTER SCHOOL	5th grade	3	16	36	46
Mosaic Preparatory Academy	5th grade	35	30	24	11

SUCCESS ACADEMY CHARTER SCHOOLS   New York State English Language Arts Test Results, 2017–2018 (Continued)

SCHOOLS HOUSED TOGETHER	CLASS GRADE LEVEL	LEVEL 1 RESULTS (Percent)	LEVEL 2 RESULTS (Percent)	LEVEL 3 RESULTS (Percent)	LEVEL 4 RESULTS (Percent)
SUCCESS ACADEMY CHARTER SCHOOL	3rd grade	0	8	71	21
PS 138 Brooklyn	3rd grade	4	13	80	2
SUCCESS ACADEMY CHARTER SCHOOL	4th grade	0	14	58	28
PS 138 Brooklyn	4th grade	4	19	50	28
SUCCESS ACADEMY CHARTER SCHOOL	5th grade	0	15	38	46
PS 138 Brooklyn	5th grade	29	21	26	25
SUCCESS ACADEMY CHARTER SCHOOL	6th grade	0	5	23	73
PS 138 Brooklyn	6th grade	33	28	20	19
SUCCESS ACADEMY CHARTER SCHOOL	3rd grade	0	4	72	24
Stem Institute of Manhattan	3rd grade	25	50	20	5
SUCCESS ACADEMY CHARTER SCHOOL	4th grade	0	1	46	53
Stem Institute of Manhattan	4th grade	22	44	22	11
SUCCESS ACADEMY CHARTER SCHOOL	6th grade	0	3	21	76
Urban Assembly Academy for Future Leaders	6th grade	52	36	12	0
SUCCESS ACADEMY CHARTER SCHOOL	7th grade	0	12	46	42
Urban Assembly Academy for Future Leaders	7th grade	41	39	19	2
SUCCESS ACADEMY CHARTER SCHOOL	8th grade	0	5	41	54
Urban Assembly Academy for Future Leaders	8th grade	26	45	24	5

Performance Levels: Level 1: Well Below Proficient   Level 2: Below Proficient   Level 3: Proficient   Level 4: Above Proficient
SOURCE: New York State Education Department

SUCCESS ACADEMY CHARTER SCHOOLS New York State English Language Arts Test Results, 2017–2018 (Continued)

SCHOOLS HOUSED TOGETHER	CLASS GRADE LEVEL	LEVEL 1 RESULTS (Percent)	LEVEL 2 RESULTS (Percent)	LEVEL 3 RESULTS (Percent)	LEVEL 4 RESULTS (Percent)
SUCCESS ACADEMY CHARTER SCHOOL	6th grade	0	6	32	63
Urban Assembly Bronx Academy of Letters	6th grade	45	31	18	6
SUCCESS ACADEMY CHARTER SCHOOL	7th grade	0	8	75	18
Urban Assembly Bronx Academy of Letters	7th grade	35	48	14	2
SUCCESS ACADEMY CHARTER SCHOOL	8th grade	0	2	36	62
Urban Assembly Bronx Academy of Letters	8th grade	37	31	21	11
SUCCESS ACADEMY CHARTER SCHOOL	3rd grade	0	7	68	25
William Floyd School	3rd grade	29	38	29	4
SUCCESS ACADEMY CHARTER SCHOOL	4th grade	0	13	50	37
William Floyd School	4th grade	24	48	26	2

Performance Levels: Level 1: Well Below Proficient Level 2: Below Proficient Level 3: Proficient Level 4: Above Proficient
SOURCE: New York State Education Department

SUCCESS ACADEMY CHARTER SCHOOLS　　New York State Mathematics Test Results, 2017–2018

SCHOOLS HOUSED TOGETHER	CLASS GRADE LEVEL	LEVEL 1 RESULTS (Percent)	LEVEL 2 RESULTS (Percent)	LEVEL 3 RESULTS (Percent)	LEVEL 4 RESULTS (Percent)
SUCCESS ACADEMY CHARTER SCHOOL	3rd grade	0	1	27	72
Benjamin Franklin School	3rd grade	24	25	28	22
SUCCESS ACADEMY CHARTER SCHOOL	4th grade	0	1	3	96
Benjamin Franklin School	4th grade	35	37	18	9
SUCCESS ACADEMY CHARTER SCHOOL	6th grade	0	0	2	98
Bronx Writing Academy	6th grade	44	23	25	8
Jordan L. Mott Junior High School	6th grade	46	34	17	2
SUCCESS ACADEMY CHARTER SCHOOL	7th grade	0	0	2	98
Bronx Writing Academy	7th grade	51	32	13	4
Jordan L. Mott Junior High School	7th grade	67	26	6	1
SUCCESS ACADEMY CHARTER SCHOOL	3rd grade	0	0	8	92
Crown Elementary School	3rd grade	41	24	27	8
SUCCESS ACADEMY CHARTER SCHOOL	4th grade	0	1	5	94
Crown Elementary School	4th grade	36	34	16	13

Performance Levels:　Level 1: Well Below Proficient　Level 2: Below Proficient　Level 3: Proficient　Level 4: Above Proficient
SOURCE: New York State Education Department

SUCCESS ACADEMY CHARTER SCHOOLS   New York State Mathematics Test Results, 2017–2018 (Continued)

SCHOOLS HOUSED TOGETHER	CLASS GRADE LEVEL	LEVEL 1 RESULTS (Percent)	LEVEL 2 RESULTS (Percent)	LEVEL 3 RESULTS (Percent)	LEVEL 4 RESULTS (Percent)
SUCCESS ACADEMY CHARTER SCHOOL	6th grade	0	0	22	78
Frederick Douglass Academy II	6th grade	50	30	20	0
Wadleigh Performing and Visual Arts	6th grade	40	36	20	4
SUCCESS ACADEMY CHARTER SCHOOL	7th grade	2	2	9	88
Frederick Douglass Academy II	7th grade	44	25	19	13
Wadleigh Performing and Visual Arts	7th grade	40	40	15	5
SUCCESS ACADEMY CHARTER SCHOOL	5th grade	0	1	20	79
Henry H. Garnet School	5th grade	62	20	15	4
SUCCESS ACADEMY CHARTER SCHOOL	3rd grade	1	0	3	96
Hernandez/Hughes School	3rd grade	29	26	29	17
SUCCESS ACADEMY CHARTER SCHOOL	4th grade	0	0	11	89
Hernandez/Hughes School	4th grade	29	39	26	6
SUCCESS ACADEMY CHARTER SCHOOL	3rd grade	0	0	21	79
Mahalia Jackson School	3rd grade	54	33	7	6
SUCCESS ACADEMY CHARTER SCHOOL	4th grade	0	5	19	76
Mahalia Jackson School	4th grade	38	31	25	6
SUCCESS ACADEMY CHARTER SCHOOL	5th grade	3	3	17	77
Mosaic Preparatory Academy	5th grade	41	32	19	8

Performance Levels: Level 1: Well Below Proficient   Level 2: Below Proficient   Level 3: Proficient   Level 4: Above Proficient

SOURCE: New York State Education Department

SUCCESS ACADEMY CHARTER SCHOOLS   New York State Mathematics Test Results, 2017–2018 (Continued)

SCHOOLS HOUSED TOGETHER	CLASS GRADE LEVEL	LEVEL 1 RESULTS (Percent)	LEVEL 2 RESULTS (Percent)	LEVEL 3 RESULTS (Percent)	LEVEL 4 RESULTS (Percent)
SUCCESS ACADEMY CHARTER SCHOOL	3rd grade	0	2	27	71
PS 138 Brooklyn	3rd grade	11	9	53	27
SUCCESS ACADEMY CHARTER SCHOOL	4th grade	0	4	15	81
PS 138 Brooklyn	4th grade	4	28	37	31
SUCCESS ACADEMY CHARTER SCHOOL	5th grade	0	1	14	85
PS 138 Brooklyn	5th grade	15	35	35	16
SUCCESS ACADEMY CHARTER SCHOOL	6th grade	0	5	9	86
PS 138 Brooklyn	6th grade	27	29	26	19
SUCCESS ACADEMY CHARTER SCHOOL	3rd grade	0	0	5	95
Stem Institute of Manhattan	3rd grade	57	22	22	0
SUCCESS ACADEMY CHARTER SCHOOL	4th grade	0	0	1	99
Stem Institute of Manhattan	4th grade	43	32	18	7
SUCCESS ACADEMY CHARTER SCHOOL	6th grade	0	0	2	98
Urban Assembly Academy for Future Leaders	6th grade	74	21	6	0
SUCCESS ACADEMY CHARTER SCHOOL	7th grade	0	0	20	80
Urban Assembly Academy for Future Leaders	7th grade	64	22	15	0

Performance Levels: Level 1: Well Below Proficient   Level 2: Below Proficient   Level 3: Proficient   Level 4: Above Proficient
SOURCE: New York State Education Department

SUCCESS ACADEMY CHARTER SCHOOLS   New York State Mathematics Test Results, 2017–2018 (Continued)

SCHOOLS HOUSED TOGETHER	CLASS GRADE LEVEL	LEVEL 1 RESULTS (Percent)	LEVEL 2 RESULTS (Percent)	LEVEL 3 RESULTS (Percent)	LEVEL 4 RESULTS (Percent)
SUCCESS ACADEMY CHARTER SCHOOL	6th grade	0	1	13	86
Urban Assembly Bronx Academy of Letters	6th grade	70	23	5	3
SUCCESS ACADEMY CHARTER SCHOOL	7th grade	0	0	12	88
Urban Assembly Bronx Academy of Letters	7th grade	63	24	9	3
SUCCESS ACADEMY CHARTER SCHOOL	3rd grade	1	3	19	77
William Floyd School	3rd grade	26	15	45	15
SUCCESS ACADEMY CHARTER SCHOOL	4th grade	0	0	6	94
William Floyd School	4th grade	40	43	14	2

Performance Levels: Level 1: Well Below Proficient   Level 2: Below Proficient   Level 3: Proficient   Level 4: Above Proficient
SOURCE: New York State Education Department

UNCOMMON SCHOOLS CHARTER SCHOOLS New York State English Language Arts Test Results, 2017–2018

SCHOOLS HOUSED TOGETHER	CLASS GRADE LEVEL	LEVEL 1 RESULTS (Percent)	LEVEL 2 RESULTS (Percent)	LEVEL 3 RESULTS (Percent)	LEVEL 4 RESULTS (Percent)
UNCOMMON SCHOOLS CHARTER SCHOOL	3rd grade	1	14	68	17
Christopher Avenue Community School	3rd grade	22	35	41	3
UNCOMMON SCHOOLS CHARTER SCHOOL	4th grade	2	18	39	41
Christopher Avenue Community School	4th grade	11	54	29	7
UNCOMMON SCHOOLS CHARTER SCHOOL	5th grade	12	37	28	23
Christopher Avenue Community School	5th grade	58	25	13	4
UNCOMMON SCHOOLS CHARTER SCHOOL	5th grade	36	30	23	11
Christopher Elementary School	5th grade	67	21	8	4
UNCOMMON SCHOOLS CHARTER SCHOOL	6th grade	17	26	25	32
Eagle Academy for Young Men II	6th grade	51	32	11	7
Mott Hall IV	6th grade	38	38	19	6
UNCOMMON SCHOOLS CHARTER SCHOOL	7th grade	16	35	35	13
Eagle Academy for Young Men II	7th grade	27	50	22	1
Mott Hall IV	7th grade	23	50	20	8
UNCOMMON SCHOOLS CHARTER SCHOOL	8th grade	12	31	43	14
Eagle Academy for Young Men II	8th grade	27	47	25	2
Mott Hall IV	8th grade	20	54	15	11

Performance Levels: Level 1: Well Below Proficient   Level 2: Below Proficient   Level 3: Proficient   Level 4: Above Proficient
SOURCE: New York State Education Department

UNCOMMON SCHOOLS CHARTER SCHOOLS New York State English Language Arts Test Results, 2017–2018 (Continued)

SCHOOLS HOUSED TOGETHER	CLASS GRADE LEVEL	LEVEL 1 RESULTS (Percent)	LEVEL 2 RESULTS (Percent)	LEVEL 3 RESULTS (Percent)	LEVEL 4 RESULTS (Percent)
UNCOMMON SCHOOLS CHARTER SCHOOL	3rd grade	2	18	63	17
George E. Wibecan Preparatory Academy	3rd grade	42	37	18	3
UNCOMMON SCHOOLS CHARTER SCHOOL	4th grade	1	11	40	47
George E. Wibecan Preparatory Academy	4th grade	48	33	14	5
UNCOMMON SCHOOLS CHARTER SCHOOL	5th grade	24	30	27	18
Gregory Jocko Jackson School	5th grade	44	32	22	2
UNCOMMON SCHOOLS CHARTER SCHOOL	6th grade	12	33	36	19
Gregory Jocko Jackson School	6th grade	53	22	20	5
UNCOMMON SCHOOLS CHARTER SCHOOL	7th grade	12	44	33	10
Gregory Jocko Jackson School	7th grade	48	35	11	7
UNCOMMON SCHOOLS CHARTER SCHOOL	8th grade	8	30	46	16
Gregory Jocko Jackson School	8th grade	36	43	17	4
UNCOMMON SCHOOLS CHARTER SCHOOL	5th grade	28	42	24	6
Herman Schreiber School	5th grade	31	29	22	17
UNCOMMON SCHOOLS CHARTER SCHOOL	5th grade	25	44	25	7
Leonard Dunkly School	5th grade	41	50	6	3

Performance Levels: Level 1: Well Below Proficient Level 2: Below Proficient Level 3: Proficient Level 4: Above Proficient

SOURCE: New York State Education Department

UNCOMMON SCHOOLS CHARTER SCHOOLS   New York State English Language Arts Test Results, 2017–2018
(Continued)

SCHOOLS HOUSED TOGETHER	CLASS GRADE LEVEL	LEVEL 1 RESULTS (Percent)	LEVEL 2 RESULTS (Percent)	LEVEL 3 RESULTS (Percent)	LEVEL 4 RESULTS (Percent)
UNCOMMON SCHOOLS CHARTER SCHOOL	6th grade	16	30	26	28
Math, Science & Technology Middle School	6th grade	44	34	13	9
UNCOMMON SCHOOLS CHARTER SCHOOL	7th grade	13	29	46	12
Math, Science & Technology Middle School	7th grade	32	33	22	13
UNCOMMON SCHOOLS CHARTER SCHOOL	8th grade	3	38	41	17
Math, Science & Technology Middle School	8th grade	18	40	28	13
UNCOMMON SCHOOLS CHARTER SCHOOL	6th grade	11	26	33	30
Middle School for Art and Philosophy	6th grade	35	39	9	18
UNCOMMON SCHOOLS CHARTER SCHOOL	7th grade	18	38	40	5
Middle School for Art and Philosophy	7th grade	41	29	28	2
UNCOMMON SCHOOLS CHARTER SCHOOL	8th grade	10	38	32	20
Middle School for Art and Philosophy	8th grade	18	43	28	11
UNCOMMON SCHOOLS CHARTER SCHOOL	5th grade	9	32	28	31
Paul Robeson School	5th grade	39	44	11	6

Performance Levels: Level 1: Well Below Proficient   Level 2: Below Proficient   Level 3: Proficient   Level 4: Above Proficient
SOURCE: New York State Education Department

UNCOMMON SCHOOLS CHARTER SCHOOLS   New York State Mathematics Test Results, 2017–2018

SCHOOLS HOUSED TOGETHER	CLASS GRADE LEVEL	LEVEL 1 RESULTS (Percent)	LEVEL 2 RESULTS (Percent)	LEVEL 3 RESULTS (Percent)	LEVEL 4 RESULTS (Percent)
UNCOMMON SCHOOLS CHARTER SCHOOL	3rd grade	3	7	31	59
Christopher Avenue Community School	3rd grade	29	26	29	16
UNCOMMON SCHOOLS CHARTER SCHOOL	4th grade	0	9	25	66
Christopher Avenue Community School	4th grade	29	39	14	18
UNCOMMON SCHOOLS CHARTER SCHOOL	5th grade	10	22	35	33
Christopher Avenue Community School	5th grade	54	33	8	4
UNCOMMON SCHOOLS CHARTER SCHOOL	5th grade	39	15	27	19
Christopher Elementary School	5th grade	76	20	4	0
UNCOMMON SCHOOLS CHARTER SCHOOL	6th grade	15	24	24	37
Eagle Academy for Young Men II	6th grade	34	29	27	10
Mott Hall IV	6th grade	68	29	3	0
UNCOMMON SCHOOLS CHARTER SCHOOL	7th grade	13	20	29	38
Eagle Academy for Young Men II	7th grade	22	42	23	14
Mott Hall IV	7th grade	55	35	10	0

Performance Levels: Level 1: Well Below Proficient   Level 2: Below Proficient   Level 3: Proficient   Level 4: Above Proficient
SOURCE: New York State Education Department

UNCOMMON SCHOOLS CHARTER SCHOOLS   New York State Mathematics Test Results, 2017–2018 (Continued)

SCHOOLS HOUSED TOGETHER	CLASS GRADE LEVEL	LEVEL 1 RESULTS (Percent)	LEVEL 2 RESULTS (Percent)	LEVEL 3 RESULTS (Percent)	LEVEL 4 RESULTS (Percent)
UNCOMMON SCHOOLS CHARTER SCHOOL	3rd grade	3	13	37	47
George E. Wibecan Preparatory Academy	3rd grade	62	24	11	3
UNCOMMON SCHOOLS CHARTER SCHOOL	4th grade	7	6	31	57
George E. Wibecan Preparatory Academy	4th grade	57	29	14	0
UNCOMMON SCHOOLS CHARTER SCHOOL	5th grade	32	21	30	17
Gregory Jocko Jackson School	5th grade	51	33	8	8
UNCOMMON SCHOOLS CHARTER SCHOOL	6th grade	12	24	39	26
Gregory Jocko Jackson School	6th grade	56	34	8	2
UNCOMMON SCHOOLS CHARTER SCHOOL	7th grade	9	19	33	39
Gregory Jocko Jackson School	7th grade	63	26	7	4
UNCOMMON SCHOOLS CHARTER SCHOOL	5th grade	37	29	27	7
Herman Schreiber School	5th grade	29	21	22	28
UNCOMMON SCHOOLS CHARTER SCHOOL	5th grade	28	33	21	18
Leonard Dunkly School	5th grade	45	36	15	3

Performance Levels: Level 1: Well Below Proficient   Level 2: Below Proficient   Level 3: Proficient   Level 4: Above Proficient
SOURCE: New York State Education Department

UNCOMMON SCHOOLS CHARTER SCHOOLS   New York State Mathematics Test Results, 2017–2018 (Continued)

SCHOOLS HOUSED TOGETHER	CLASS GRADE LEVEL	LEVEL 1 RESULTS (Percent)	LEVEL 2 RESULTS (Percent)	LEVEL 3 RESULTS (Percent)	LEVEL 4 RESULTS (Percent)
UNCOMMON SCHOOLS CHARTER SCHOOL	6th grade	10	36	31	23
Math, Science & Technology Middle School	6th grade	51	28	13	8
UNCOMMON SCHOOLS CHARTER SCHOOL	7th grade	15	18	27	40
Math, Science & Technology Middle School	7th grade	36	38	23	4
UNCOMMON SCHOOLS CHARTER SCHOOL	6th grade	26	35	23	16
Middle School for Art and Philosophy	6th grade	50	36	12	2
UNCOMMON SCHOOLS CHARTER SCHOOL	7th grade	13	33	25	29
Middle School for Art and Philosophy	7th grade	66	26	9	0
UNCOMMON SCHOOLS CHARTER SCHOOL	5th grade	14	18	40	28
Paul Robeson School	5th grade	44	39	11	6

Performance Levels: Level 1: Well Below Proficient   Level 2: Below Proficient   Level 3: Proficient   Level 4: Above Proficient
SOURCE: New York State Education Department

AGGREGATE TEST SCORES

New York City Public Schools
New York State Public Schools

NEW YORK STATE ENGLISH LANGUAGE ARTS TEST RESULTS, 2017–2018

NEW YORK CITY PUBLIC SCHOOLS

CLASS GRADE LEVEL	LEVEL 1 RESULTS (Percent)	LEVEL 2 RESULTS (Percent)	LEVEL 3 RESULTS (Percent)	LEVEL 4 RESULTS (Percent)
3rd grade	17	30	44	9
4th grade	18	31	29	22
5th grade	31	29	23	16
6th grade	27	23	21	29
7th grade	25	32	29	14
8th grade	15	33	28	24

Performance Levels: Level 1: Well Below Proficient   Level 2: Below Proficient   Level 3: Proficient   Level 4: Above Proficient
SOURCE: New York State Education Department

NEW YORK STATE MATHEMATICS TEST RESULTS, 2017–2018

NEW YORK CITY PUBLIC SCHOOLS

CLASS GRADE LEVEL	LEVEL 1 RESULTS (Percent)	LEVEL 2 RESULTS (Percent)	LEVEL 3 RESULTS (Percent)	LEVEL 4 RESULTS (Percent)
3rd grade	24	21	29	26
4th grade	26	25	21	28
5th grade	33	24	21	22
6th grade	34	25	20	21
7th grade	34	25	21	20
8th grade	36	30	18	17

Performance Levels: Level 1: Well Below Proficient   Level 2: Below Proficient   Level 3: Proficient   Level 4: Above Proficient
SOURCE: New York State Education Department

NEW YORK STATE ENGLISH LANGUAGE ARTS TEST RESULTS, 2017–2018

NEW YORK STATE PUBLIC SCHOOLS

CLASS GRADE LEVEL	LEVEL 1 RESULTS (Percent)	LEVEL 2 RESULTS (Percent)	LEVEL 3 RESULTS (Percent)	LEVEL 4 RESULTS (Percent)
3rd grade	18	32	43	7
4th grade	19	33	29	18
5th grade	33	30	22	14
6th grade	28	23	22	27
7th grade	29	31	28	12
8th grade	19	33	27	21

Performance Levels: Level 1: Well Below Proficient   Level 2: Below Proficient   Level 3: Proficient   Level 4: Above Proficient
SOURCE: New York State Education Department

NEW YORK STATE MATHEMATICS TEST RESULTS, 2017–2018

NEW YORK STATE PUBLIC SCHOOLS

CLASS GRADE LEVEL	LEVEL 1 RESULTS (Percent)	LEVEL 2 RESULTS (Percent)	LEVEL 3 RESULTS (Percent)	LEVEL 4 RESULTS (Percent)
3rd grade	24	22	31	23
4th grade	26	26	23	25
5th grade	33	24	23	21
6th grade	31	25	23	22
7th grade	33	25	23	18
8th grade	39	31	18	12

Performance Levels: Level 1: Well Below Proficient   Level 2: Below Proficient   Level 3: Proficient   Level 4: Above Proficient
SOURCE: New York State Education Department

APPENDIX II: STUDENT DEMOGRAPHIC DATA

2017–2018 School Year

APPENDIX II: STUDENT DEMOGRAPHIC DATA

SCHOOLS HOUSED TOGETHER	BLACK STUDENTS Percent	HISPANIC STUDENTS Percent	WHITE STUDENTS Percent	ASIAN STUDENTS Percent
ACADEMIC LEADERSHIP CHARTER SCHOOL	41	57	0	0
Mother Hale Academy	42	55	0	3
ACHIEVEMENT FIRST CHARTER SCHOOL	87	7	1	0
Adrian Hegeman School	73	13	1	12
ACHIEVEMENT FIRST CHARTER SCHOOL	28	70	2	1
Alejandrina B. De Gautier School	27	71	2	0
ACHIEVEMENT FIRST CHARTER SCHOOL	78	19	0	1
Ernest S. Jenkyns School	59	34	4	2
ACHIEVEMENT FIRST CHARTER SCHOOL	71	26	0	3
Margaret S. Douglas Junior High School	49	30	3	17
ACHIEVEMENT FIRST CHARTER SCHOOL	97	2	0	0
New Heights Middle School	84	10	4	1
ACHIEVEMENT FIRST CHARTER SCHOOL	26	72	0	1
Philippa Schuyler Junior High School	36	57	2	4

SOURCE: New York State Education Department

APPENDIX II: STUDENT DEMOGRAPHIC DATA

SCHOOLS HOUSED TOGETHER	BLACK STUDENTS Percent	HISPANIC STUDENTS Percent	WHITE STUDENTS Percent	ASIAN STUDENTS Percent
ACHIEVEMENT FIRST CHARTER SCHOOL	81	16	0	1
Roberto Clemente School	66	28	3	2
BRONX CHARTER SCHOOL FOR BETTER LEARNING	82	12	2	2
Seton Falls School	59	37	2	0
BRONX GLOBAL LEARNING INSTITUTE FOR GIRLS CHARTER SCHOOL (THE SHIRLEY RODRIGUEZ-REMENESKI SCHOOL)	25	71	1	0
Concourse Village Elementary School	36	58	3	2
BROOKLYN CHARTER SCHOOL	81	16	1	2
Carter G. Woodson School	48	49	2	0
BROOKLYN URBAN GARDEN CHARTER SCHOOL	39	35	16	3
Carroll Gardens School for Innovation	21	39	33	5
CHILDREN'S AID COLLEGE PREP CHARTER SCHOOL	49	47	1	1
PS 211 Bronx	18	81	0	0
Math, Science & Technology Through Arts	33	67	0	0
COMMUNITY PARTNERSHIP CHARTER SCHOOL	77	15	2	4
Benjamin Banneker School	67	30	4	0
COMMUNITY PARTNERSHIP CHARTER SCHOOL	73	21	0	1
Johann DeKalb School	73	19	4	0

SOURCE: New York State Education Department

APPENDIX II: STUDENT DEMOGRAPHIC DATA

SCHOOLS HOUSED TOGETHER	BLACK STUDENTS Percent	HISPANIC STUDENTS Percent	WHITE STUDENTS Percent	ASIAN STUDENTS Percent
DR. RICHARD IZQUIERDO HEALTH AND SCIENCE CHARTER SCHOOL	26	70	2	0
Bronx Latin School	19	76	3	0
EAST HARLEM SCHOLARS ACADEMY II CHARTER SCHOOL	37	58	0	3
Central Park East I School	22	31	32	5
EMBER CHARTER SCHOOL	81	17	1	0
Clara Cardwell School	82	12	1	3
EXPLORE SCHOOLS CHARTER SCHOOL	75	20	1	2
Brooklyn Arts and Science Elementary School	52	34	10	3
EXPLORE SCHOOLS CHARTER SCHOOL	78	21	0	1
Ebbets Field Middle School	59	27	4	9

SOURCE: New York State Education Department

APPENDIX II: STUDENT DEMOGRAPHIC DATA

SCHOOLS HOUSED TOGETHER	BLACK STUDENTS Percent	HISPANIC STUDENTS Percent	WHITE STUDENTS Percent	ASIAN STUDENTS Percent
EXPLORE SCHOOLS CHARTER SCHOOL	92	5	1	1
Isaac Bildersee Junior High School	84	7	6	3
EXPLORE SCHOOLS CHARTER SCHOOL	87	9	1	1
MS 394 Brooklyn	74	18	1	7
EXPLORE SCHOOLS CHARTER SCHOOL	87	9	0	0
Parkside Preparatory Academy	77	14	2	4
EXPLORE SCHOOLS CHARTER SCHOOL	88	9	0	1
Ryder Elementary School	86	9	5	0
FUTURE LEADERS INSTITUTE CHARTER SCHOOL	80	15	2	1
Young Diplomats Magnet Academy	60	31	4	1
GIRLS PREP CHARTER SCHOOL	46	47	2	1
East Side Community School	13	52	20	11
GIRLS PREP CHARTER SCHOOL	50	44	1	2
Island School	28	67	2	2
GIRLS PREP CHARTER SCHOOL	37	61	0	0
Paul L. Dunbar Middle School	40	58	1	0

SOURCE: New York State Education Department

APPENDIX II: STUDENT DEMOGRAPHIC DATA

SCHOOLS HOUSED TOGETHER	BLACK STUDENTS Percent	HISPANIC STUDENTS Percent	WHITE STUDENTS Percent	ASIAN STUDENTS Percent
HYDE LEADERSHIP CHARTER SCHOOL	33	65	1	0
Hunts Point School	23	72	1	2
HYDE LEADERSHIP CHARTER SCHOOL	73	26	0	1
Phyllis Wheatley School	53	40	4	3
ICAHN CHARTER SCHOOL	51	43	1	4
Albert G. Oliver School	58	37	1	1
ICAHN CHARTER SCHOOL	55	42	1	0
Crotona Park West School	58	38	2	2
ICAHN CHARTER SCHOOL	32	60	1	5
Van Nest Academy	14	63	15	7
KIPP CHARTER SCHOOL	10	89	1	0
Alexander Humboldt School	3	95	0	1
KIPP CHARTER SCHOOL	15	82	1	0
Maria Teresa School	4	94	1	0
Patria Mirabal School	12	84	3	1

SOURCE: New York State Education Department

APPENDIX II: STUDENT DEMOGRAPHIC DATA

SCHOOLS HOUSED TOGETHER	BLACK STUDENTS Percent	HISPANIC STUDENTS Percent	WHITE STUDENTS Percent	ASIAN STUDENTS Percent
KIPP CHARTER SCHOOL	28	71	0	0
New Design Middle School	55	42	2	0
KIPP CHARTER SCHOOL	88	7	0	2
School of Integrated Learning	81	14	0	3
KIPP CHARTER SCHOOL	43	54	1	0
William Lloyd Garrison School	23	72	2	1
Lou Gehrig School	27	70	2	0
MANHATTAN CHARTER SCHOOL	15	70	2	11
Amalia Castro School	9	86	0	3
NEW AMERICAN ACADEMY CHARTER SCHOOL	95	2	1	1
Langston Hughes School	91	5	2	1
SOUTH BRONX CLASSICAL CHARTER SCHOOL	39	58	1	2
Entrada Academy	16	78	1	3
School of Performing Arts Middle School	32	63	1	2
SOUTH BRONX CLASSICAL CHARTER SCHOOL	44	54	0	0
Jonathan D. Hyatt School	41	55	1	0

SOURCE: New York State Education Department

APPENDIX II: STUDENT DEMOGRAPHIC DATA

SCHOOLS HOUSED TOGETHER	BLACK STUDENTS Percent	HISPANIC STUDENTS Percent	WHITE STUDENTS Percent	ASIAN STUDENTS Percent
SUCCESS ACADEMY CHARTER SCHOOL	59	41	0	0
Benjamin Franklin School	53	46	1	0
SUCCESS ACADEMY CHARTER SCHOOL	62	35	1	3
Bronx Writing Academy	32	64	1	2
Jordan L. Mott Junior High School	22	74	2	1
SUCCESS ACADEMY CHARTER SCHOOL	88	10	1	0
Crown Elementary School	81	14	1	2
SUCCESS ACADEMY CHARTER SCHOOL	77	16	3	1
Frederick Douglass Academy II	63	33	0	0
Wadleigh Performing and Visual Arts	46	48	1	0
SUCCESS ACADEMY CHARTER SCHOOL	73	20	2	3
Henry H. Garnet School	65	33	2	0
SUCCESS ACADEMY CHARTER SCHOOL	62	30	4	3
Hernandez/Hughes School	37	56	3	1
SUCCESS ACADEMY CHARTER SCHOOL	68	28	1	1
Mahalia Jackson School	46	44	7	2

SOURCE: New York State Education Department

APPENDIX II: STUDENT DEMOGRAPHIC DATA

SCHOOLS HOUSED TOGETHER	BLACK STUDENTS Percent	HISPANIC STUDENTS Percent	WHITE STUDENTS Percent	ASIAN STUDENTS Percent
SUCCESS ACADEMY CHARTER SCHOOL	66	30	0	1
Mosaic Preparatory Academy	49	40	0	8
SUCCESS ACADEMY CHARTER SCHOOL	77	17	3	1
PS 138 Brooklyn	82	10	5	2
SUCCESS ACADEMY CHARTER SCHOOL	66	31	2	1
Stem Institute of Manhattan	45	45	6	4
SUCCESS ACADEMY CHARTER SCHOOL	64	31	2	2
Urban Assembly Academy for Future Leaders	56	35	2	2
SUCCESS ACADEMY CHARTER SCHOOL	56	40	1	1
Urban Assembly Bronx Academy of Letters	41	56	3	0
SUCCESS ACADEMY CHARTER SCHOOL	66	26	4	1
William Floyd School	49	47	1	1
UNCOMMON SCHOOLS CHARTER SCHOOL	83	15	1	0
Christopher Avenue Community School	70	27	1	0
UNCOMMON SCHOOLS CHARTER SCHOOL	66	30	1	0
Christopher Elementary School	73	23	3	0

SOURCE: New York State Education Department

APPENDIX II: STUDENT DEMOGRAPHIC DATA

SCHOOLS HOUSED TOGETHER	BLACK STUDENTS Percent	HISPANIC STUDENTS Percent	WHITE STUDENTS Percent	ASIAN STUDENTS Percent
UNCOMMON SCHOOLS CHARTER SCHOOL	84	11	0	0
Eagle Academy for Young Men II	89	8	0	0
Mott Hall IV	86	12	0	1
UNCOMMON SCHOOLS CHARTER SCHOOL	83	13	0	3
George E. Wibecan Preparatory Academy	66	28	2	5
UNCOMMON SCHOOLS CHARTER SCHOOL	84	14	1	0
Gregory Jocko Jackson School	66	32	1	0
UNCOMMON SCHOOLS CHARTER SCHOOL	95	4	0	0
Herman Schreiber School	92	3	0	3
UNCOMMON SCHOOLS CHARTER SCHOOL	21	79	0	0
Leonard Dunkly School	42	55	0	0
UNCOMMON SCHOOLS CHARTER SCHOOL	66	29	0	1
Math, Science & Technology Middle School	72	20	2	1
UNCOMMON SCHOOLS CHARTER SCHOOL	93	3	0	0
Middle School for Art and Philosophy	86	9	2	1
UNCOMMON SCHOOLS CHARTER SCHOOL	86	9	1	3
Paul Robeson School	79	14	0	4

SOURCE: New York State Education Department

APPENDIX III: SPECIAL STUDENTS DATA

2017–2018 School Year

APPENDIX III: SPECIAL STUDENTS DATA

SCHOOLS HOUSED TOGETHER	ENGLISH LANGUAGE LEARNERS Percent	STUDENTS WITH DISABILITIES Percent	ECONOMICALLY DISADVANTAGED Percent
ACADEMIC LEADERSHIP CHARTER SCHOOL	13	10	93
Mother Hale Academy	10	31	99
ACHIEVEMENT FIRST CHARTER SCHOOL	no data	23	84
Adrian Hegeman School	22	16	91
ACHIEVEMENT FIRST CHARTER SCHOOL	13	16	88
Alejandrina B. De Gautier School	13	30	97
ACHIEVEMENT FIRST CHARTER SCHOOL	2	13	79
Ernest S. Jenkyns School	11	36	94
ACHIEVEMENT FIRST CHARTER SCHOOL	2	11	84
Margaret S. Douglas Junior High School	15	25	94
ACHIEVEMENT FIRST CHARTER SCHOOL	no data	15	77
New Heights Middle School	6	31	89
ACHIEVEMENT FIRST CHARTER SCHOOL	4	17	87
Philippa Schuyler Junior High School	5	16	83

SOURCE: New York State Education Department

APPENDIX III: SPECIAL STUDENTS DATA

SCHOOLS HOUSED TOGETHER	ENGLISH LANGUAGE LEARNERS Percent	STUDENTS WITH DISABILITIES Percent	ECONOMICALLY DISADVANTAGED Percent
ACHIEVEMENT FIRST CHARTER SCHOOL		16	91
Roberto Clemente School	no data	32	95
BRONX CHARTER SCHOOL FOR BETTER LEARNING	3	8	76
Seton Falls School	9	35	91
BRONX GLOBAL LEARNING INSTITUTE FOR GIRLS CHARTER SCHOOL (THE SHIRLEY RODRIGUEZ-REMENESKI SCHOOL)	17	14	90
Concourse Village Elementary School	14	25	93
BROOKLYN CHARTER SCHOOL	5	9	84
Carter G. Woodson School	11	43	89
BROOKLYN URBAN GARDEN CHARTER SCHOOL	3	23	61
Carroll Gardens School for Innovation	4	41	49
CHILDREN'S AID COLLEGE PREP CHARTER SCHOOL	no data	24	78
PS 211 Bronx	22	26	93
Math, Science & Technology Through Arts	18	30	98
COMMUNITY PARTNERSHIP CHARTER SCHOOL	no data	13	90
Benjamin Banneker School	no data	26	96
COMMUNITY PARTNERSHIP CHARTER SCHOOL	no data	21	87
Johann DeKalb School	no data	46	88

SOURCE: New York State Education Department

APPENDIX III: SPECIAL STUDENTS DATA

SCHOOLS HOUSED TOGETHER	ENGLISH LANGUAGE LEARNERS Percent	STUDENTS WITH DISABILITIES Percent	ECONOMICALLY DISADVANTAGED Percent
DR. RICHARD IZQUIERDO HEALTH AND SCIENCE CHARTER SCHOOL	10	28	94
Bronx Latin School	18	31	95
EAST HARLEM SCHOLARS ACADEMY II CHARTER SCHOOL	4	25	89
Central Park East I School	no data	20	40
EMBER CHARTER SCHOOL	7	17	85
Clara Cardwell School	no data	31	97
EXPLORE SCHOOLS CHARTER SCHOOL	4	32	78
Brooklyn Arts and Science Elementary School	11	38	77
EXPLORE SCHOOLS CHARTER SCHOOL	8	21	79
Ebbets Field Middle School	23	30	98

SOURCE: New York State Education Department

APPENDIX III: SPECIAL STUDENTS DATA

SCHOOLS HOUSED TOGETHER	ENGLISH LANGUAGE LEARNERS Percent	STUDENTS WITH DISABILITIES Percent	ECONOMICALLY DISADVANTAGED Percent
EXPLORE SCHOOLS CHARTER SCHOOL			
Isaac Bildersee Junior High School	6	28	77
	21	27	82
EXPLORE SCHOOLS CHARTER SCHOOL			
MS 394 Brooklyn	4	30	80
	8	17	87
EXPLORE SCHOOLS CHARTER SCHOOL			
Parkside Preparatory Academy	no data	11	70
	10	18	91
EXPLORE SCHOOLS CHARTER SCHOOL			
Ryder Elementary School	5	20	79
	18	34	81
FUTURE LEADERS INSTITUTE CHARTER SCHOOL			
Young Diplomats Magnet Academy	7	12	91
	no data	29	92
GIRLS PREP CHARTER SCHOOL			
East Side Community School	no data	17	77
	no data	32	61
GIRLS PREP CHARTER SCHOOL			
Island School	no data	20	76
	21	37	89
GIRLS PREP CHARTER SCHOOL			
Paul L. Dunbar Middle School	2	23	86
	26	26	95

SOURCE: New York State Education Department

APPENDIX III: SPECIAL STUDENTS DATA

SCHOOLS HOUSED TOGETHER	ENGLISH LANGUAGE LEARNERS Percent	STUDENTS WITH DISABILITIES Percent	ECONOMICALLY DISADVANTAGED Percent
HYDE LEADERSHIP CHARTER SCHOOL	6	21	92
Hunts Point School	23	31	96
HYDE LEADERSHIP CHARTER SCHOOL	8	16	91
Phyllis Wheatley School	18	33	100
ICAHN CHARTER SCHOOL	no data	10	74
Albert G. Oliver School	6	32	76
ICAHN CHARTER SCHOOL	no data	11	93
Crotona Park West School	14	30	96
ICAHN CHARTER SCHOOL	4	13	67
Van Nest Academy	4	22	75
KIPP CHARTER SCHOOL	15	21	89
Alexander Humboldt School	31	14	98
KIPP CHARTER SCHOOL	6	17	93
Maria Teresa School	37	24	99
Patria Mirabal School	33	25	91

SOURCE: New York State Education Department

APPENDIX III: SPECIAL STUDENTS DATA

SCHOOLS HOUSED TOGETHER	ENGLISH LANGUAGE LEARNERS Percent	STUDENTS WITH DISABILITIES Percent	ECONOMICALLY DISADVANTAGED Percent
KIPP CHARTER SCHOOL			
New Design Middle School	4	29	93
	6	39	91
KIPP CHARTER SCHOOL			
School of Integrated Learning	no data	21	90
	7	26	94
KIPP CHARTER SCHOOL			
William Lloyd Garrison School	2	20	90
Lou Gehrig School	15	31	91
	33	26	99
MANHATTAN CHARTER SCHOOL			
Amalia Castro School	9	29	79
	10	46	98
NEW AMERICAN ACADEMY CHARTER SCHOOL			
Langston Hughes School	no data	21	82
	4	24	84
SOUTH BRONX CLASSICAL CHARTER SCHOOL			
Entrada Academy	no data	5	87
School of Performing Arts Middle School	40	23	98
	17	32	97
SOUTH BRONX CLASSICAL CHARTER SCHOOL			
Jonathan D. Hyatt School	no data	13	92
	9	25	97

SOURCE: New York State Education Department

APPENDIX III: SPECIAL STUDENTS DATA

SCHOOLS HOUSED TOGETHER	ENGLISH LANGUAGE LEARNERS Percent	STUDENTS WITH DISABILITIES Percent	ECONOMICALLY DISADVANTAGED Percent
SUCCESS ACADEMY CHARTER SCHOOL	7	15	80
Benjamin Franklin School	16	26	99
SUCCESS ACADEMY CHARTER SCHOOL	no data	9	79
Bronx Writing Academy	28	26	96
Jordan L. Mott Junior High School	36	24	98
SUCCESS ACADEMY CHARTER SCHOOL	no data	16	79
Crown Elementary School	4	30	94
SUCCESS ACADEMY CHARTER SCHOOL	no data	17	79
Frederick Douglass Academy II	no data	48	95
Wadleigh Performing and Visual Arts	7	28	94
SUCCESS ACADEMY CHARTER SCHOOL	no data	20	82
Henry H. Garnet School	27	29	96
SUCCESS ACADEMY CHARTER SCHOOL	no data	20	79
Hernandez/Hughes School	13	31	92
SUCCESS ACADEMY CHARTER SCHOOL	6	19	89
Mahalia Jackson School	23	26	97

SOURCE: New York State Education Department

APPENDIX III: SPECIAL STUDENTS DATA

SCHOOLS HOUSED TOGETHER	ENGLISH LANGUAGE LEARNERS Percent	STUDENTS WITH DISABILITIES Percent	ECONOMICALLY DISADVANTAGED Percent
SUCCESS ACADEMY CHARTER SCHOOL	no data	34	88
Mosaic Preparatory Academy	no data	53	92
SUCCESS ACADEMY CHARTER SCHOOL	no data	14	77
PS 138 Brooklyn	9	19	96
SUCCESS ACADEMY CHARTER SCHOOL	3	15	80
Stem Institute of Manhattan	16	35	94
SUCCESS ACADEMY CHARTER SCHOOL	no data	17	81
Urban Assembly Academy for Future Leaders	6	35	92
SUCCESS ACADEMY CHARTER SCHOOL	no data	14	80
Urban Assembly Bronx Academy of Letters	14	33	96
SUCCESS ACADEMY CHARTER SCHOOL	no data	19	80
William Floyd School	14	27	98
UNCOMMON SCHOOLS CHARTER SCHOOL	no data	11	88
Christopher Avenue Community School	5	27	98
UNCOMMON SCHOOLS CHARTER SCHOOL	13	16	93
Christopher Elementary School	no data	53	97

SOURCE: New York State Education Department

APPENDIX III: SPECIAL STUDENTS DATA

SCHOOLS HOUSED TOGETHER	ENGLISH LANGUAGE LEARNERS Percent	STUDENTS WITH DISABILITIES Percent	ECONOMICALLY DISADVANTAGED Percent
UNCOMMON SCHOOLS CHARTER SCHOOL	2	13	84
Eagle Academy for Young Men II	no data	30	84
Mott Hall IV	no data	39	89
UNCOMMON SCHOOLS CHARTER SCHOOL	3	13	81
George E. Wibecan Preparatory Academy	13	36	90
UNCOMMON SCHOOLS CHARTER SCHOOL	no data	16	89
Gregory Jocko Jackson School	11	33	95
UNCOMMON SCHOOLS CHARTER SCHOOL	no data	18	79
Herman Schreiber School	no data	20	85
UNCOMMON SCHOOLS CHARTER SCHOOL	11	33	84
Leonard Dunkly School	no data	34	89
UNCOMMON SCHOOLS CHARTER SCHOOL	3	16	72
Math, Science & Technology Middle School	5	38	90
UNCOMMON SCHOOLS CHARTER SCHOOL	2	16	71
Middle School for Art and Philosophy	8	32	94
UNCOMMON SCHOOLS CHARTER SCHOOL	no data	13	77
Paul Robeson School	no data	32	100

SOURCE: New York State Education Department

NOTES

PREFACE

1. T. Rees Shapiro, "Vanished Glory of an All-Black High School," *Washington Post*, January 19, 2014, p. B6.

2. "Cuomo's Good Charter Fight," *Wall Street Journal*, April 17, 2019, p. A14.

CHAPTER 1: COMPARISONS AND COMPARABILITY

1. David Osborne, *Reinventing America's Schools: Creating a 21st Century Education System* (New York: Bloomsbury, 2017), Chapters 7, 8; Center for Research on Education Outcomes, *Charter School Performance in New York City* (Stanford: Center for Research on Education Outcomes, 2017); Thomas J. Kane, *Let the Numbers Have Their Say: Evidence on Massachusetts' Charter Schools* (Cambridge, Massachusetts: Harvard University Center for Education Policy Research, 2016).

2. "State of the Teachers Union," *Wall Street Journal*, July 6, 2017, p. A14. Charter schools were also called a "failed experiment" by Diane Ravitch, "The Miseducation of Liberals," *New Republic*, June 2017, p. 17.

3. Glenn Sacks, "Charter Schools' Success Is an Illusion," *Wall Street Journal*, August 27, 2019, p. A15.

4. "Public charter schools are publicly funded schools that are typically governed by a group or organization under a legislative contract (or charter) with the state, district, or other entity. Traditional public schools include all publicly funded schools other than public charter schools." Ke Wang, Amy Rathbun and Lauren Musu, *School Choice in the United States: 2019* (Washington: U.S. Department of Education, National Center for Education Statistics, 2019), p. 1.

5. Ibid., pp. 16, 17.

6. See, for example, Abigail Thernstrom and Stephan Thernstrom, *No Excuses: Closing the Racial Gap in Learning* (New York: Simon and Schuster, 2003), pp. 1–23.

7. Stan J. Liebowitz and Matthew L. Kelly, "Fixing the Bias in Current State K-12 Education Rankings," *Policy Analysis*, Number 854 (November 13, 2018), pp. 3–4.

8. Ibid., p. 3.

9. Similarity or comparability are ultimately subjective terms. But, in this context, it should at a minimum mean that a majority of students in both charter schools and traditional public schools with whom they are being compared are either black or Hispanic. For those who prefer more stringent standards, specific percentages are provided in the Appendix for every school in our sample, whether charter school or traditional public school.

10. A tabulation of the New York State Education Department data for the New York City students in our sample showed that, in school year 2017–2018, there were 22,298 students who were tested in mathematics and 23,969 students who were tested in English Language Arts.

CHAPTER 2: CHARTER SCHOOL RESULTS

1. See Appendix II.

2. See Appendix III.

3. Because the discussion in this chapter will be primarily comparisons of students in different grades in different buildings, third-graders in one building will not be lumped together with third-graders in another building. That would defeat the purpose of recognizing that differences exist between

buildings— or the neighborhoods where the buildings are located— as well as differences between charter schools and traditional public schools. If, for example, there are third-graders, fourth-graders and fifth-graders in five different buildings housing a particular charter school's classes, there will be said to be 15 "grade levels" of students in that particular charter school in those particular buildings and their test score results will be listed separately. That way, we can recognize differences in test score results from building to building, as well as from charter school to traditional public school, and within each of these categories of schools. This definition of "grade levels" is a definition created for this particular study, as distinguished from all the other definitions created by the New York State Education Department.

4. "New York Attacks Success," *Wall Street Journal*, August 23, 2017, p. A14.

5. See Appendix III.

6. Eva Moskowitz, *The Education of Eva Moskowitz: A Memoir* (New York: HarperCollins, 2017), p. 32.

7. Daniel Bergner, "Class Warfare," *New York Times Magazine*, September 7, 2014, p. 62.

8. See Appendix III.

9. See Appendix III.

10. "Cuomo's Good Charter Fight," *Wall Street Journal*, April 17, 2019, p. A14.

11. See, for example, Diana Lambert, "Charter Schools Facing New Oversight," *Mercury News* (San Francisco Bay Area), February 25, 2019, pp. B1 ff; Laura Waxmann, "State Legislation Could Give School District More Leverage Against Charter Schools," *San Francisco Examiner*, August 8, 2019, p. 4; Richard Cano, "California Charter Schools, Unions Call a Truce In an Epic Battle as Newsom Brokers a Deal," *Mercury News* (San Francisco Bay Area), August 29, 2019, pp. B1 ff; Dustin Gardiner, "Major Changes Ahead for State's Charter Schools,"

San Francisco Chronicle, August 29, 2019, p. C3; Taryn Luna, "State Brokers Deal on Charter Schools," *Los Angeles Times*, August 29, 2019, pp. B1 ff; "Charter Compromise Could Prove Ominous," *San Diego Union-Tribune*, August 30, 2019, p. 6; Ruben Navarrette, Jr., "California Bill Would Allow Students to Defy, Disrupt with Impunity," *Mercury News* (San Francisco Bay Area), September 8, 2019, p. A17; Kate Hardiman, "New California Law Bans School Suspensions for Defiant Students," *Washington Examiner*, September 12, 2019; "Charters to Face New Era of Open Hostility," *San Diego Union-Tribune*, October 5, 2019, p. 8. See also the following press releases, all downloaded from the website of the Office of the Governor of California Gavin Newsom: "Governor Newsom Signs Long-Discussed Charter School Transparency Legislation," March 5, 2019; "Governor Newsom Issues Legislative Update," September 9, 2019; "Governor Newsom Signs Charter School Legislation," October 3, 2019.

12.   See, for example, "Carranza's Poisonous Lie," *New York Post*, February 2, 2019, p. 16; Selim Algar, "Lift the Cap: Success Earns Academy $10M from Feds," *New York Post*, April 17, 2019, p. 8; Eliza Shapiro, "A Reckoning on Charters, from Within," *New York Times*, July 6, 2019, pp. A1 ff; Julia Marsh, "De Blasio Shouts That He 'Hates' Charter Schools at Campaign Event," *New York Post*, July 8, 2019. A condensed account appeared in the print edition: Julia Marsh, "Blas: I'm a Charter Hater," *New York Post*, July 9, 2019, p. 4; Karl Zinsmeister, "Education Reform Will Weather the Left's Assault," *Wall Street Journal*, September 3, 2019, p. A17; Karl Zinsmeister, "The Counterrevolution Against School Reform," *Philanthropy*, Fall 2019, p. 4; Sean Parnell, "Encouraging Events in Donor Privacy," *Philanthropy*, Fall 2019, p. 8.

CHAPTER 3: HOSTILITY

1. Frederick M. Hess, "New York Is Shutting the Door on Schools that Deliver for Kids," *New York Post*, March 7, 2019.

2. U.S. Bureau of the Census, *Public Education Finances: 2015* (Washington: U.S. Government Printing Office, 2017), p. 37.

3. Ke Wang, Amy Rathbun and Lauren Musu, *School Choice in the United States: 2019* (Washington: U.S. Department of Education, National Center for Education Statistics, 2019), p. 2.

4. Ibid., p. 14.

5. Matthew Kaminski, "The Weekend Interview with Eva Moskowitz: Teachers Union Enemy No. 1," *Wall Street Journal*, February 15, 2014, p. A15.

6. Chester E. Finn, Jr., Bruno V. Manno and Brandon L. Wright, *Charter Schools at the Crossroads: Predicaments, Paradoxes, Possibilities* (Cambridge, Massachusetts: Harvard Education Press, 2016), p. 65; Frederick M. Hess, "New York Is Shutting the Door on Schools that Deliver for Kids," *New York Post*, March 7, 2019.

7. See, for example, C.J. Szafir and Cori Petersen, "Cross Country: This Building Is for Sale (but Not to a Charter School)," *Wall Street Journal*, November 10, 2018, p. A11; C.J. Szafir, "Cross Country: The Vacant School Buildings That Made Milwaukee Infamous," *Wall Street Journal*, January 25, 2014, p. A13; "The 'Progressive' War on Kids," *Wall Street Journal*, February 1, 2014, p. A12; David Hunn, "Ban on Sale of Schools Stirs Anger," *St. Louis Post-Dispatch*, February 10, 2009, p. A1.

8. Myron Lieberman and Charlene K. Haar, *Public Education as a Business: Real Costs and Accountability* (Lanham, Maryland: Scarecrow Press, 2003), p. 54, note 11.

9. Mike Antonucci, "How Much Do Unions Spend on Politics?" *Education Next*, Winter 2016, p. 29; Terry M. Moe, *Special Interest: Teachers Unions and America's*

Public Schools (Washington: Brookings Institution Press, 2011), pp. 281, 283, 288, 289; Alicia Mundy, "Teachers Unions Give Broadly," *Wall Street Journal*, July 13, 2012, p. A4.

10. Barbara Ross, Ben Chapman, and Stephen Rex Brown, "2 Wins for Charters," *New York Daily News*, April 18, 2014, p. 10.

11. See, for example, Katie Lannan, "Campaign Eyes $1.5 Billion More for Education," *Lowell Sun*, December 14, 2018; Howard Blume, "UTLA Turns Focus to Charters," *Los Angeles Times*, December 22, 2018, pp. B1, B6; "Toughening Up on Charter Schools, Finally," *Los Angeles Times*, April 29, 2019, p. A9; "The Union Routs Students in Chicago," *Wall Street Journal*, November 1, 2019, p. A14.

12. Todd Ziebarth, *Measuring Up to the Model: A Ranking of State Public Charter School Laws*, 10th annual edition (Washington: National Alliance for Public Charter Schools, 2019), pp. 4, 5, 8.

13. "With New Report, Pressure Mounts on Gov. Newsom to Break Silence on Charter School Legislation," *Torrance Daily Breeze*, June 16, 2019.

14. *Hearing Before the Subcommittee on Constitution, Civil Rights and Human Rights of the Committee of the Judiciary, United States Senate*, One Hundred Twelfth Congress, Second Session, December 12, 2012, pp. 527–528, 530; Rachel M. Cohen, "Rethinking School Discipline," *The American Prospect*, Fall 2016, pp. 87–88; Teresa Watanabe and Howard Blume, "Disorder in the Classroom," *Los Angeles Times*, November 8, 2015, pp. A1 ff.

15. Motoko Rich, "Charter Schools Are Improving, a Study Says," *New York Times*, June 25, 2013, p. A15.

16. Joel Klein, "Scenes from the New York Education Wars," *Wall Street Journal*, May 10, 2011, p. A15.

17. Selim Algar, "Lift the Cap: Success Earns Academy $10M from Feds," *New York Post*, April 17, 2019, p. 8; "Cuomo's Good Charter Fight," *Wall Street Journal*, April 17, 2019, p. A14.

18. Daniel Bergner, "Class Warfare," *New York Times Magazine*, September 7, 2014, p. 67.

19. Al Baker and Javier C. Hernandez, et al., "Mayor and Operator of Charter Schools Do Battle in Albany," *New York Times*, March 5, 2014, p. A24.

20. Daniel Bergner, "Class Warfare," *New York Times Magazine*, September 7, 2014, p. 68.

21. Kate Taylor, "At Charters, High Scores and Polarizing Tactics," *New York Times*, April 7, 2015, pp. A1 ff; "Learning to Share," *New York Daily News*, August 30, 2015, p. 34.

22. Eliza Shapiro, "Gift of $16 Million Will Help Pay for Dozens of New City Schools," *New York Times*, October 3, 2019, p. A25.

23. "Denver's Education Stakes," *Wall Street Journal*, October 30, 2019, p. A16.

24. Karl Zinsmeister, "The Counterrevolution Against School Reform," *Philanthropy*, Fall 2019, p. 4.

25. Lori Higgins, "Snyder Signature Impacts Fight Over Detroit School," *Detroit Free Press*, January 27, 2018, p. A4.

26. Ben DeGrow and Jarrett Skorup, "Detroit Prep," *Impact*, March/April 2018, p. 9.

27. Ibid.

28. Ibid., p. 11; C.J. Szafir and Cori Petersen, "Cross Country: This Building Is for Sale (but Not to a Charter School)," *Wall Street Journal*, November 10, 2018, p. A11.

29. Ben DeGrow and Jarrett Skorup, "Detroit Prep," *Impact*, March/April 2018, p. 10.

30. Lori Higgins, "Detroit Might Reclaim Facilities: Some Charter Schools' Leases Run Out at End of School Year," *Detroit Free Press*, January 1, 2019, pp. A1 ff.

31. Lori Higgins, "Detroit's Schools Are Worst in U.S. Again: Tests Show Performance Deficits in Math, Reading," *Detroit Free Press*, April 10, 2018, p. A7.

32. "Who's Afraid of Betsy DeVos?" *Wall Street Journal*, January 14, 2017, p. A12.

33. See, for example, Motoko Rich, "Charter Schools Are Improving, a Study Says," *New York Times*, June 25, 2013, p. A15; Jonathan Kozol, "Vote 'No' on Charter Schools," *Boston Globe*, November 1, 2016, p. A10; Diane Ravitch, "Resegregation," *New Republic*, October 14, 2010, p. 42.

34. Thomas Ott, "Charter Backer Upset by Plan for Old Schools," *Cleveland Plain Dealer*, March 9, 2011, p. B2.

35. Ibid.

36. Alexis Huicochea, "TUSD Approves Sale of Reynolds Elementary School for $1.4 Million," *Arizona Daily Star*, February 9, 2016.

37. Hank Stephenson, "TUSD Racing to Beat Law that Curbs Control Over Sale of Closed Schools," *Arizona Daily Star*, May 11, 2018, pp. A1 ff.

38. Ibid.

39. C.J. Szafir, "Cross Country: The Vacant School Buildings That Made Milwaukee Infamous," *Wall Street Journal*, January 25, 2014, p. A13.

40. "The 'Progressive' War on Kids," *Wall Street Journal*, February 1, 2014, p. A12.

41. "Milwaukee's Public School Barricade," *Wall Street Journal*, August 14, 2018, p. A14.

42. Lauren FitzPatrick, "CPS to List 40 Vacant Schools, Mostly from 2013 Mass Closings," *Chicago Sun-Times*, January 12, 2017.

43. David Osborne, *Reinventing America's Schools: Creating a 21st Century Education System* (New York: Bloomsbury, 2017), p. 137.

44. Mary Shaffner, "Many Students, Not Enough Bricks," *Washington Post*, July 1, 2018, p. C4.

45. Arika Herron and James Briggs, "IPS Rejects Bid for High School Site: District May Struggle to Get Better Deal for Broad Ripple HS Building," *Indianapolis Star*, June 17, 2018, pp. A1 ff.

46. Eva Moskowitz, *The Education of Eva Moskowitz: A Memoir* (New York: HarperCollins, 2017), p. 139.

47. "Learning to Share," *New York Daily News*, August 30, 2015, p. 34.

48. Howard Blume, "A Tug of War Over Empty Classrooms," *Los Angeles Times*, July 9, 2019, p. A1.

49. Maggie Angst, "Bullis Charter School, Los Altos School District Strike Deal After Nearly a Decade of Negotiations," *Mercury News* (San Francisco Bay Area), April 6, 2019, p. B1.

50. Jeremiah Grace, "Charter Schools Deserve Support," *Fairfield Citizen News*, June 10, 2016, p. A10.

51. Zach Murdock, "Charter School Faces Tough Climb," *New-Times Danbury*, October 7, 2018, p. A4.

52. Anthony Johnson, "Academy Hopes to Fulfill Promise to San Jose Families," *Mercury News* (San Francisco Bay Area), July 20, 2018, p. A8.

53. See, for example, Sharon Noguchi, "San Jose Unified Rejects Charter School-Tech Museum Partnership," *Mercury News* (San Francisco Bay Area), June 2, 2017; Sharon Noguchi, "Santa Clara County School Board Deadlocks, Rejects Charter School," *Mercury News* (San Francisco Bay Area), September 7, 2017; Sharon Noguchi, "Elementary, Middle Schools Headed to San Jose," *Mercury News* (San Francisco Bay Area), January 22, 2018; *Promise Public Schools, Inc. v. San Jose Unified School*

District, Case No. 18CV325491, Superior Court of the State of California, County of Santa Clara, June 14, 2018; Emily DeRuy, "Charter School Delays Opening Over Location," *Mercury News* (San Francisco Bay Area), July 31, 2018, p. 6B; Leonardo Castañeda, "Charter School Seeking Classroom Space Sues San Jose Unified—Again," *Mercury News* (San Francisco Bay Area), January 3, 2019.

54.   Jason Riley, "A Charter-School Principal Won't Go to Prison," *Wall Street Journal*, May 1, 2019, p. A17.

55.   *American Indian Model Schools v. Oakland Unified School District*, filed June 23, 2014, Court of Appeal of the State of California, First Appellate District, Division Two, A139652 (Alameda County Superior Court No. RG13680906); Jill Tucker, "3 Charter Schools Win Reprieve from Closure," *San Francisco Chronicle*, June 25, 2014, p. D3.

56.   Doug Oakley, "Oakland's American Indian Model Schools Can Stay Open, Judge Rules," *Oakland Tribune*, July 30, 2014.

57.   Lauren Streib and Ian Yarett, "Top 100 Public High Schools," *Newsweek*, May 28, 2012, p. 36.

58.   Andrew J. Coulson, "OUSD Made Wrong Decision to Close American Indian Charter Schools," *Contra Costa Times*, March 25, 2013.

CHAPTER 4: ACCOUNTABILITY

1.   Joel Klein, "Scenes from the New York Education Wars," *Wall Street Journal*, May 10, 2011, p. A15. "The teachers' contract alone ran 77,841 words, which is 4 times as long as Shakespeare's 154 sonnets, 5 times as long as Albert Einstein's paper on the general theory of relativity, 10 times as long as the United States Constitution (including all 27 amendments), 59 times as long as the Declaration of Independence, and 286 times as

long as the Gettysburg Address. Placed end to end, its pages would be taller than the United States Capitol Building and about two-thirds the height of the Washington Monument." Eva Moskowitz, *The Education of Eva Moskowitz: A Memoir* (New York: HarperCollins, 2017), p. 245.

2.   *California Education Code* (Thomson Reuters, 2018).

3.   Jennifer Medina, "Deal Reached to Fix Teacher Discipline Process," *New York Times*, April 16, 2010, pp. A1 ff.

4.   Steven Brill, "The Rubber Room," *The New Yorker*, August 31, 2009, p. 30.

5.   Ibid., p. 32.

6.   Joel Klein, "Scenes from the New York Education Wars," *Wall Street Journal*, May 10, 2011, p. A15.

7.   Ibid.

8.   Jennifer Medina, "Suspended Teachers Will No Longer Face Strange Kind of Limbo," *New York Times*, June 29, 2010, p. A24.

9.   Ibid.

10. Liana Loewus, "'Absent Reserve' Teachers Heading Back to New York City Classrooms," *Education Week*, November 14, 2017, pp. 4–5. All of these hundreds of teachers were not put back to full-time teaching duties immediately. Subsequent events in this episode were covered in Marcus A. Winters, "Cross Country: There's One Thing Worse Than Paying Bad Teachers Not to Work," *Wall Street Journal*, February 10, 2018, p. A11; Susan Edelman, "DOE Keeping 930 Teachers $tuck (stuck) in Limbo," *New York Post*, October 20, 2019, p. 4.

11. "A School Reform Landmark," *Wall Street Journal*, June 11, 2014, p. A14.

12. Barbara Wood, "District Spends $584K to Dismiss Teacher," *The Almanac* (Menlo Park, Atherton, Portola Valley, Woodside), May 17, 2017, pp. 5–6.

13. See, for example, "To Improve Schools, End the 'Dance of the Lemons,'" *USA Today*, June 17, 2014, p. A6; Beth Barrett, "LAUSD's Dance of the Lemons," *LA Weekly*, February 11, 2010; Peter M. Szeremeta, "Squeezing Public Schools' Lemons: Theorizing an Adequacy Challenge to Teacher Tenure," *Washington & Lee Law Review*, Vol. 73, Issue 3 (Summer 2016), pp. 1601–1654; Michael Goodwin, "Schools' Bitter Fruit," *New York Post*, January 22, 2012, p. 9; Jessica Terrell, "Official Says Laws Shield Bad Teachers," *Orange County Register*, February 7, 2014.

14. Diane Ravitch, *Reign of Error: The Hoax of the Privatization Movement and the Danger to America's Public Schools* (New York: Vintage Books, 2014), p. 127.

15. "Cuomo's Stand and Deliver," *Wall Street Journal*, January 24, 2015, p. A12.

16. Diane Ravitch, *Reign of Error*, p. 127; Diane Ravitch, *The Death and Life of the Great American School System: How Testing and Choice Are Undermining Education*, revised and expanded edition (New York: Basic Books, 2016), p. 185.

17. Diane Ravitch, *Reign of Error*, p. 73.

18. Ibid., p. 7.

19. Ibid., pp. 61–62.

20. Diane Ravitch, "Settling for Scores," *New Republic*, January/February 2018, p. 65.

21. Ibid., p. 67.

22. Ibid.

23. Daniel Koretz, *The Testing Charade: Pretending to Make Schools Better* (Chicago: University of Chicago Press, 2017), p. 197.

24. Diane Ravitch, *Reign of Error*, p. 235.

25. David Osborne, *Reinventing America's Schools: Creating a 21st Century Education System* (New York: Bloomsbury, 2017), p. 130.

26. "Some are run like military boot camps." Diane Ravitch, *Reign of Error*, p. 159.

27. Charles Sahm, "What Explains Success at Success Academy?" *Education Next*, Summer 2015, p. 26.

28. Lance Izumi, *Choosing Diversity: How Charter Schools Promote Diverse Learning Models and Meet the Diverse Needs of Parents and Children* (San Francisco: Pacific Research Institute, 2019), p. 156; Robert Pondiscio, *How the Other Half Learns: Equality, Excellence, and the Battle Over School Choice* (New York: Penguin Random House, 2019), p. 128.

29. Robert Pondiscio, *How the Other Half Learns*, p. 136.

30. See, for example, David Osborne, "The Big Lie About Charter Schools," *Wall Street Journal*, November 20, 2019, p. A17; Randi Weingarten and Fred Albert, "Public Support for Public Schools," *Charleston Gazette-Mail*, June 17, 2019, p. A4; Derrick Johnson, "Charter Schools Underserve Students of Color," *Wall Street Journal*, May 23, 2019, p. A18.

31. Diane Ravitch, *The Death and Life of the Great American School System*, revised and expanded edition, pp. xix, xxix, 155.

32. Chester E. Finn, Jr., Bruno V. Manno and Brandon L. Wright, *Charter Schools at the Crossroads: Predicaments, Paradoxes, Possibilities* (Cambridge, Massachusetts: Harvard Education Press, 2016), p. 103.

33. Ibid.

34. Jay Mathews, *Work Hard. Be Nice: How Two Inspired Teachers Created the Most Promising Schools in America* (Chapel Hill: Algonquin Books of Chapel Hill, 2009), p. 91.

35. Ibid., p. 112. See also pp. 93, 94–97.

36. Stephen Chapman, "The Kansas City Plan Is a Decisive Failure," *St. Louis Post-Dispatch*, September 7, 1993, p. 7B; Michael Warder, "Rule of Law: Keep Tax-Happy Judges Away from School Boards," *Wall Street Journal*, December 21, 1994, p. A15; Blake Hurst, "End of an Illusion," *The American*

Enterprise, June 2000, pp. 44–45; Dennis Farney, "Crash Course: Can Big Money Fix Urban School Systems?" *Wall Street Journal*, January 7, 1992, p. A1.

37.   Michael Warder, "Rule of Law: Keep Tax-Happy Judges Away from School Boards," *Wall Street Journal*, December 21, 1994, p. A15.

38.   Stephen Chapman, "The Kansas City Plan Is a Decisive Failure," *St. Louis Post-Dispatch*, September 7, 1993, p. 7B.

39.   See, for example, Charles T. Clotfelter, *After Brown: The Rise and Retreat of School Desegregation* (Princeton: Princeton University Press, 2004), p. 16; Abigail Thernstrom and Stephan Thernstrom, *No Excuses: Closing the Racial Gap in Learning* (New York: Simon and Schuster, 2003), pp. 151–156, 158; Bob Herbert, "In Search of Magic," *New York Times*, March 21, 2002, p. A37; "A Visionary School Plan in Maryland," *New York Times*, April 30, 2002, p. A28; Jonathan Kozol, "Malign Neglect," *The Nation*, June 10, 2002, pp. 20, 22–23; Jesse Levin, et al., *What Does It Cost to Educate California's Students? A Professional Judgement Approach* (Stanford: Policy Analysis for California Education and Stanford University, 2018); Jason Richwine, "The Myth of Racial Disparities in Public School Funding," Heritage Foundation *Backgrounder*, No. 2548, April 20, 2011, pp. 1–6; Marcus A. Winters, "Savage Exaggerations: Worshipping the Cosmology of Jonathan Kozol," *Education Next*, Spring 2006, pp. 71–75; Stephan Thernstrom and Abigail Thernstrom, *America in Black and White: One Nation, Indivisible* (New York: Simon & Schuster, 1997), pp. 351–352, 355; Andrew J. Coulson, "State Education Trends: Academic Performance and Spending over the Past 40 Years," Cato Institute *Policy Analysis*, No. 746 (March 18, 2014); Eric A. Hanushek, "What Matters for Student Achievement," *Education Next*, Spring 2016, pp. 18–26; Lauren Musu-Gillette, et al., *Status and Trends in the Education of Racial and Ethnic Groups 2017* (Washington: U.S. Department of Education, National Center for Education Statistics, 2017), pp. 46, 48, 50, 52.

40.   See, for example, Abigail Thernstrom and Stephan Thernstrom, *No Excuses*, Chapter 8; Andrew J. Coulson, "State Education

Trends: Academic Performance and Spending over the Past 40 Years," Cato Institute *Policy Analysis*, No. 746 (March 18, 2014); Eric A. Hanushek, "What Matters for Student Achievement," *Education Next*, Spring 2016, pp. 18–26.

41. *Hearings Before the Subcommittee on Education of the Committee on Labor and Public Welfare, United States Senate*, Nineteenth Congress, First Session, July 24, 25, 26, 1967 (Washington: Government Printing Office, 1967), p. 990.

42. Ibid., p. 994.

43. Michael Kelly, "'F' for School Reform," *Washington Post*, April 11, 2001, p. A27.

44. Walter Williams, "Breaking Down Baltimore," *Daily Press* (Newport News, VA), August 10, 2019, p. A7.

45. See, for example, June Kronholz, "California's Districts of Choice," *Education Next*, Summer 2014, pp. 38–45; Kristen Taketa, "SDUSD Weighs Family Choice Balance," *San Diego Union-Tribune*, May 6, 2019, pp. A1 ff.

46. Daniel Bergner, "Class Warfare," *New York Times Magazine*, September 7, 2014, p. 62.

47. See, for example, Diane Ravitch, *Reign of Error*, pp. 298, 325; Diane Ravitch, *The Death and Life of the Great American School System*, revised and expanded edition, p. xxxix.

48. Diane Ravitch, *Reign of Error*, pp. 108–110.

49. Susan Edelman, "'It's Not Burger King. You Can't Have It Your Way,'" *New York Post*, September 8, 2019, p. 10; Success Academy, "Scaling Excellence: 2019 New York State Exams," downloaded from the website of Success Academy.

CHAPTER 5: STUDENT DIFFERENCES

1.   Ana Amélia Freitas-Vilela, et al., "Maternal Dietary Patterns During Pregnancy and Intelligence Quotients in the Offspring at 8 Years of Age: Findings from the ALSPAC Cohort," *Maternal & Child Nutrition*, Vol. 14, Issue 1 (January 2018), pp. 1–11; Ingrid B. Helland, et al., "Maternal Supplementation with Very-Long-Chain n-3 Fatty Acids During Pregnancy and Lactation Augments Children's IQ at 4 Years of Age," *Pediatrics*, Vol. 111, No. 1 (January 2003), pp. e39–e44.

2.   William D. Altus, "Birth Order and Its Sequelae," *Science*, Vol. 151 (January 7, 1966), pp. 44, 48.

3.   Ibid., p. 45.

4.   See, for example, Daniel S.P. Schubert, Mazie E. Wagner, and Herman J.P. Schubert, "Family Constellation and Creativity: Firstborn Predominance Among Classical Music Composers," *The Journal of Psychology*, Vol. 95, No. 1 (1977), pp. 147–149; *Astronauts and Cosmonauts: Biographical and Statistical Data*, Revised August 31, 1993, Report Prepared by the Congressional Research Service, Library of Congress, Transmitted to the Committee on Science, Space, and Technology, U.S. House of Representatives, One Hundred Third Congress, Second Session, March 1994 (Washington: U.S. Government Printing Office, 1994), p. 19. See also Julia M. Rohrer, Boris Egloff, and Stefan C. Schmukle, "Examining the Effects of Birth Order on Personality," *Proceedings of the National Academy of Sciences*, Vol. 112, No. 46 (November 17, 2015), p. 14225; Lillian Belmont and Francis A. Marolla, "Birth Order, Family Size, and Intelligence," *Science*, Vol. 182, No. 4117 (December 14, 1973), p. 1098; Sandra E. Black, Paul J. Devereux and Kjell G. Salvanes, "Older and Wiser? Birth Order and IQ of Young Men," *CESifo Economic Studies*, Vol. 57, 1/2011, pp. 103–120.

5.   See, for example, Robert J. Gary-Bobo, Ana Prieto and Natalie Picard, "Birth Order and Sibship Sex Composition as Instruments in the Study of Education and Earnings," Discussion Paper No. 5514 (February 2006), Centre for Economic Policy Research, London, p. 22; Daniel S.P.

Schubert, Mazie E. Wagner, and Herman J.P. Schubert, "Family Constellation and Creativity: Firstborn Predominance Among Classical Music Composers," *The Journal of Psychology*, Vol. 95, No. 1 (1977), p. 148; *Astronauts and Cosmonauts*, p. 19; Richard D. Lyons, "Each Astronaut Is an Only Child," *New York Times*, December 24, 1968, p. 7.

6. Arthur R. Jensen, *Genetics and Education* (New York: Harper & Row, 1972), p. 143.

7. R.G. Record, Thomas McKeown and J.H. Edwards, "An Investigation of the Difference in Measured Intelligence between Twins and Single Births," *Annals of Human Genetics*, Vol. 34, Issue 1 (July 1970), pp. 18, 19, 20.

8. See, for example, Maggie Gallagher, "Fatherless Boys Grow Up Into Dangerous Men," *Wall Street Journal*, December 1, 1998, p. A22; James Bartholomew, *The Welfare State We're In* (London: Biteback Publishing, 2013), pp. 291, 294; Barbara Maughan and Frances Gardner, "Families and Parenting," *A New Response to Youth Crime*, edited by David J. Smith (London: Routledge, 2010), p. 250; Stephen Baskerville, "Is There Really a Fatherhood Crisis?" *The Independent Review*, Vol. 8, No. 4 (Spring 2004), pp. 485–486; Kathleen M. Ziol-Guest, Greg J. Duncan, and Ariel Kalil, "One-Parent Students Leave School Earlier," *Education Next*, Spring 2015, pp. 36–41; David T. Lykken, "Psychopathic Personality: The Scope of the Problem," *Handbook of Psychopathy* (New York: Guilford Press, 2006), pp. 7, 8.

9. Malcolm Gladwell, *Outliers: The Story of Success* (New York: Little, Brown and Company, 2008), pp. 111–112.

10. "Choose Your Parents Wisely," *The Economist*, July 26, 2014, p. 22.

11. Betty Hart and Todd R. Risley, *Meaningful Differences in the Everyday Experience of Young American Children* (Baltimore: Paul H. Brookes Publishing Co., 1995), pp. 123–124, 125–126, 128, 198–199, 247.

12.   See, for example, Thomas Sowell, *Wealth, Poverty and Politics*, revised and enlarged edition (New York: Basic Books, 2016), pp. 396–402.

13.   For data and analysis, see Thomas Sowell, *Discrimination and Disparities*, revised and enlarged edition (New York: Basic Books, 2019), pp. 24, 96 and p. 252, endnote 22.

14.   For a survey of the social and economic impact of geographic differences, see Thomas Sowell, *Wealth, Poverty and Politics*, revised and enlarged edition, pp. 17–81. For a classic treatise on the subject, see Ellen Churchill Semple, *Influences of Geographic Environment* (New York: Henry Holt and Company, 1911).

15.   Theodore Dalrymple, *Life at the Bottom: The Worldview That Makes the Underclass* (Chicago: Ivan R. Dee, 2001), p. 69. See also pp. 158, 188.

16.   Ibid., p. 69.

17.   Ibid., p. 70.

18.   "A New Kind of Ghetto," *The Economist*, November 9, 2013, p. 10.

19.   Dr. Philip Kirby and Carl Cullinane, "Class Differences: Ethnicity and Disadvantage," The Sutton Trust, *Research Brief*, Edition 14, November 2016, p. 3.

20.   The London *Daily Mail* reported: "Across all disadvantaged pupils, white British children had the poorest performance at the age of 16 last year— with only 28 per cent getting good grades, according to the Sutton Trust, an education think tank. In comparison, 74 per cent of similarly hardup Chinese children got good grades." Eleanor Harding, "GSCE Pupils from Poor Chinese Families Do Three Times Better Than Whites," *Daily Mail*, November 10, 2016, p. 32. See also Natalie Perera and Mike Treadway, *Education in England: Annual Report 2016* (London: Centre Forum, 2016), p. 7; "Poor, White and Bottom of the Class," *The Week*, August 2, 2014, p. 13; Oliver Kamm, "We Can't Rely on the Market Alone to Close the Ethnicity Pay Gap," *The Times* (London), July 12, 2019, p. 39; "Black

Britons: The Next Generation," *The Economist*, January 30, 2016, p. 47.

21. See, for example, Monica Anderson, "A Rising Share of the U.S. Black Population Is Foreign Born," Pew Research Center, Washington, DC, April 9, 2015, pp. 17, 18; Pew Research Center, "The Rise of Asian Americans," updated edition, April 4, 2013, p. 10.

22. Theodore Dalrymple, *Life at the Bottom*, p. 68.

23. James Bartholomew, *The Welfare of Nations* (Washington: The Cato Institute, 2016), p. 92.

24. Ibid., p. 103.

25. Roland G. Fryer and Paul Torelli, "An Empirical Analysis of 'Acting White'," *Journal of Public Economics*, Vol. 94, No. 5–6 (June 2010), p. 380n.

26. Roland G. Fryer, "'Acting White': The Social Price Paid by the Best and Brightest Minority Students," *Education Next*, Winter 2006, p. 56.

27. Roland G. Fryer and Paul Torelli, "An Empirical Analysis of 'Acting White'," *Journal of Public Economics*, Vol. 94, No. 5–6 (June 2010), p. 381.

28. Roland G. Fryer, "'Acting White': The Social Price Paid by the Best and Brightest Minority Students," *Education Next*, Winter 2006, p. 54.

29. Theodore Dalrymple, *Life at the Bottom*, p. 158.

30. T. Rees Shapiro, "Vanished Glory of an All-Black High School," *Washington Post*, January 19, 2014, p. B6.

31. Henry S. Robinson, "The M Street High School, 1891–1916," *Records of the Columbia Historical Society*, Washington, D.C., Vol. LI (1984), p. 122; *Report of the Board of Trustees of Public Schools of the District of Columbia to the Commissioners of the District of Columbia: 1898–99* (Washington: Government Printing Office, 1900), pp. 7, 11.

32.   Mary Gibson Hundley, *The Dunbar Story: 1870–1955* (New York: Vantage Press, 1965), pp. 75, 78; Mary Church Terrell, "History of the High School for Negroes in Washington," *Journal of Negro History*, Vol. 2, No. 3 (July 1917), p. 262.

33.   Alison Stewart, *First Class: The Legacy of Dunbar, America's First Black Public High School* (Chicago: Lawrence Hill Books, 2013), p. 97.

34.   Ibid., p. 124.

35.   Ibid., p. 155.

36.   Jervis Anderson, "A Very Special Monument," *The New Yorker*, March 20, 1978, p. 100.

37.   Alison Stewart, *First Class*, p. 99; "The Talented Black Scholars Whom No White University Would Hire," *Journal of Blacks in Higher Education*, No. 58 (Winter 2007/2008), p. 81.

38.   Jervis Anderson, "A Very Special Monument," *The New Yorker*, March 20, 1978, p. 100.

39.   The years were 1953 through 1959. Editors of Sports Illustrated, *Sports Illustrated Almanac 2015* (New York: Sports Illustrated Books, 2014), pp. 44–45.

40.   See, for example, "A Misguided Attack on Charter Schools," *New York Times*, October 13, 2016, p. A24; "New York Attacks Success," *Wall Street Journal*, August 23, 2017, p. A14; Jonathan Kozol, "Vote 'No' on Charter Schools," *Boston Globe*, November 1, 2016, p. A10.

41.   Diane Ravitch, "The Charter Mistake," *Los Angeles Times*, October 1, 2013, p. A15.

42.   Diane Ravitch, *Reign of Error: The Hoax of the Privatization Movement and the Danger to America's Public Schools* (New York: Vintage Books, 2014), p. 298.

43.   Jonathan Kozol, *The Shame of the Nation: The Restoration of Apartheid Schooling in America* (New York: Broadway Paperbacks, 2005), p. 36.

44. Roland G. Fryer, "'Acting White': The Social Price Paid by the Best and Brightest Minority Students," *Education Next*, Winter 2006, pp. 57, 58.

45. Jonathan Kozol, *The Shame of the Nation*, p. 229.

46. Gary Orfield, "Foreword," Erica Frankenburg, Genevieve Siegel-Hawley and Jia Wang, *Choice Without Equity: Charter School Segregation and the Need for Civil Rights Standards* (Los Angeles: Civil Rights Project at UCLA, 2010), p. 1.

47. Ibid., p. 2.

48. *Random House Webster's College Dictionary* (New York: Random House, 1991), p. 1214.

49. Tomas Monarrez, Brian Kisida and Matthew Chingos, "Do Charter Schools Increase Segregation?" *Education Next*, Fall 2019, p. 71.

50. See, for example, Jonathan Kozol, *The Shame of the Nation*, pp. 9, 22, 216; Jonathan Kozol, "Vote 'No' on Charter Schools," *Boston Globe*, November 1, 2016, p. A10; Diane Ravitch, *The Death and Life of the Great American School System: How Testing and Choice Are Undermining Education*, revised and expanded edition (New York: Basic Books, 2016), pp. xxxix–xl, 269; "A Misguided Attack on Charter Schools," *New York Times*, October 13, 2016, p. A24; "New York Attacks Success," *Wall Street Journal*, August 23, 2017, p. A14.

51. Eliza Shapiro, "Then as New, a Fight over School Segregation," *New York Times*, April 15, 2019, p. A20.

52. Leonard Buder, "Board Asks Defeat of a Bill Retaining 4 Specialized Schools' Entrance Tests," *New York Times*, May 17, 1971, p. 26.

53. Heather Mac Donald, "How Gotham's Elite High Schools Escaped the Leveller's Ax," *City Journal*, Spring 1999, p. 74.

54. Malcolm Gladwell, *Outliers*, pp. 111–112.

55. Fernand Braudel, *A History of Civilizations*, translated by Richard Mayne (New York: The Penguin Press, 1994), p. 17.

56. Thomas Sowell, *Discrimination and Disparities*, revised and enlarged edition, Chapter 3.

57. See, for example, Diane Ravitch, *Slaying Goliath: The Passionate Resistance to Privatization and the Fight to Save America's Public Schools* (New York: Alfred A. Knopf, 2020), p.277; Jonathan Kozol, "Vote 'No' on Charter Schools," *Boston Globe*, November 1, 2016, p. A10.

58. Diane Ravitch, *The Death and Life of the Great American School System*, revised and expanded edition, p. 243.

59. Julia M. Klein, "The Rigors of Success," *The Pennsylvania Gazette*, September-October 2018, p. 54.

60. Jay P. Greene, "The Union War on Charter Schools," *Wall Street Journal*, April 16, 2009, p. A15.

61. Will Dobbie and Roland G. Fryer, Jr., "The Medium-Term Impacts of High-Achieving Charter Schools," *Journal of Political Economy*, Vol. 123, No. 5 (October 2015), p. 985.

62. Diane Ravitch, "The Miseducation of Liberals," *New Republic*, June 2017, p. 17.

63. See, for example, Center for Research on Education Outcomes, *Urban Charter School Study: Report on 41 Regions* (Stanford: Center for Research on Education Outcomes, 2015); Max Eden, *Lifting the Massachusetts Cap on Charter Schools: Pro and Con* (New York: Manhattan Institute, 2016); Marcus A. Winters, *New York City's Charter Schools: What the Research Shows* (New York: Manhattan Institute, 2018); Ray Domanico, *Lift the Cap: Why New York City Needs More Charter Schools* (New York: Manhattan Institute, 2019); Julian R. Betts and Y. Emily Tang, "The Effects of Charter Schools on Student Achievement," *School Choice at the Crossroads: Research Perspectives*, edited by Mark Berends, R. Joseph Waddington, and John Schoenig (New York: Routledge, 2019), pp. 69–91.

64. Chester E. Finn, Jr., Bruno V. Manno and Brandon L. Wright, *Charter Schools at the Crossroads: Predicaments, Paradoxes,*

Possibilities (Cambridge, Massachusetts: Harvard Education Press, 2016), p. 127.

65. Diane Ravitch, *Reign of Error*, p. 175.

66. "Lift the Cap: The Charter Difference," *New York Post*, March 18, 2019, p. 22.

67. Abigail Thernstrom and Stephan Thernstrom, *No Excuses: Closing the Racial Gap in Learning* (New York: Simon and Schuster, 2003), pp. 138, 139.

68. Ibid., p. 140.

69. Jay Mathews, *Work Hard. Be Nice: How Two Inspired Teachers Created the Most Promising Schools in America* (Chapel Hill: Algonquin Books of Chapel Hill, 2009), p. 23.

70. Ibid., p. 172.

71. Ibid., p. 210.

72. Samuel Casey Carter, *No Excuses: Lessons from 21 High-Performing, High-Poverty Schools* (Washington: The Heritage Foundation, 2000), p. 86.

73. Robert Pondiscio, *How the Other Half Learns: Equality, Excellence, and the Battle Over School Choice* (New York: Penguin Random House, 2019), p. 148.

74. Kate Hardiman, "New California Law Bans School Suspensions for Defiant Students," *Washington Examiner*, September 12, 2019; Ruben Navarrette, Jr., "California Bill Would Allow Students to Defy, Disrupt with Impunity," *Mercury News* (San Francisco Bay Area), September 8, 2019, p. A17; Nina Agrawal, "Ban on School Suspensions Grows," *Los Angeles Times*, September 11, 2019, p. B3.

75. Katherine Kersten, "Mollycoddle No More," *Minneapolis Star Tribune*, March 20, 2016, p. OP 1.

76. Madeline Will, "When Students Assault Teachers, Effects Linger," *Education Week*, February 14, 2018, p. 1.

77.   Max Eden, *School Discipline Reform and Disorder: Evidence from New York City Public Schools, 2012–2016* (New York: Manhattan Institute, 2017), Executive Summary.

78.   Ibid., pp. 17, 18, 24.

79.   Lauren Musu-Gillette, et al., *Indicators of School Crime and Safety: 2017* (Washington: National Center for Education Statistics, U.S. Department of Education, and Bureau of Justice Statistics, Office of Justice Programs, U.S. Department of Justice, 2018), p. 50.

80.   Max Eden, *School Discipline Reform and Disorder*, p. 11.

81.   Gail Heriot and Alison Somin, "The Department of Education's Obama-Era Initiative on Racial Disparities in School Discipline: Wrong for Students and Teachers, Wrong on the Law," *Texas Review of Law & Politics*, Vol. 22, No. 3 (Spring 2018), p. 498.

82.   James Bartholomew, *The Welfare State We're In*, p. 218; Nicola Woolcock, "Pregnant Teacher 'Punched by Pupil,'" *Daily Telegraph* (London), March 19, 2002.

83.   Gordon Rayner, "No Remorse as Boy Who Killed Teacher in Class Faces Life in Jail," *Daily Telegraph* (London), November 4, 2014, p. 1.

84.   Department of Education in New York City.

85.   Eva Moskowitz, *The Education of Eva Moskowitz: A Memoir* (New York: HarperCollins, 2017), p. 220.

86.   *Hearing Before the Subcommittee on Constitution, Civil Rights and Human Rights of the Committee of the Judiciary, United States Senate*, One Hundred Twelfth Congress, Second Session, December 12, 2012, pp. 527–528, 530; Rachel M. Cohen, "Rethinking School Discipline," *The American Prospect*, Fall 2016, pp. 87–88.

CHAPTER 6: DANGERS

1.   David Osborne, *Reinventing America's Schools: Creating a 21st Century Education System* (New York: Bloomsbury, 2017), p. 290.

2.   "Cuomo's Good Charter Fight," *Wall Street Journal*, April 17, 2019, p. A14.

3.   See, for example, Diane Ravitch, *Reign of Error: The Hoax of the Privatization Movement and the Danger to America's Public Schools* (New York: Vintage Books, 2014), pp. 298, 325; Diane Ravitch, *The Death and Life of the Great American School System: How Testing and Choice Are Undermining Education*, revised and expanded edition (New York: Basic Books, 2016), p. xxxix.

4.   Robert Pondiscio, *How the Other Half Learns: Equality, Excellence, and the Battle Over School Choice* (New York: Penguin Random House, 2019), p. 40.

5.   See, for example, David Osborne, *Reinventing America's Schools*, pp. 116–123, 165–166.

6.   Had that flight begun at home plate on a baseball diamond, it would have landed just short of second base. Nor did it matter how many other planes around the world had failed to get off the ground. Once the Wright brothers' plane lifted itself into the air and moved forward under its own power, that was decisive for proving what could be done. See Stephen Kinzer, "Dayton Claims Its Airspace," *New York Times*, June 22, 2003, p. TR8; Jennifer Oldham and Ashley Surdin, "Jet Fans Flock to LAX to Watch Big Bird Land," *Los Angeles Times*, March 20, 2007, p. A16.

7.   California Legislative Counsel's Digest, Assembly Bill No. 1505, Chapter 486, Approved by Governor October 3, 2019.

8.   James L. Highsaw, Jr. and William C. Burt, "Competition Under the Civil Aeronautics Act," *Louisiana Law Review*, Vol. 6, No. 2 (May 1945), pp. 149–150; Donald Tomaskovic-Deveu and Dustin Avent-Holt, *Relational Inequalities: An Organizational Approach* (New York: Oxford University Press, 2019), p. 205.

9.	Elizabeth E. Bailey, "Airline Deregulation: Confronting the Paradoxes," *Regulation*, Summer 1992, pp. 18–25; Robert Peterson, "Impacts of Airline Deregulation," *TR News*, May-June 2018, pp. 10–17.

10.	Thomas Gale Moore, "Unfinished Business in Motor Carrier Deregulation," *Regulation*, Summer 1991, pp. 49, 50.

11.	Thomas Gale Moore, "Trucking Deregulation," *The Fortune Encyclopedia of Economics*, edited by David R. Henderson (New York: Warner Books, 1993), pp. 433–437.

12.	Thomas Hazlett, "The Untold Story of FCC Regulation," *Cato Policy Report*, May/June 2018, p. 9.

13.	In 1962, the Federal Communications Commission ruled that "an application by a cable operator to expand its service could not be granted without a hearing on the economic impact of the proposed expansion on a local television station. The Commission denied the application after determining that outside signals from a cable system would have an economic impact on the local television station in question." Mark A. Conrad, "The Saga of Cable TV's 'Must Carry' Rules: Will a New Phoenix Rise from the Constitutional Ashes?" *Pace Law Review*, Vol. 10, Issue 1 (Winter 1990), p. 14.

14.	California Legislative Counsel's Digest, Senate Bill No. 419, Chapter 279, Approved by Governor September 9, 2019.

15.	Susan Edelman, "'It's Not Burger King. You Can't Have It Your Way,'" *New York Post*, September 8, 2019, p. 10.

16.	See, for example, Thomas Sowell, *Inside American Education: The Decline, the Deception, the Dogmas* (New York: Free Press, 1993), Chapters 3 and 4; Peter C. Myers, "Black Lives Matter Comes to the Classroom," *City Journal*, Summer 2019, pp. 92–100.

17.	As Senator Edward Brooke, a Dunbar alumnus, put it: "Negro History Week was observed, and in American history they taught about the emancipation of the slaves and the struggle for equality and civil rights. But there was no demand by students for more, no real interest in Africa and its heritage. We knew about Africa as we knew about Finland." Jervis Anderson, "A Very Special Monument," *The New Yorker*, March 20, 1978, p. 105.

18. "Brown Makes His Final Mark on California Education," *Ukiah Daily Journal*, October 10, 2018, p. 6; Peter C. Myers, "Black Lives Matter Comes to the Classroom," *City Journal*, Summer 2019, pp. 92–100; Williamson Evers, "California Wants to Teach Your Kids That Capitalism Is Racist," *Wall Street Journal*, July 30, 2019, p. A17.

19. Diana Lambert, "Charter Schools Facing New Oversight," *Mercury News* (San Francisco Bay Area), February 25, 2019, pp. B1 ff.

20. *National Association for the Advancement of Colored People v. Alabama ex rel. Patterson, Attorney General*, 357 U.S. 449 (1958) at 462–463.

21. Eva Moskowitz, *The Education of Eva Moskowitz: A Memoir* (New York: HarperCollins, 2017), p. 88.

22. NAACP, *Task Force on Quality Education: Hearing Report* (Baltimore: NAACP, 2017). See also "The NAACP's Disgrace," *Wall Street Journal*, October 17, 2016, p. A14; Derrick Johnson, "Charter Schools Underserve Students of Color," *Wall Street Journal*, May 23, 2019, p. A18.

23. Walter F. Murphy, "The South Counterattacks: The Anti-NAACP Laws," *The Western Political Quarterly*, Vol. 12, No. 2 (June 1959), p. 376; *NAACP v Patty*, 159 F. Supp. 503 (E.D. Va. 1958), 526.

24. Louis Freedberg, "Panel Faces Deadline to Recommend Reforms of State Charter School Law," *Mercury News* (San Francisco Bay Area), April 22, 2019, pp. B1 ff.

25. Sean Parnell, "Encouraging Events in Donor Privacy," *Philanthropy*, Fall 2019, p. 8.

26. Eliza Shapiro, "A Reckoning on Charters, from Within," *New York Times*, July 6, 2019, p. A1.

27. Ibid., p. A18.

28. Julia Marsh, "De Blasio Shouts That He 'Hates' Charter Schools at Campaign Event," *New York Post*, July 8, 2019. A condensed account appeared in the print edition: Julia Marsh, "Blas: I'm a Charter Hater," *New York Post*, July 9, 2019, p. 4.

29. Eva Moskowitz, *The Education of Eva Moskowitz*, p. 282.

30. Selim Algar, "Lift the Cap: Success Earns Academy $10M from Feds," *New York Post*, April 17, 2019, p. 8.

31. Eliza Shapiro, "Gift of $16 Million Will Help Pay for Dozens of New City Schools," *New York Times*, October 3, 2019, p. A25.

32. Dana Goldstein, "Year in Education: Stalled Test Scores, Increased College Costs," *New York Times*, December 28, 2019, p. A9; Jason L. Riley, "Sanders Chooses Teachers Unions Over Black Voters," *Wall Street Journal*, May 22, 2019, p. A17.

33. "Denver's Education Stakes," *Wall Street Journal*, October 30, 2019, p. A16.

34. Paul Sampson, "Program Aimed at Problems Caused by Differences in Ability of Students," *Washington Post-Times Herald*, July 19, 1955, p. 17.

35. Luther P. Jackson, "Second Precinct High Scholastic Qualities Eroded," *Washington Post-Times Herald*, June 30, 1960, p. D1.

36. David Osborne, *Reinventing America's Schools*, p. 118. See also, Alison Stewart *First Class: The Legacy of Dunbar, America's First Black Public High School* (Chicago: Lawrence Hill Books, 2013), p. 225.

37. Louise Daniel Hutchison, *Anna J. Cooper: A Voice from the South* (Washington: The Smithsonian Institution Press, 1981), pp. 58, 59.

38. Robert N. Mattingly, *Autobiographic Memories 1897–1954: M Street-Dunbar High School* (Washington, 1974), p. 9.

39.   Ibid. He was the son of a slave, and he entered Amherst in 1902, one year before the 40th anniversary of the Emancipation Proclamation. (Jervis Anderson, "A Very Special Monument," *The New Yorker*, March 20, 1978, p. 114.) Yet today, more than a century after he graduated from Amherst, the "legacy of slavery" is still being invoked by some to try to explain away today's social problems. Incidentally, in 1903 one of Mattingly's high school classmates became the first graduate of the same high school to enter Harvard. Henry S. Robinson, "The M Street High School, 1891–1916," *Records of the Columbia Historical Society*, Washington, D.C., Vol. LI (1984), p. 122.

40.   Mary Gibson Hundley, *The Dunbar Story: 1870–1955* (New York: Vantage Press, 1965), p. 75.

41.   Ibid., p. 78; Mary Church Terrell, "History of the High School for Negroes in Washington," *Journal of Negro History*, Vol. 2, No. 3 (July 1917), p. 262.

42.   David Osborne, *Reinventing America's Schools*, p. 118.

43.   Karl Zinsmeister, "The Counterrevolution Against School Reform," *Philanthropy*, Fall 2019, p. 6.

44.   Edmund Burke, *Speeches and Letters on American Affairs* (London: J.M Dent & Sons, Ltd., 1961), p. 109.

INDEX

INDEX